THE GREAT WILLIAM

THE

GREAT WILLIAM

Writers Reading Shakespeare

THEODORE LEINWAND

THE UNIVERSITY OF CHICAGO PRESS

CHICAGO & LONDON

THEODORE LEINWAND

is professor of English at the University of Maryland.

The University of Chicago Press, Chicago 60637
The University of Chicago Press, Ltd., London
© 2016 by The University of Chicago
All rights reserved. Published 2016.
Printed in the United States of America

25 24 23 22 21 20 19 18 17 16   1 2 3 4 5

ISBN-13: 978-0-226-36755-2 (cloth)
ISBN-13: 978-0-226-36769-9 (e-book)
DOI: 10.7208/chicago/9780226367699.001.0001

Library of Congress Cataloging-in-Publication Data

Names: Leinwand, Theodore B., author.
Title: The great William : writers reading Shakespeare / Theodore Leinwand.
Description: Chicago ; London : The University of Chicago Press, 2016. | Includes bibliographical
references and index.
Identifiers: LCCN 2015038291 | ISBN 9780226367552 (cloth : alk. paper) |
ISBN 9780226367699 (e-book)
Subjects: LCSH: Shakespeare, William, 1564–1616—Criticism and interpretation—History. |
Shakespeare, William, 1564–1616—Influence. | Shakespeare, William, 1564–1616—Appreciation.
Classification: LCC PR2965 .L45 2016 | DDC 822.3/3—dc23 LC record available at
http://lccn.loc.gov/2015038291

♾ This paper meets the requirements of ANSI/NISO Z39.48-1992 (Permanence of Paper).

CONTENTS

ACKNOWLEDGMENTS

A longtime reader of Shakespeare, I have been moved by the intensity, intelligence, and affection shown by the seven Shakespeare readers that I discuss in this book. Spending time in their archives, looking over their shoulders as they write in the margins of their Shakespeare editions, as well as in their notebooks, journals, and letters, has been a great pleasure. Also rewarding has been the advice and encouragement that I have received from Jonathan Auerbach, Amanda Bailey, Kent Cartwright, William Cohen, Michael Collier, Neil Corcoran, Stephen Donadio, Neil Fraistat, Ivy Goodman, Kenneth Gross, John Haffenden, John Irwin, Robert Levine, Elizabeth Loizeaux, William Loizeaux, J. D. McClatchy, Kevin Nesline, Howard Norman, Stanley Plumly, Adele Seeff, Christopher Reid, James Shapiro, Anita Sherman, Jeffrey Skoblow, Richard Strier, Joshua Weiner, and Frank Whigham. Randy Petilos and Alan Thomas, my editors at the University of Chicago Press, have been a great pleasure to work with. So too, Mary Corrado at the Press, and my copy editor, Nick Murray.

At Emory University's Manuscripts, Archives, and Rare Book Library, Steve Ennis, David Faulds, Sara Logue, and Kathy Shoemaker were of great assistance to me; at the Charles Olson Research Collection, Archives and Special Collections at the Thomas J. Dodd Research Center at the University of Connecticut, Melissa Watterworth; at the Literary Manuscripts Collection, University of Minnesota Libraries, Kathryn Hujda; at the Department of Special Collections and University Archives, Stanford University Libraries, Peter Whidden and Tim Noakes; at the Folger Shakespeare Library, Betsy Walsh; and at the London Metropolitan Archives, David Luck. What was once the University of Maryland's Graduate Research Board, now its Research and Scholarship Awards, has several times generously supported my research.

Most of all, I am indebted to Joan, Sarah, and Jesse. From near and far, each of them kept me company as I wrote this book.

An earlier version of chapter 1 appeared as "Shakespeare, Coleridge, Intellecturition" in *Studies in Romanticism* 46, no. 1 (2007), 77–104. The author acknowledges the Trustees of Boston University. An earlier version of chapter 2 appeared originally in *The Kenyon Review*, Spring 2002, Volume XXIV, Number 2. An earlier version of chapter 3 appeared in *The Yale Review* 93 (April 2005); an earlier version of chapter 4 appeared in *New England Review* 32, no. 4 (2011–12); an earlier version of chapter 5 appeared in *The Hopkins Review* 2, no. 3 (2009); and an earlier version of chapter 7 appeared in *New England Review* 30, no. 2 (2009).

The author acknowledges The Society of Authors as the Literary Representative of the Estate of Virginia Woolf. *The Virginia Woolf Manuscripts: From the Henry W. and Albert A. Berg Collection of the New York Public Library* is cited with permission of the New York Public Library, Astor, Lenox, and Tilden Foundations. *Virginia Woolf Manuscripts in the Monks House Papers University of Sussex* is cited with permission of the University of Sussex.

Works by Charles Olson published during his lifetime are held in copyright by the Estate of Charles Olson. Previously unpublished works by Charles Olson are under copyright by the University of Connecticut Libraries, used by permission, and are held at the University of Connecticut in the Charles Olson Research Collection, Archives and Special Collections at the Thomas J. Dodd Research Center.

The John Berryman Papers (MSS 43) are cited with permission courtesy of the Literary Manuscripts Collection, University of Minnesota Libraries, Minneapolis, and the copyright holder, Kate Donahue.

The Allen Ginsberg papers are cited with permission of the Department of Special Collections and University Archives, Stanford University Libraries. Excerpts from the Allen Ginsberg Papers by Allen Ginsberg, copyright [1975, 2015][1980, 2015][1976, 2015][1980, 2015] by the Allen Ginsberg Trust, are used by permission of The Wylie Agency LLC.

The Ted Hughes Collection (MSS 644) is cited with permission courtesy of the Manuscripts, Archives, and Rare Book Library, Emory University, and reprinted with permission of the copyright holder, Carol Hughes. © Estate of Ted Hughes and reprinted by permission of the Estate. Property of the Estate of Ted Hughes, Faber and Faber Ltd., publishers.

All Shakespeare citations are from *William Shakespeare: The Complete Works*, edited by Stephen Orgel and A. R. Braunmuller (New York: Penguin Books, 2002).

INTRODUCTION

The first *Complete Works* of Shakespeare that I owned I purchased in 1970. It was the 1942 New Cambridge Edition edited by William Allan Neilson and Charles Jarvis Hill. In blue ink, I wrote quite a bit both in and beyond the margins of the thirty-one plays I read that year and the next. I still have my Neilson and Hill, with four strips of blue electrical tape compensating for its broken binding. I even wrote a dedication on the recto of its heavy-stock first blank page: "to Edwin Barrett," the charismatic professor who led me through those plays. If marginalia, or *adversaria*, are signs of admiration and self-assertion, response and argument, collaboration and rivalry (at times, in Coleridge's case, notes for the friends who asked him to annotate their books), then I was conversing in one way or another with Shakespeare, with Barrett, very occasionally with Neilson and Hill, and most often with myself. Used copies of Shakespeare's plays sold online and in bookstores all over the world demonstrate that scores of readers have similar marginal conversations.

Some ten years later, when I started teaching, I put aside my Neilson and Hill edition and ordered for my classes the readily available *Complete Pelican Shakespeare*. Then, about four years along, something occurred in one of my classes that led me to write a short paper entitled "Ner and Por, or Teaching Shakespeare." A student had turned in a paper in which she used the abbreviated speech prefixes that she kept seeing as she read through *The Merchant of Venice* in the familiar two-column *Complete Works* format, rather than the unabridged Nerissa and Portia that appear in the editors' Dramatis Personae. Her paper got me interested in the effects the editions from which we read Shakespeare's plays have on our reading and comprehension, and on our pleasure, too. I knew that there was a long-standing discussion of quartos versus folios, of original spelling versus modernization, and of verse and prose lineation. But my paper pertained more obviously to all readers, novices and experts alike. I wondered about the effects of the size, weight, and quality of Shakespeare editions (hardcover *Complete Works* versus individual plays in paperback, bindings, paper stock, cover design, font and type size), and about page layout (size of margins, one column or the two that give rise to shortened speech prefixes, annotations and glosses alongside the text or below it). Long before I learned that Keats read Shakespeare in both folio and duodecimo editions, I wondered about the effect of reading from an edition that could be held in one hand as opposed to an edition that required a desk or a lap.

Starting with the Ner and Por paper, when I first became self-conscious about what actually transpired when I read Shakespeare, then fast forwarding to the moment when I was rereading Keats's letters and discovered that he inserted a sonnet ("On sitting down to read King Lear once again") in the blank space between *Hamlet* and *King Lear* in his folio edition of the plays, I was led to undertake a study of the experiences of writers whose Shakespeare reading has an intensity, acuity, and complexity that is at once moving and instructive. The case studies in *The Great William: Writers Reading Shakespeare* describe, compare, and interpret what occurred when Samuel Taylor Coleridge, John Keats, Virginia Woolf, Charles Olson, John Berryman, Allen Ginsberg, and Ted Hughes read Shakespeare. Each chapter is more of an essay than an argument, and each of them is addressed to Shakespeare readers no less than literary scholars, since everyone who reads Shakespeare submits and resists, exults and chafes, in his or her own way. With occasional exceptions, mine is not, then, a study of the influence of Shakespeare on these writers, although there are many excellent books and articles of this sort. Instead, I have tried to stay "close to the nose" (as Ginsberg might have put it), as close as possible to each writer in the act of reading.[1] My evidence of choice is the marginalia in their copies of the plays and poems, and in every case but one (Woolf), I bring marginalia to bear to a greater or lesser extent. I also rely extensively on notebooks, notepapers, journals and diaries, unpublished manuscripts, memoirs and remembrances, published essays, paintings and drawings, teaching notes, recordings of readings, and classroom recordings to fill out the picture. Some of the archives are so extensive that I hardly could peruse even the Shakespeare-related papers (Berryman); some of the Shakespeare material that I came upon has drawn almost no comment (Keats's and much of Coleridge's writings are the predictable exceptions); and sometimes Shakespeare editions (like one that belonged to Ted Hughes) were off limits to me. There is a long and frustrating list of writers whose copies of Shakespeare I could not locate or learned were unmarked (Karl Marx, Joseph Conrad, Mark Twain, Oscar Wilde, D. H. Lawrence, Frank Harris, H. D., Wyndham Lewis, Anne Sexton, among many others). Finally, there is one disappointing omission: Louis Zukofsky was deeply interested in Shakespeare and his Shakespeare editions are extensively annotated. But Zukofsky's heir warned me that, while he could not stop me from examining these volumes, he would not permit me to quote from or publish anything penned by his father and archived at the Harry Ransom Center at the University of Texas.

The energy and conviction of these seven writers' engagements with Shakespeare are palpable. Each of them experienced a host of pleasures but more than a few vexations. James Boswell records Dr. Johnson having said that "the progress which the understanding makes through a book, has more pain than pleasure in it." Berryman wrote to Mark Van Doren that "*Lear*'s renovation is going on rapidly & ruins me altogether for anything else. I am willing, however, to be destroyed in this cause."[2] Ginsberg, a consistently amused Shakespeare reader, betrays not even a hint of anxiety in relation to the Bard.[3] Olson wrote to Robert Creeley that reading Shakespeare made him "wild" and "giddy." Keats half-jokingly told John Hamilton Reynolds that Shakespeare "overwhelms a genuine Lover of Poesy with all manner of abuse." Woolf wrote in her diary that "the pliancy of [Shakespeare's] mind was so complete that he could furbish out any train of thought; &, relaxing lets fall a shower of such unregarded flowers. Why then should anyone else attempt to write?" Not just poignant, these writers' responses are, as we would expect, consistently revealing. Hughes assiduously works out his "tragic equation" (his "skeleton key" to Shakespeare plays) over the course of twenty years, both in manuscripts and letters, and in one after another graphic template inked and doodled on over-sized pages of notes. There was never a moment when he was not aware that his thesis would expose him to ridicule, but he kept at in a steadfast, methodical way. Olson unexpectedly confirms the validity of his "Projective Verse" manifesto when he describes for Creeley his excitement about the prosody of the late plays. Ginsberg has an idea about what he called the "mouthing that Shakespeare presents for an actor"—he seems to have hit upon it when he read *The Tempest* out loud in a Naropa classroom. When they read Shakespeare, these writers are almost never half-hearted or casual. They are urgent and deeply sincere; each of them has something at stake in the encounter.

Before Shakespeare seeps into what a writer writes, and even if that writing is immune to Shakespeare's influence, there is the reading itself, the silent or out loud enunciation, the sense-making, the pauses and skips, the pages turned back to, the lines anticipated, and quite often, the marks or comments—sometimes just a word, sometimes the equivalent to a paragraph—made in margins or notebooks.[4] At the same time, there is exhilaration, confusion, delight, exhaustion, astonishment, and reflection. On the title page of a volume of Schelling's, Coleridge wrote, "[a] book, I value, I reason & quarrel wit[h] as with myself when I am reasoni[ng]."[5] The multiple volumes of the Bollingen Coleridge marginalia testify to this; but Coleridge's Shakespeare marginalia were by no means always cerebral. In the margins of Theobald's 1773 edition of *Measure for Measure*, we come across "horrible" and "disgusting" (*CM*, 4.693). Coleridge's exasperation with William Warburton's editorial interventions ranges from impatience to sarcastic dismissal. Although some writers' discursive Shakespeare responses have gotten a good deal of attention (say, W. H. Auden on Hal and Falstaff or T. S. Eliot on *Hamlet*), it is not surprising that writers themselves often pay attention to Shakespeare at the level of the phrase or the word. Keats wrote that he "look[ed] upon fine phrases like a lover."[6] In his 1980 Naropa Basic Poetics class, Ginsberg was so tickled by a phrase from Sonnet 116 ("[Time's] bending sickle's compass come") that he kept repeating it, even humorously riffing on it. He loved its "funny syncopation." We have no recording of Virginia Woolf reading Shakespeare, but in one of her notebooks, she wrote that *Coriolanus*'s "close-packed elliptical style" was "not easy to read."[7] In her diary she wrote that she was amazed by Shakespeare's "stretch & speed & word coining power."[8]

The famous eighteenth-century editor Lewis Theobald did not think that Shakespeare would have allowed *The Winter's Tale*'s Paulina to call Leontes a fool. Coleridge disagreed because his "ear feels it Shakespearian" and because "the involved grammar is Shakespearian" (*CM*, 4.707). In my chapter on Berryman, I discuss the fifteen- and eighteen-hour days over the course of two years that he spent editing *King Lear*. Certainly he had to come up with his own account of the divergences between the quarto and folio versions of the play, but he also had to wrestle with one word of the play after the next after the next. When he took on notorious cruxes, Berryman entered fully into the fray, so I will pause over one instance because it provides a tightly focused example of how a poet read Shakespeare with a combination of ardor and almost madcap tenacity. I take the risk of pushing my reader down a rabbit hole with Berryman because what we find there is a limiting case (what mathematicians call a degenerate case) but also a generic case (indicative of the scrupulous ways these writers construed Shakespeare). Even to skim the minutiae that follow in this example is to get a taste of Berryman's breathtaking zeal. The case in point is Edgar's description of his father with the Old Man in act 4, scene 1 of *King Lear*, where Gloucester is said to be "poorlie, leed" in Quarto 1A, "parti, eyed" in Quarto 1B, and "poorely led" in Quarto 2 and the 1623 Folio. "Poorely led," Berryman wrote to Mark Van Doren, his adored and admired Columbia professor, is "the feeblest phrase in Shak, I suppose."[9] Berryman does not say why he believes this to be the case; but I would guess that it was Berryman the poet-connoisseur, not the scholar-editor, who felt this way. His rhetoric heated up some two weeks later, when he wrote to Van Doren that he "hate[s] to see you tormented by 'poorly led,' though it's companionable to know that someone besides myself can feel the fever." Having been meticulously testing variants, he told his former teacher that there were "half a dozen recent possibilities fighting for my faith" (227). "Poorly led" is beside the point at this painful moment in the play; it is indistinct, it is banal, or so I imagine Berryman thinking. But even if this is so, it could hardly have been the whole story for Berryman. For one thing, he knew that there are times when, on a particular (Edgar-like?) character's behalf, Shakespeare might strive for flat-footedness. Coleridge reconciled himself to this when he read the early scenes of *King Lear* and came upon a moment when Shakespeare seems to hold his imagination in check. For another, like a host of prior commentators, Berryman knew that whoever "corrected" the QA compositor's "poorlie, leed" to give us QB's "parti,eyd" must have seen something in his copy that we will never see. Whatever this was, Berryman was confident that it did not pertain to Gloucester's or to the Old Man's socioeconomic status but to Gloucester's eyes.

For Berryman, eyes had in their favor their "general dramatic relevance (Gloucester's plight consisting except for dishevelment only in blindness)" (229). So for starters, he proposed "bloody-eyed," pointing to the uncontroversially Shakespearean "hollow-ey'd" in *The Comedy of Errors* and "bloody-fac'd" in *2 Henry 4*, along with "bloody sceptred" in *Macbeth*. He also liked the idea that his emendation anticipated Edgar's "Bless thy sweet eyes, they bleed" (just over forty lines later), and he would have noticed "my father with his bleeding rings" in 5.3. At one point in his correspondence on the crux, Berryman refers to Shakespeare's "sixteen" combinations with "eyed" (246), so he knew that his conjecture had plenty of cognates. But he still wanted what he called a "clearer case" (229; Gloucester's "case of eyes" makes one wonder about Berryman's grim wordplay). "Unhappily," he sighed to Van Doren, "I can't escape a suspicion that 'parti-eyed' may have been intended, meaning perhaps 'striped with blood' (& egg)—on the analogy of 'parti-coloured'" (229). Writing about eight months later, in this instance to the great bibliographer W. W. Greg, Berryman put forward another conjecture. Still certain that the word ends in "-ey'd," he now tried to tame "this savage passage" with "emptie-eyd" (237). Berryman acknowledged that this new offering side-steps whatever "chaos the copy had" (237), but in its favor was Kent's "empty-hearted" in 5.1, not to mention Morocco's "carrion Death, within whose empty eye" in *The Merchant of Venice*. Not even two weeks later, the renowned author of *The Variants in the First Quarto of "King Lear": A Bibliographical and Critical Inquiry* demurred (239). Undeterred, Berryman waited a decent interval of time—about three months—and then wrote back to Greg with a letter that unceremoniously begins: "I wonder if this can be it: 'My father, pearly-ey'd'"? (245). Berryman and Greg had been corresponding with one another about numerous Lear questions both large and small, but the savage passage was now simply "it."

In favor of "pearly" was the fact that "pearl" was "a thin white film or opacity over the eye: a kind of cataract" (245). Berryman thought that this got him closer to "parti-ey'd" and to Q's Third Servant's "flax and whites of eggs" (although Greg could not see how pearl pertains to flax [247]). Berryman liked the fact that "pearly-ey'd" "enriches the [play's] destruction of sight imagery." And he was particularly happy to play as his trump card his conviction that his (or Shakespeare's) pearl was "hovering under Edgar's 'his bleeding rings, Their precious stones new lost'" (246). No doubt he was pleased when Greg responded, "I like the way you connect it up with the imagery and the 'precious stones'" (247).

This Berryman editorial excursus cannot be said to have taken us very far from the moment of reading Shakespeare if we remember that every time he returned to the text—and he did so hundreds of times—the crux stared him in the face. Doggedness like Berryman's may or may not be what first comes to mind when we think about one writer reading another (or one composer listening to the music of another), but a moment's thought tells us that local, technical, and professional matters are bound to count for a great deal in such circumstances. So, too, do *grands récits* or schemas such as the ones I describe in my Hughes and Olson chapters. Artists', if not scholars', so-called idiosyncratic responses to works of art are not only tolerated, they are celebrated. However, the case studies in this volume, including those in which eccentricity raises its head, are ballasted by an intensity of consideration of Shakespeare's writing that puts paid to any thought of unconsidered theorizing. Even the passion, the distress, the anger, and the excitement revealed in the Shakespeare marginalia, notes, and commentary of Coleridge, Keats, Olson, Woolf, Berryman, and Hughes typically derive from deeply considered responses to what they found on the page. If Hughes was by turns testy and ferocious in defense of his argument that a "patterned force field"—an astonishingly reticulated myth of a great goddess—can explain Shakespeare's plays from *All's Well That Ends Well* to *The Tempest*, it was because so much was at stake for him. He believed that powerful aftershocks of the Reformation were still being felt in England.[10] Hence, he found nothing hyperbolic in his certainty that "any discussion about the book [*Shakespeare and the Goddess of Complete Being*] is not about Shakespeare or me—it's about importance of spiritual tradition versus unimportance of it, importance of imaginative life or censorship of the same, . . . the survival of group culture versus the suicide of group culture, depth and reality of psychological life versus Academic orthodoxy. . . . Whether the Civil War is still being fought or isn't."[11] As for the quality of his evidence, he conceded that while scholars might not call it scholarship, his "book is logical in the way that algebra is logical . . . logical like a detective novel."[12] When an Olson or Berryman or Hughes reads and comments on Shakespeare, the rules of scholarship obtain, but differently.

For example, in many instances, there is very little premium put on objectivity or disinterestedness by the latter-day writer or by that writer's Shakespeare. Hughes's Shakespeare is a fanatical Catholic, a prophet, and a shaman, and Hughes himself an enthusiast.[13] Berryman's Shakespeare, also Ginsberg's, is usually indistinct from the speaker of the Sonnets. With utter confidence, Berryman insists that "connexions, now illuminating, now mysterious, between the artist's life and his work . . . [are] denied only by very young persons or writers whose work perhaps really does bear no relation to their lives, *tant pis pour eux*."[14] Ginsberg told his students that the Sonnets are Shakespeare's "novel," "drama," and "love story," but he also explained that the sequence confirms that Shakespeare "found someone who really answers the call of his heart . . . somebody that really turns him on . . . went to bed with him . . . a young kid, apparently."[15] Finding Shakespeare's autobiography in his writing is but the mirror image of finding one's own autobiography in the *Complete Works*. Coleridge famously has a "smack of Hamlet" himself, and Olson wrote in the margin of his Kittredge edition of *Hamlet* that "the trouble with Hamlet [is that] he could never add any thing to me, for I was he."[16] Virginia Woolf's take on this sort of identification is shrewd, and less self-indulgent: "To write down one's impressions of *Hamlet* as one reads it year after year, would be virtually to record one's own autobiography, for as we know more of life, so Shakespeare comments upon what we know."[17]

In other instances, Shakespearean objectivity and disinterestedness are the coin of the realm. Keatsian "negative capability" is one example; another is Hazlitt's often-cited remark that Shakespeare "seemed scarcely to have an individual existence of his own, but to borrow that of others at will."[18] Detachment is the hallmark of Olson's analysis of Shakespeare's verse in plays like *Pericles* and *The Two Noble Kinsmen*. The adjectives that Olson uses to describe this verse range from "sacred" to "mechanical" and "artificial." The verse is not, he argues, evocative of individual selves or characters—it is unmistakably, intentionally "unrealistic" and impersonal. "Choric verse," as he called it, is less expressive than it is obdurate; it is indifferent to "any dramatic exigency, either of a person or the situation in which the person finds himself." From what he heard on the page, Olson made his way to his remarkable account of the differences that generations of readers have noticed as they pass from the verse of the great tragedies to that of the romances. According to Olson, Shakespeare turned from the dead end that was secularism and subjective lyric drama to the objective "flatness" and "dryness" of the verse of "*rites de passage*."[19]

Such Shakespearean objectivity correlates with acoustics as much as comprehension. Like Olson, Coleridge recognizes a passage as Shakespearean because of what his "ear feels." In *Julius Caesar*, well along in the speech Antony makes after he shakes hands with the conspirators, Coleridge paused when he came upon this:

> Pardon me, Julius. Here was thou bayed, brave hart;
> Here didst thou fall, and here thy hunters stand
> Signed in thy spoil and crimsoned in thy lethë.
> O world, thou was the forest to this hart;
> And this indeed, O world, the heart of thee.
> How like a deer stricken by many princes
> Dost thou here lie!

(3.1.205–11)

Coleridge drew a large parenthesis around "O world . . . thee" and wrote "I doubt these Lines." While no one else appears ever to have had Coleridge's doubts, he objected not because the lines "are vile; but first on account of the Rhythm which is not Shakespearian but just the very *Tune* of some old Play, from which the Actor might have interpolated thatem." In other words, everything about these two lines *sounds* wrong to Coleridge. From what he heard, he moved on to a second and then a third objection: the lines interrupt "the flow of the Passion, & (what is with me still more decisive) the Shakespearian Link of Association." To test this, Coleridge writes, we have only to read the passage without these lines to see that Shakespeare never put them in it. Having done this, we are ready for Coleridge's determinative point. As I show in my Coleridge chapter, he was singularly interested in Shakespeare's method of composition ("How is it done?" he asked in one of his Shakespeare lectures).[20] Writing in the margins as he read, he laid the groundwork upon which his methodological conclusion rests: "Conceits he [Shakespeare] has; but they not only rise out of some *word* in the Lines before, but they *lead* to the Thought in the Lines following. Here it is a mere alien: Ant. forgets an image—when he is even touching it; & then recollects it when the Thought last in his mind must have led him away from it" (*CM*, 4.734–75). Shakespeare's "manner of connection," Coleridge wrote in the margin of *All's Well That Ends Well*, proceeds "by unmarked influences of association from some preceding metaphor. This it is which makes his style so peculiarly vital and organic" (*CM*, 4.701). As if in real time, we learn that before he could *know* that the hart in the forest violated organic form, Coleridge first had to *hear* a tune.

All of these examples, and the case studies that follow, prompt consideration of the inductive and deductive aspects of reading and interpretation. In this instance, Coleridge appears to be working up or outward, proceeding inductively from the evidence that he has heard. But his principle of "Association" does not feel merely Shakespearean. It seems to be on the shelf, waiting to be applied when he adjudicates something puzzling in the text. Ginsberg apparently had to hear Shakespeare's verse spoken in his own voice before he could construe it, as if what he read solicited recitation. But Ginsberg's own prosody is based on breathing, what he called "voweled breath," so it is not surprising that he would by method and habit "mouth" Shakespeare's words. Under the rubric "SOME DIFFERENT CONSIDERATIONS IN MINDFUL ARRANGEMENT OF OPEN VERSE FORMS ON THE PAGE," he listed "Units of mouth phrasing (pause within the same breath)."[21] The question of induction versus deduction applies as well to the comprehensive arguments that Hughes and Olson develop. Both poets would have it that their understanding of what Shakespeare is pursuing emerged from what they find on the page; but it is difficult not to imagine them confirming their a priori schema even as they read. The case studies in *The Great William: Writers Reading Shakespeare* are filled with moments when Shakespeare's language and themes serve (un)acknowledged agendas as well as moments of discovery and surprise, of yielding to the text. It is not easy to say when these writers' (or our own) Shakespeare reading is, or could be, genuinely dialectical.

Nor is it easy to determine how well at any given moment Keats, or Woolf, or Berryman knew that his or her marginalia, notebooks, journals, and letters were destined for the public sphere. Of course their poems, novels, and essays were composed for public consumption, but even when Coleridge was annotating for a particular book owner, what he penned in margins must have felt different to him from what he spoke in a lecture hall. To immerse oneself in a writer's more or less private writing about Shakespeare is inevitably to learn something new about that writer's life and mind, about that writer's art, and, not least, about Shakespeare's writing. Regarding Berryman, for example, I pay least attention to his poetry, a fair bit of attention to his life, more attention still to what John Haffenden has called Berryman's Shakespeare, and in the end, attention to what I call Shakespeare's Berryman (as Woolf writes, Shakespeare comments on us). In general, and to the extent that they are distinguishable, it is each writer's Shakespeare reading that preoccupies me, as opposed to each writer him or her-self. In numerous instances we learn something memorable about these writer/readers, but the most portable insights are about Shakespeare's art. When Henry/Hal advises Falstaff, "Make less thy body hence, and more thy grace" (5.5.55), Berryman responds, *One might argue, even, that this word "grace" is too often at Shakespeare's disposal for this kind of situation—Caliban you remember promises to be wiser thereafter and "seek for grace."*[22] The imputation that Shakespeare is culpable of ethical finessing, that Shakespeare might be facile, is bracing. One wants to test this by deploying one's own fudge detector across the length and breadth of the canon. Speaking of ethics, Hughes offers an astute summary judgment of his own. On the page at the end of *Richard 3* in his Collins Clear-Type Press edition of *The Complete Works of William Shakespeare*, he wrote that "morality was an impulse not a system in Shakespeare." Here, too, one begins mentally to race through the canon to assess the validity of the assertion (even as one suspects that Hughes is speaking aspirationally about himself). While Keatsian "negative capability" says something about Keats, it more interestingly prompts us to think about Shakespeare, about his works, and about ourselves as readers of them.

The Great William: Writers Reading Shakespeare is a testament to the impressive learning and research that these writers marshaled. Berryman set out to read everything that he assumed Shakespeare had read and every English play known to have been written between 1570 and 1614. Coleridge draws on his voluminous reading when he comments on the plays; and Ted Hughes bases what he calls Shakespeare's "archetypal plot" on hermeticism from occult Neo-platonism all the way up to *The White Goddess*. Poets steeped in poetics respond to Shakespeare's craft; pitch, meter, accent, each of these unsurprisingly plays a role in how they read Shakespeare.[23] Their understanding of poetics extends as well to a presumption like Ginsberg's, that Shakespeare subscribed *avant la lettre* to William Carlos Williams's dictum, "no ideas but in things." But there is an equally important phenomenological cast to these case studies, by which I mean that I am particularly interested in the affective or psychosomatic components of latter-day writers' Shakespeare reading. At issue at these moments is not how Shakespeare influences their writing but what Shakespeare "does" to them. Implicitly, at least, I want to speak to the connection any reader of Shakespeare may feel with these seven readers of Shakespeare. One does not have to be Keats to feel that as we read, Shakespeare "overwhelms" us—"genuine Lover[s] of Poesy" that we are—"with all manner of abuse." "The vigour of the [Shakespeare's] language is too overwhelming," writes Woolf.[24] There are so many words and so many of them count for so much that, for us too, awe competes with bewilderment and fatigue.

Of course, we are by no means always *in extremis*. Like Ginsberg, we are tickled and amused. Like Olson, we are jazzed; in the margin of his copy of *The Two Noble Kinsmen*, we find "wow" and "dotty verse! Crazy." At the same time that *The Great William: Writers Reading Shakespeare* presses into service available sources to determine where, when, and how its subjects read Shakespeare, it gestures toward how all of us read Shakespeare. Virginia Woolf envied and resented the way her brother Thoby "possessed himself" of Shakespeare, his "casual, rough and ready" way with the Bard. A woman at home, not university, "a breaker off of single words . . . a note taker," Woolf had to find her own way to read Shakespeare.[25] And so do we.

At least this is what a dozen years of on and off work on these case studies tells me. I sometimes set myself a ridiculous test: with my eyes closed I open a *Complete Works* to any page and put my finger on any line. Then I am supposed to demonstrate and confirm (for whom, it is not clear) that every line in every play has some value, hides or displays some treasure. Of course, this is foolish.[26] More salutary would be to watch someone like Berryman write in the margins of the Sonnets. His copy of W. G. Ingram and Theodore Redpath's *Shakespeare's Sonnets* is replete with scribbled "poors" and "mediocres" and "trivials." It is a relief to know that someone so profoundly engaged in his Shakespeare reading now and then finds the need to ward off "the great William," as Woolf puts it. Trained to be scholarly, analytical, and pedagogical when I think about Shakespeare, I nonetheless keep reading him for the same reason that Woolf says her brother Thoby read Shakespeare. He "took his bearings" from Shakespeare, made his works into equipment for living. Shakespeare provides me with both a social and a private currency. Like many others, I think through the plays and poems, sometimes talk in their words. I bend Lear's "reason not the need" (2.4.264) into a justification for one of my unjustifiable purchases, thereby dragging Shakespearean tragedy into my pedestrian, everyday life. I keep coming back to "I love [you] . . . / According to my bond, no more nor less" (1.1.92–

93) to articulate my relationship with a difficult parent, even though after a hundred readings, I still do not quite understand what Cordelia is saying. What reading Shakespeare continues to do to and for me is to clarify and complicate, startle and confound; it reminds me of the necessity and so the inevitability of interpretation; and it fills my ears with words and sounds that, although they are unmistakably his, have become ours.

I

SAMUEL TAYLOR COLERIDGE'S
"IMPELLING THOUGHTS"
ABOUT SHAKESPEARE

Hundreds and hundreds of pages of the Bollingen *Collected Works of Samuel Taylor Coleridge* are given over to Coleridge's notes, comments, reflections, marginalia, and lectures on Shakespeare. These testify *en masse* to the remarkable gregariousness of Coleridge the Shakespearean. The poems and plays, like so much else that Coleridge read, sponsored earnest, lifelong pedagogical relations between Coleridge and his family, friends, readers, and audiences.[1] It fell to Coleridge first to understand, then to explain Shakespeare. What he read, he could not help but talk about. And talk about.[2] He is relentlessly analytical, even when he experiences pleasure. Indeed, analysis itself was a source of pleasure: the best poetry stimulates the best reader to "be carried forward . . . by the pleasure-able [*sic*] activity of mind excited by the attractions of the journey itself."[3] Time and again, where there is evidence of Coleridgean pathos, hard on its heels, even antecedent to it, there may be found a measure of logos and a dose of ethos. In his notes on interleaved sheets in the two-volume Ayscough edition of *The Dramatic Works of William Shakespeare* (1807) which he took with him into the lecture room at the Crown and Anchor Tavern, Coleridge's initial response to Iago observing Cassio take Desdemona "by the palm," then planning to "ensnare" him in "as little a web as this," is a burst of sheer enthusiasm: "O excellent."[4] This is the stock in trade of a huge warehouse filled with Shakespeare marginalia; it expresses either knowing connoisseurship or it is the unselfconscious gasp of sudden recognition, the utter delight familiar to every reader of Shakespeare. However, no sooner does this pleasurable shiver register than Coleridge probes its cause. To write, "O excellent. The importance given to fertile trifles . . ." is for Coleridge to begin to expose the logic—the compositional strategy—that intensifies the shudder. The wit of the playwright, no less than the villain's, consists of making terrors of trifles. Then Coleridge extends his gloss just one phrase further ("O excellent. The importance given to fertile trifles, made fertile by the villainy of the observer—"), now acknowledging the ethical dimension of his own, perhaps also Shakespearean, pathos. Coleridge's pulse appears to quicken to the fecundity of villainy, but the full glossarial trajectory—from felt impression to analysis to evaluation—is the distinguishing mark of the reader Coleridge at work. He may ask what a Shakespearean passage means; he often asks what a particular editorial crux actually says; but implicitly or explicitly, he most wants to know "[h]ow is it done?" (John Payne Collier's notes).[5]

Here is another instance: not much farther along in the play, reading in 3.3, Coleridge writes, "Divine!" (*CM*, 4.868) in response to the way Othello's "If she be false, O, then heaven mocks itself!" cues Desdemona's entrance. Once again, because of the pressure of a pedagogical imperative, an exclamation is not suffered to stand alone, as it undoubtedly would in the margin of any casually annotated volume of the plays. Coleridge has to explain. His exclamation point measures the duration of feeling before it gives way to clarification: "Divine! the effect of innocence & the [bitter/better?] [? genius]" (the conjectures are Foakes's in *CLect*, 2.319; Jackson and Whalley give "better genius" without comment in *CM*). Coleridge infers that his involuntary affect, his !, has been triggered by a Shakespearean display of technical virtuosity (the exquisite collision between Othello and innocence plus better genius, or between Desdemona's innocence and Othello's bitter genius) enacted by characters who for Coleridge are always "a medium for value."[6]

While Coleridge's experience of the pleasures of a Shakespearean text has a genuine affective component, he responds as if pleasure were a prompt, or a heuristic. According to James Dykes Campbell's transcription of J. Tomalin's notes on Coleridge's November 28, 1811, lecture in the Great Room of the London Philosophical Society, Coleridge read the description of the horse and then of the hare in *Venus and Adonis*. He commented that "auditors w^d perceive that there was accuracy of description blended with the fervour of the poet's mind, thereby communicating pleasure to the reader" (*CLect*, 1.252). The path to pleasure traverses (Tomalin's version of) Coleridge's precise and logical ("thereby") account. As befits someone who valued "*every thing . . . in its place*" and the ability "to contemplate not *things* only, or for their own sake alone, but . . . the *relations* of things, either their relations to each other, or to the observer, or to the state and apprehension of the hearers," he begins by applauding Shakespearean method, or discrimination ("accuracy of description").[7] Coleridge's Shakespeare, famously, always exercises judgment. To Shakespeare's "accuracy" Coleridge joins "fervour," but notably, this is *mental* fervor. The door is barred against

Shakespeare as "a sort of beautiful Lusus Naturae, a delightful Monster—wild indeed, without taste or Judgment, but like the inspired Ideots of so much venerated in the East."[8] In the lecture sentence from which I have quoted, we do make our way to the reader's pleasure, but it is a telos that serves primarily as an opportunity to inquire into its source. John Payne Collier's 1811 notes confirm that insofar as poetry is concerned, "Pleasurable excitement was its origin & object" (*CLect*, 1.207). Pleasure-giving poetry begins with "constant activity of mind, arising from the poet himself" (Tomalin's notes transcribed by Campbell, *CLect*, 1.222). For the reader, it produces "a highly pleasurable Whole, of which each part shall communicate for itself a distinct & conscious pleasure" (*CN*, 3:4111). This is just one version of what was axiomatic for Coleridge, that a poem "must be one, the parts of which mutually support and explain each other"; that the poet "diffuses a tone and spirit of unity, that blends, and (as it were) *fuses*, each into each"; that the imagination reduces "multitude into unity of effect" and depends upon imitation to express "sameness and difference" (*BL*, 2:10–14 and 256). Our *cognition* of a poem's or a poet's success according to these criteria determines whether or not we experience pleasure, that is to say, "pleasureable activity of mind" (*BL*, 2:11).[9] If a poem is "a rationalized dream" (*CN*, 2:2087), then the poetic imagination, first and foremost a "power . . . put in action by the will and understanding," always remains "under their . . . controul" (*BL*, 2:12). The poet, then, is only ever a "great poet" if a "profound philosopher" (again and again, Coleridge insists that Shakespeare, a "philosophical aristocrat," was "no automaton of genius, no passive vehicle of inspiration" [*CLect*, 2.272; *BL*, 2:19; cf. *CN*, 3:4115]). And the reader repays the philosophical poet with "perpetual activity of attention"—what Coleridge called "intellectual pleasure" (*BL*, 2:15; *CN*, 3:4111) and experienced as "intellecturition" (*CM*, 1.653).

George Whalley, the first Bollingen editor of Coleridge's marginalia, points out that this neologism appears in one of Coleridge's notes in the margin of the *Works of Jacob Behmen* [Jakob Böhme], a four-volume edition that was a gift from Thomas De Quincey (*CM*, 1.lix). Coleridge summons multiple languages, even devising a nonce word, as he tries to describe something that is "*haud Jam Intelligens neque Intellectus*" ("this not-yet Intelligent [Intellecting] nor Intelligible [Intellected]"—*CM*, 1.653, n. 122[4]). Here is the series of synonyms that unfurls in the margin: "perpetual Intellecturition, a ποθοζ [pothos], Sehnsucht, Yearning, Ceres" (*CM*, 1.653). "Intellecturition" combines activity of the mind with desire (in his essay on the "*Prometheus* of Aeschylus," Coleridge refers to "ποθοζ or desire" [*CM*, 1.665, n. 140[4]]), with love (ποθοζ is synonymous with "*the being in love*" in one of Coleridge's marginal notes in Joseph Ritson's *A*

Select Collection of English Songs [*CM*, 4.292]), with longing, and with appetite (according to Friedrich Schelling, who had read Böhme, Ceres stood for languor plus *sucht*, or for "hunger" [*CM*, 1.665, n. 140⁴]). Whalley adds a "sexual component," arguing that for Coleridge, "the only way of rendering the feel of intellecturition is in a sexual image" (*CM*, 1.601, n. 52²). The reader engaged in intellecturition reaches out, longing for the sustaining pleasures of intellectual intercourse, for table talk that consists mostly of nu*r*ture (giving), but also a degree of self-serving nut*rition* (taking). The solitary act of reading is largely a pretext for the social, extroverted arts of conversation and lecturing. The primacy of intelligence in intellecturition answers to the mental activity that for Coleridge was the greatest pleasure and the necessary imposition for which reading was responsible. But intellecturition also entails outward- or other-directed activity that extends beyond mere talk to pedagogy. Coleridge's homemade abstract noun tallies with his yearning for someone with whom to talk, better still, someone who would just listen to him. Seamus Perry quotes Bryan Waller Procter, who thought that talking was for Coleridge "like laying down part of his burden." Coleridge no less than his critics could see the connection between himself and the Ancient Mariner. As Perry sympathetically notes, "[t]his is the act of uttering as a desperate '*out*ering, getting rid of'' (*CN*, 4:4954), an attempt to evade the prison of the unhappy self and make contact with a redeeming world without: 'Have Mercy on me, O something *out* of me!' (*CN*, 2:2453)."[10]

At one point in 1803, Coleridge told his brother that for three years, he had been reading at least eight hours a day (*CM*, 1.lxxxi). All of this appears to have been reading *for*—not merely for himself, or for knowledge or for pleasure, but for knowledge and pleasure that he could convey to others (this despite the fact that when he was twenty-four years old, he imagined himself as "a library-cormorant" who "seldom read except to amuse myself").[11] Kathleen Coburn, the first Bollingen editor of Coleridge's voluminous notebooks, quotes from an autobiographical fragment written by Coleridge two years before his death, when he was sixty years old. In what is called the "Folio Notebook," Coleridge begins with his childhood, passes on to his father's death, and then to his years at Christ's Hospital school. He remembers that a stranger gave him borrowing privileges at a circulating library in King's Street, Cheapside, and that he "*read thro* the whole Catalogue, folios and all . . ." He describes how his "whole Being was with eyes closed to every object of *present* sense—to crumple myself up in a sunny Corner, and read, read, read,—finding myself in Rob. Crusoe's Island, finding a Mountain of Plum Cake, and eating out a room for myself, and then eating it into the shapes of Chairs & Tables—Hunger and Fancy—".[12] Because what struck me when I first read this was what Coburn calls Coleridge's "solitariness," I was brought up short when I found Coburn shrewdly asking us to notice that "the plum-cake room had tables and chairs, in the plural, for *sociability*."[13] Books, Coleridge wrote in his notebook, were his "dear, very dear, Companions"; yet he often felt a "pang that the Author is not present . . . At times, I become restless: for my nature is very social" (*CN*, 2:2322). Even for the boy, there was something missing: someone to join him in table talk, or, at least, to pull up a chair and listen to what Coleridge had to say about what he had been reading.

In notes on "our Shakespear" that appear to date from 1811 or 1812, Coleridge wrote "that I have been <almost> daily reading him since I was ten years old" (*CLect*, 1.429). However, there does not seem to be any evidence that he took pleasure in reading Shakespeare with or out loud to others. What excited and motivated him was what he derived from his reading, what it led him to think and then to say. Even his earliest Shakespeare reading looks grim. The Reverend James Boyer, master of the upper grammar school at Christ's Hospital, required students to memorize Shakespeare and Milton. What Coleridge remembers, early in *Biographia Literaria*, is not the memorization *per se*, but the "time and trouble [it took] to *bring up* [what he had memorized], so as to escape his censure" (*BL*, 1.4). If this does, after all, conjure a kind of reading community, then it represents a benchmark level of Shakespearean negative sociability for Coleridge. There is no evidence of pleasure—Coleridge seems to have associated Boyer with vulnerable bottoms at least as much as with book learning—in fact, it may be that reading and reciting Shakespeare, as opposed to talking about what he read in Shakespeare, never satisfied Coleridge.[14] In John Payne Collier's notes, taken at an 1811 lecture on *The Tempest*, we find Coleridge refusing to "pass from the character of a lecturer into a mere reciter" (*CLect*, 1.366). When Henry Crabb Robinson complained in a letter to his brother about Coleridge's lectures that "C. can^t be induced to read Shakespear" (1.410), Crabb Robinson revealed what would please him but decidedly not his friend. And if we can credit De Quincey's jaundiced report, then "amongst Coleridge's accomplishments, good reading was not one; he had neither voice (so, at least, *I* thought), nor management of voice." (1.148). Coleridge's bent was pedagogy, not oratory. He was a professional lecturer—an educator who lectured on education as well as on literature—not an actor.

At times, then, there must have been what we now call a "disconnect" between what Coleridge set out to do in his lectures and what he accomplished. This gap between intention and effect has all of the hallmarks—rapture, abstraction, and self-absorption—of Coleridge attempting conversation. In Crabb Robinson's 1811 letter, he describes Coleridge's "pretended lectures" as "immethodical rhapsodies" (*CLect*, 1.409; Coleridge himself acknowledged that the *Biographia* was so "immethodical a miscellany" [*BL*, 1:64]). De Quincey, who appears to have attended Coleridge's second lecture in 1808, complained that the "passages he read, moreover, in illustrating his doctrines, were generally unhappily chosen, because chosen at haphazard" (*CLect*, 1.148). Crabb Robinson recorded in his diary that Lamb made fun of Coleridge for delivering a "lecture [supposedly on *Romeo and Juliet*] in the character of the nurse" (*CLect*, 1.283). But as far back as 1804, when he was first contemplating a series of Shakespeare lectures, Coleridge wrote to Sir George Beaumont that he would prepare by reading

> each scene of each play . . . as if it were the whole of Shakespere's Works—the sole thing extant. I ask myself what are the characteristics—the Diction, the Cadences, and metre, the character, the passion, the moral or metaphysical Inherencies, & fitness for theatric effect, and in what sort of Theatres—all these I write down with great care & precision of Thought & Language— / and when I have gone thro' the whole, I then shall collect my papers, & observe, how often such & such Expressions recur / & thus shall not only know what the Characteristics of Shakespere's Plays are, but likewise what proportion they bear to each other. (*CL*, 2:1054)

"Each . . . each . . . care & precision . . . collect . . . recur . . . proportion"—if this is anything, it is methodical. Coleridge describes a quasi-scientific collection of evidence, an orderly reading process that would enable him to produce proofs. We hear more of this sort in a much later letter, from 1819: "during a course of lectures, I faithfully employ *all* the intervening days in collecting and digesting the materials" (*CLect*, 2.346). On the one hand, meticulous data harvesting, on the other, rhapsody. There are several ways to explain this, the first of which is straightforward. R. A. Foakes, the editor of the Bollingen *Lectures*, argues that at first, the Coleridge who was "afflicted . . . by illness, opium-addiction, and other problems" frequently improvised and digressed. However, "[f]rom 1813 onwards he seems to have prepared with some care almost every lecture . . . he followed his notes . . . his later lectures were probably more obviously coherent and better organised than many of the early ones" (1.li). According to this version, Coleridge "consolidated and improved his technique" (1.liii). A second explanation—Coleridge's own (although Foakes finds it "untrustworthy" [1:i])—may be found in the same letter from 1819. There is indeed, as we have seen, a process of "collecting and digestion," of "consideration," and there are "study" and "principle"; but then Coleridge writes that "before I had proceeded twenty minutes, I have been obliged to push the MSS. away, and give the subject a new turn." So much for following his notes. "I know almost as little as any one of my audience . . . what they ["the words, illustrations, &c."] will be five minutes before the lecture begins." In fact, he crows, his auditors used to "threaten" him when they saw his sheaf of notes, "declaring they never felt so secure of a good lecture as when they perceived that I had not a single scrap of writing before me" (2.346–47).

Needless to say, all of Coleridge's lectures were not identical in style. He might work "without book" (*CLect*, 1.l) in one, read directly from notes in another. Any one lecture might mix methods. C. R. Leslie, who, unlike De Quincey, found Coleridge's voice "deep, and musical," lamented that "Coleridge's lectures were, unfortunately, extemporaneous." James Gillman, sounding like Coleridge himself, wrote that he "lectured from his notes, which he had carefully made; yet it was obvious, that his audience was more delighted when, putting his notes aside, he spoke extempore" (1.li, liii). Since both of these responses are from 1818–19, we have reason to doubt Foakes's increasingly coherent, improved-technique scenario. Given what we know of Coleridge, a third and more plausible explanation might take the form of Foakes's own observation that, although Coleridge "liked to boast of his ability to speak impromptu, the evidence suggests that he proceeded by a mixture of careful preparation and spontaneous development, backed up of course by years of reading and thinking about topics he dealt with and often by previous experience of speaking on them" (1.l).

Still, we should put some pressure on Foakes's casual use of the word *mixture*. To mix premeditation with spontaneity, method with rhapsody—no easy thing to do—is to accomplish precisely what Coleridge understood to be Shakespearean. The "deep Feeling & exquisite sense of Beauty" that Coleridge attributed to Shakespeare, he insisted were under "the command" of Shakespeare's "*own Will*." What Shakespeare felt and makes us feel derive from his "force of Contemplation" (*CN*, 3:3290). Shakespeare "first studied, deeply meditated, understood minutely—the knowledge become habitual gradually wedded itself with his habitual feelings, & at length gave him that wonderful Power" (*CN*, 3:4115; cf. the more famous version of this, in *BL*, 2:19). This does a nice job of describing the premeditated aspect of Coleridge's lectures on Shakespeare; but there is also an unforced and unscripted Shakespeare. Responding to lines describing the flight of Adonis from Venus, Coleridge argues for a Shakespearean *sprezzatura*, admiring his ability to bring together images and feelings "without effort & without discord." The answering response to this on a reader's part is "almost [to] lose the consciousness of words" (*CN*, 3:3290). As for spontaneity, just as Coleridge ascribes what is "notorious" and incorrigible about his penchant for speaking off the cuff to "*my nature*" (*CLect*, 2.347), or to what, according to John Payne Collier, Coleridge said "came warm from the heart" (*CLect*, 1.xlvi–xlvii), so "Chance & his powerful Instinct" (*CN*, 3:3290) never quite quit Shakespeare as sources of inspiration. Notwithstanding contemplation and aggregation, one might be "Great" at what one did by a "sort of Instinct" (*CN*, 3:3288) after all. One might be a "vehicle of inspiration," just not a "passive vehicle," "possessing," not "possessed by[,] the spirit" (*BL*, 2:19).

Coleridge wrote and lectured, on Shakespeare and much more, because he needed the income. Necessity trumped his fear that his audience would be filled with those he christened "Theomammonists" (*CL*, 2:1042). That he believed that he was getting a generally enthusiastic response, and that he was attracting paying audiences and mostly respectful notices in the press, must have provided further incentive. But his lectures were also a public, performative way to channel what he read, to vent his "impelling thoughts," thoughts which were "crowd[ing] each other to death" (*CM*, 1.lx). George Whalley writes that "reading was for Coleridge a strenuous activity, and that almost anything he took up to read could instantly arouse his mind to intense reflective and organising energy" (1.lx). The recurrent question for Coleridge was, what to do with all of this energy. When he finds a *semblable*, as Whalley points out was the case with Sir Thomas Browne, he admires him because "[a] library was a living world to him." "I have never read a book [*Religio Medici*], in which I felt greater similarity to my own *make* of mind" (1.758; cf. 1.lxi). Coleridge wrote to Sara Hutchinson that, like himself, Browne "loved to contemplate and *& discuss* his own Thought & Feelings" (1.763; my emphasis). He found "exquisite" the "gravity with which he [Browne] records contradictory opinions" (1.758). But Whalley is right to emphasize the Coleridgean insistence on organization. What was true for poetry was true for Coleridge the thinker: thoughts no less than poetic parts are laudable to the extent that they relate to one another and to some whole. Browne could live with contradictions, or with parts, but as Keats pointed out, this was more of a trial for Coleridge. And once again, Coleridge knew it. Throughout his life he acknowledged that when it came to organization, he fell short. He knew that like Browne, and in spite of his own desires, he was more apt to survey than to arrange. This recognition stands behind the admission that the *Biographia* is immethodical and it informs what Coleridge wrote in the Prospectus of *The Friend*:

I have employed almost the whole of my Life in acquiring, or endeavouring to acquire, useful Knowledge by Study, Reflection, Observation,
and by cultivating the Society of my Superiors in Intellect, both at Home
and in foreign Countries. You know too, that at different Periods of my
Life I have not only planned, but collected the Materials for, many Works
on various important Subjects: so many indeed, that the Number of my
unrealized Schemes, and the mass of my miscellaneous Fragments, have
often furnished my Friends with a Subject of Raillery, and sometimes of
Regret and Reproof. Waiving the Mention of all private and accidental
Hindrances, I am inclined to believe, that this Want of Perseverance has
been produced in the Main by an Over-activity of Thought, modified by a
constitutional Indolence, which made it more pleasant to me to continue
acquiring, than to reduce what I had acquired to a regular Form. Add too,
that almost daily throwing off my Notices and Reflections in desultory
Fragments, I was still tempted onward by an increasing Sense of the Im-
perfection of my Knowledge, and by the Conviction, that, in Order fully
to comprehend and develope any one Subject, it was necessary I should
make myself Master of some other, which again as regularly involved a
third, and so on, with an ever-widening Horizon. (*Friend*, 2.16)

"Over-activity of Thought"—Coleridge's benign version of thoughts crowding one another to death—and fragmentation are at odds with "regular Form."
If we can judge from some notes that follow the heading "Shakespere," printed
by Foakes as supplemental to the 1808 lecture series, then Coleridge conceived
of Shakespeare in similar terms. For Shakespeare, too, there was "difficulty
in arranging & disciplining the crowd of Thoughts which from that Matrix
rush in to enlist themselves" (*CLect*, 1.126). These crowding thoughts are no
less intense than they are for Coleridge, but Shakespeare's genius is to manage
them, to bring method to bear, to arrange and to discipline. In Shakespeare, the
"[h]eterogeneous united as in Nature" (*CLect*, 1.127). In Shakespeare, centrif-
ugal forces (he "becomes all things") are compensated for by centripetal forces
("yet for ever remaining himself") (*BL*, 2:20).
    Coleridge's Shakespeare annotations, notebook entries, and lectures consti-
tute a fragmented homage to the "harmonized Chaos" that he found in each
of Shakespeare's works (*CLect*, 2.224; not in reference to Shakespeare but to
"the perfect Form"). It is as if the uncanny blend of Shakespearean parts and
principles, of "*detail*" and "general construction," indemnified miscellaneity in
Coleridge, or as if discipline in the former counterbalanced disarray in the latter

(*BL*, 1:22n). With Coleridge, "[i]f one thought leads to another, so often does it blot out another"; in the best of circumstances, "[h]owever irregular and desultory his talk, there is *method* in the fragments" (*CN*, 3:3342; *Friend*, 1.449). With Shakespeare, there is more than method, or a "Link of Association" (*CM*, 4.734); there is always one "great purpose" (Collier's 1812 lecture notes; *CLect*, 1.390). Coleridge was constitutionally (and self-consciously) unsuited to stanching the flood of his "[h]ints & first Thoughts" (*CN*, 3:3881). Shakespeare could resolve "many circumstances ~~by~~ into one moment of thought to produce that ultimate end of human Thought, and human Feeling, Unity" (*CN*, 3:3247). Coleridge could, however, follow Shakespeare's lead. When Shakespeare brings "forward no subject which he does not moralize or intellectualize" (*CM*, 4.810), Coleridge tries to match him, intellectualization for intellectualization. And Coleridge takes pleasure in this, pleasure of the sort that was afforded him by Luther's *Colloquia Mensalia*, which "*potenziate[d]*" his thought (see *CM*, 1.ci). Pleasurable thought, or thoughtful pleasure, these constituted a satisfactory response to, and a way to acknowledge, Shakespeare's pervasive and "excellent Judgement" (*CM*, 4.810). They also occasionally might have enabled Coleridge to assuage his "desperate desire for a kind of imaginative wholeness and philosophical unity."[15]

The best way to get a feel for how Coleridge read Shakespeare is to look at the responses he left in the margins of the editions he read from, as well as to pursue what might at times have been his reading notes, and what he or note-takers have left us as a record of his lectures.[16] I began with two snippets of *Othello* marginalia and will return to more of this sort of evidence after setting out a few of the familiar, more general principles typically associated with Coleridge's account of Shakespeare. For one thing, Coleridge was committed to reading the plays not simply as poetry but as dramatic poetry. In the course of reading *Timon of Athens*, he laments that "Editors are all of them ready enough to cry out against Shakespear's laxities & licences of Style, forgetting that he is not merely a Poet but a *dramatic* Poet—that when the Head & Heart are swelling with fullness, a man does not ask himself whether he has grammatically *arranged*, but only whether (context taken in) he has *conveyed*, his meaning" (*CM*, 4.723). Shakespeare's heart may swell, but as I have already noted, Coleridge makes him out to be predominantly a poet of judgment, not instinct (not "immortal in his own Despite" [*CN*, 3:3288]). A corollary of this is Coleridge's recognition that Shakespeare always discriminates, that his drama is "an *imitation* of reality not a *Copy*" (*CM*, 4.780). With this distinction in mind Coleridge would refer to words and images that were "shakespearianized" (*CN*, 2:2274) and compare Shakespeare to Proteus, "able to become by power of Imagination another Thing . . . yet still the God felt to be there" (*CN*, 3:3247). Coleridge further observed in regard to Shakespeare's characters that they are hybrids, "*genera* intensely individualized": "class-characteristics . . . are so modified and particularized in each person of the Shakespearean Drama, that life itself does not excite more distinctly that sense of individuality which belongs to real existence" (*CLect*, 2.273 and *BL*, 2:33n). As John Payne Collier's report on one of Coleridge's 1811 lectures has it, "The characters were drawn rather from meditation than from observation, or rather by observation which was the child of meditation" (*CLect*, 1.306).

These are some of Coleridge's oft-repeated insights into reading Shakespeare. They, and quite a few more, have been noted; some have been absorbed into the realm of the "taken for granted," others have been modified, challenged, or dismissed out of hand. Coleridge's experience of reading Shakespeare, the ways he grappled with what was always for him Shakespeare's myriad-mindedness, has been less often noticed. Of course, he was neither the first nor the last reader to doubt his or her own competence when confronted with Shakespeare's writing. Take that adjective "myriad-minded." It appears in the notebooks, lectures, and the *Biographia Literaria*. In the latter instance, Coleridge begins chapter 15 by announcing his plans to apply the principles that he has been adducing to the "purposes of practical criticism" (*BL*, 2:13). Even *this* now-famous phrase, to the extent that it has to do with Coleridge reading Shakespeare in particular, is itself worth thinking about. Principles, critical analysis, practical criticism, all of these are to be brought to bear on Shakespeare, as if the Shakespearean text were spread out for examination and anatomization on a dissection table (in which case Coleridge again would be emulating Shakespeare, whom he described as "a comparative Anatomist" [*CLect*, 2.151]). The way to cope with, to tame, or simply to make sense of the "myriad" in "myriad-minded" is to conduct a thorough "investigation" according to set "principles": "[i]n this investigation, I could not, I thought, do better, than keep before me the earliest work of the greatest genius, that perhaps human nature has yet produced, our *myriad-minded** Shakespeare" (*BL*, 2:13). In his asterisked note, Coleridge explains that he has "borrowed" the phrase from the Greek—from a Greek monk's characterization of a Patriarch of Constantinople—because "it seems to belong to Shakespeare." This we can trace further back to 1801, to a brief notebook entry in which we first find Coleridge aligning the "hyperbole from Naucratius's

Panegyric of Theodorus Studites" with "Shakespeare?" (*CN*, 1:1070 and note). While there are good reasons to credit Coleridge's commitment to Shakespearean myriad-mindedness, we may still ask after the "perhaps" in the passage from *BL*, the "seems to" in his footnote, and the question mark after "Shakespeare" in the earlier note. Are such minuscule reservations evidence of resistance, of a will to withhold something—anything—from Shakespeare? How does one hold one's own in the face of (or against) Shakespeare?[17]

In a passage in Coleridge's notes, cancelled with a vertical line, that Foakes associates with one of the 1818 Shakespeare lectures, we again come upon "the myriad-minded man" (*CLect*, 2.112). And here, too, otherwise unremarkable encomia tell us something about Coleridge, as well as Coleridge's Shakespeare. In his lecture notes, Coleridge writes that what he plans to say "this evening" will require "~~my bes truest efforts~~." Even "Powers tenfold greater than mine would be incommensurate to the solution," would "leave a wide chasm, which our Love and Wonder alone can fill up"—as if after all is said and done, principles and investigation are beside the point. "Feeble ~~would every~~ will my voice be ~~that would~~ to my own ears, while I speak of Shakespear: and superflous [*sic*] must all praises be of the myriad-minded man whom all English Hearts feel to be above praise" (*CLect*, 2.112). Is any investigation sufficient unto Shakespeare? Will any praise satisfy the Shakespeare whose "*Genius*," still in 1833, Coleridge was associating with "Protean metempsychosis of the same idea, in an endless ~~nu~~ succession & multiplication of facts and incidents" (*CM*, 6.6811)? What with tenfold greater powers and a wide chasm on one side, feebleness and recourse to love and wonder ("wonder" becomes "Admiration" on the next sheet of paper) on the other, the odds are against us. Shakespeare comes at Coleridge not simply with his myriadness (which must, as Kathleen Coburn writes, pertain to "Coleridge's favourite 'unity in multeity'" [*CN*, 1:1070n]), but with the full force of his mind. If "consciousness of the Poet's Mind must be diffused over that of the Reader," then Coleridge must contend with its enveloping breadth (its myriadness, its diffusion) no less than its intensity (*CLect*, 1.86). Because Shakespeare is the "poet, whose mighty mind demands my utmost efforts," Coleridge asks his audience for "encouragement from your sympathy" in light of the "difficulty" of "the subject" (*CLect*, 2.112). H. H. Carwardine's notes confirm that at the 1818 lecture, Coleridge acknowledged that "[m]y words are indeed feeble when I speak of that myriad minded man who all artists feel above all praise" (*CLect*, 2.119). If not praise, then, perhaps analysis.

Always, for Coleridge, it is the mind that is put to the test.[18] According to the transcription of Tomalin's notes from an 1811 lecture, Coleridge explained that "[t]here was, in truth, an energy in the age, an energy of thinking, which gave writers of the reigns of Elizabeth & James, the same energy. . . . [T]he chief object . . . was to make the reader think—not to make him understand at once, but to show him rather that he did not understand, or to make him review, & re-meditate till he had placed himself upon a par with the writer" (*CLect*, 2.229). Here is an indication of what Coleridge may have expected of his audiences, not just in response to Shakespeare, but to himself: "[t]he effort & at first the very painful Effort of really *thinking*" (*CLect*, 1.187). And here, too, is an indication of what Coleridge felt, what he must have suffered and thrilled to, when he read Shakespeare. It is the optimistic version of what we find in his notebook, in notes that appear to anticipate a lecture in 1808 (Coleridge reminds himself to speak the following words in "a *low quiet voice*"): "I am deeply convinced, that no man, however wide his Erudition, however patient his antiquarian researches, can possibly understand, or be worthy of understanding, the writing of Shakespere" (*CLect*, 1.78). Reading Shakespeare, and the thinking concomitant to it, threatens exhaustion. If understanding is foreclosed, then how does one succeed as an analyst? Worse still, having expended energy and effort, then having endured pain, we still may find ourselves demeaned, having fallen well short of understanding Shakespeare. One memorable articulation of our thought process appears in *The Friend* (2.48–49):

> Alas! Legitimate reasoning is impossible without severe thinking, and thinking is neither an easy nor an amusing employment. The reader, who would follow a close reasoner to the summit and absolute principle of any one important subject, has chosen a Chamois-hunter for his Guide. Our Guide will, indeed, take us the shortest way, will save us many a wearisome and perilous wandering, and warn us of many a mock road that had formerly led himself to the brink of chasms and precipices, or at best in an idle circle to the spot from whence he started; but he cannot carry us on his shoulders; we must strain our own sinews, as he has strained his; and make firm footing on the smooth rock for ourselves, by the blood and toil of our own feet.

Coleridge does not quite strip reasoning or reading of pleasure when he writes that they are anything but amusing and easy. "Amusing" is the appropriate pejorative for that which is not really even reading. In *Biographia Literaria*, he recommends transferring "*amusement* . . . from the *genus*, reading," to "the indulgence of sloth" (1.34n). There is still a possibility of pleasure, but it accrues to those who have the stamina for "blood and toil." This would not be the Coleridge who "seldom read except to amuse" himself (*CL*, 1:260). Instead, cue the Coleridge who filled the margins of books, at least four editions of Shakespeare among them; the Coleridge who gave dozens and dozens of lectures on literature, many on Shakespeare; or the public intellectual Coleridge of *Table Talk*, *The Friend*, *The Watchman* and many more expressions of his restless mind.

On the title page of his copy of Schelling's *System des transcendentalen Idealismus*, Coleridge wrote, "[a] book, I value, I reason & quarrel wit[h] as with myself when I am reasoni[ng]" (*CM*, 4.453). When it came to reading Shakespeare, most quarrels Coleridge might have had with the playwright he displaced onto his editors. Warburton and Theobald really take their lumps; something like Keats's mostly good-humored but sometimes exasperated marginal mockery of Dr. Johnson crops up frequently. "Theobald *thinks*! But Sh. thought far better" (*CM*, 4.732). "Honest dull Theobald" (*CM*, 4.710). Responding to a Warburton emendation that Theobald adopts in the eight volume *Works* (1773) that Coleridge marked up, probably for J. J. and Mary Morgan (and for his 1808–1812 lectures), Coleridge wrote: "*Oh! Oh! Oh!* Lord have mercy on poor Shakspere!—& on Mr. W————n's mind's Eye!" (*CM*, 4.690). Apparently dull Warburton had emended "following" to "follying" because he was unable to imagine Titania's votaress "following" a "sail upon the land." Of course, Coleridge himself very frequently "corrected" the play he was reading, and many modern editors have dismissed any number of his emendations. The tenor of Coleridge's editorial commentary stretches from utter certainty ("There can be no doubt" [*CM*, 4.812]; "I do not hesitate to read . . ." [*CM*, 4.813]) to confidence ("More probably . . ." [*CM*, 4. 813]; "I rather think" [*CM*, 4.744]) to mere preference ("I should have preferred" [*CM*, 4.812]) to uncertainty ("I do not understand this, but I suspect . . ." [*CM*, 4.782]). Something more than impatience or mere annoyance can be felt when Coleridge takes on Theobald for accepting Warburton's decision to go with "Iudean" as opposed to "Indian": "[t]hus it is for no-poets to comment on the greatest of Poets!" Coleridge harrumphs. "To make Othello say, that he who had killed his wife was like Herod, who had killed his!—O how many beauties in this one Line were impenetrable by the *thought*-swarming ever *idea*less Warburton!" (*CM*, 4.748). It was easier and required less gumption to deride Warburton than to contend with the possibility that the Folio's "Iudean" is Shakespearean. Here and in general, Coleridge is most in his element when he is explaining, tutoring, or simply reasoning in the margins. The Iudean/Indian comment proceeds as follows: "Othello wishes to excuse himself on the score of ignorance; & yet not to excuse himself—to excuse himself by accusing. This struggle of feeling is finely conveyed in the word '*base*' which is applied to the *rude* Indian not in his own character, but as the momentary representative of Othello's." Although *accuse* bumping up against *excuse* has the feel of wit, I do not think that this is quite so polished. The three clauses in the first of these sentences sound more like Coleridge following Shakespeare's sail from the shore. Warburton's putative ignorance triggers a glimpse of Othello's; and yet Othello, tragic where Warburton is comic, makes of his very excuse a "momentary" self-accusation. Starting with "excuse," Coleridge reasons his way to "accusing." Coleridge can amuse himself when he reads Warburton or Theobald reading Shakespeare. When he goes at the "greatest of Poets" on his own, his thinking turns, as he would have it, more severe.

Coleridge could see the Ancient Mariner in himself and he recognized in Sir Thomas Browne his "own *make* of mind." With regard to reasoning, Coleridge famously asserted that "I have a smack of Hamlet myself, if I may say so"—of the Hamlet, that is, "who all the play seems reason itself" (*TT*, 2.61). While reasoning is the hallmark of Coleridge's Shakespeare marginalia, it is noteworthy that Coleridge's smack of Hamlet extends to the cognitive bifurcation that he attributes to Hamlet. On the interleaved sheets in the Ayscough Shakespeare, Coleridge comments on Hamlet's response to Claudius's revelry (Coleridge seems to have been annotating for James Gillman and for the lecture room). He first acknowledges Hamlet's "ratiocinative meditativeness," then he explains that the "co-presence of Horatio, Marcellus and Bernardo is most judiciously contrived." They make Hamlet's "impetuous eloquence perfectly intelligible" (*CM*, 4.844–45). Reason and eloquence, virtuous in their own right, may be at least partly contingent upon auditors. As Coleridge imagines the moment in 1.4, at the back of Hamlet's mind—"*a tergo*"—there is a "knowledge, the *unthought-of* consciousness, the *Sensation*, of human Auditors, of Flesh and Blood Sympathists" who both support and stimulate Hamlet. Meanwhile, the "*front* of the Mind, the whole Consciousness of the Speaker, is filled by the solemn Apparition" (*CM*, 4.845). This too, I think pertains to Coleridge's smack of Hamlet. Coleridge reads with the front of his mind filled by a solemn Shakespearean apparition at the same time that he derives, and requires, support from a cadre of lecture-goers like the ones whose encouraging sympathy he requested in 1818 (*CLect*, 2.112). No less than Hamlet's, Coleridge's reasoning is an "inward brooding . . . abstracted from external things." But again like Hamlet's, it is performative, abetted by auditors and by a lecturer's or a table-talker's "desire to escape from . . . inward thoughts" (from the *Bristol Gazette* report of Coleridge's 1813 *Hamlet* lecture [*CLect*, 1.544–45]).

We can observe Coleridge's self-consciously histrionic but nonetheless analytical style almost alongside Hamlet's. In the Ayscough Shakespeare, Coleridge developed the following substantial note in response to Hamlet's "A little more than kin, and less than kind":

> A little more than kin yet less than kind—Play on words—[due] either to 1. exuberant activity of mind, as in Shakespear's higher Comedy. 2. Imitation of it as a fashion which has this to say for it—why is not this now better than groaning?—or 3 contemptuous Exultation in minds vulgarized and overset by their success—Milton's Devils—Or 4 as the language of resentment, in order to express Contempt—most common among the lower orders, & origin of Nick-names—or lastly as the language of suppressed passion, especially of hardly smothered dislike.—3 of these combine in the present instance . . . (*CM*, 4.842)

George Whalley reminds us that Coleridge himself was "a keen punster" who "defended Shakespeare's much-criticised use of puns on several occasions" (*CM*, 4.842). In this instance, I think that it is the unexpected compression of mental activity and affect ("passion") that attracts Coleridge. And that he aims not so much to defend as ostentatiously to unpack it. How does one explain Hamlet's simultaneous comic lightness of expression and tragic eruption of contempt? Like the graveyard Hamlet who, exuberant though with "modesty enough," presses forward when Horatio demurs, Coleridge carefully, logically, and ever so slightly ridiculously works his way through five different glosses. Then—the faint sign of self-ridicule and the mark of Hamlet—he tugs on the carpet and admits that only "3 of these combine in the present instance." Which three? "I understand you not, my lord." "What dost thou mean by this?" Given that the comment that I have cited ends with Coleridge responding to a query of Richard Farmer's in the Ayscough *Hamlet*—"and doubtless Farmer is right in supposing the equivocation carried on into too much in the *Son*"—we may imagine Coleridge catching sight of his own blend of reason and equivocation. Another smack of Hamlet, perhaps. In the "Essays on the Principles of Method" in *The Friend*, where Coleridge refers to Hamlet's lines about dead Alexander as a "wayward meditation," he also speaks of the potential for "exuberance of mind" to interfere with "*forms* of Method" when there is an absence of a "*leading*

Thought" (*Friend*, 1.454–55). Coleridge's five enumerated options in response to *kin* and *kind* signal method; that he proffers no "leading thought" points to what he calls "want of Method" (1.454). Subtracting two (unspecified) options puts him somewhere betwixt and between. His multiple choices border on but skirt the "excess" that Hamlet, "meditative to excess" (1.452), flaunts. In *The Friend*, in his own if not in Hamlet's defense, Coleridge parenthetically remarks of "meditative excess" that "with due abatement and reduction, [it] is distinctive of every powerful and methodizing intellect" (1.452). Not much further on, he invokes "our 'myriad-minded Bard'" (1.453). In Hamlet and in Coleridge, the excessive, the wayward, the immethodical, myriad, and exuberant contend with method, with "just proportion . . . union and interpenetration" (1.457). That there is a synthesis in sight only for Shakespeare must be what makes us feel that we are more like Hamlet, or for that matter, Coleridge, than the Bard.

Which is not to say that Coleridge annotates or lectures with ingratiation in mind. He is no more a sentimentalist than is Shakespeare. In the Theobald edition, he responds to the murder of Lady Macduff and her son with a mixture of relief and shrewd consideration. "This Scene," he writes, "dreadful as it is, is still a relief because a variety, . . ." Here, as often, we sense that Coleridge may not yet know where he is heading. "Because" begins to effect a transition from pathos (dread and relief) to logos (variety), but the predictable dose of Coleridgean tutelage begins only with the repetition of "because." And even then, I think he surprises us, maybe even himself: "because a variety, because domestic/." Having found his way to domesticity, a full explanation may now follow: "because domestic/ Something in the domestic affections always soothing because associated with the only real pleasures of life" (*CM*, 4.729). In lecture notes transcribed by Ernest Hartley Coleridge, Samuel Taylor writes of "the sweet scene between Lady Macduff and the Child" and of Shakespeare's "fondness for children" (*CLect*, 1.528). The Theobald marginalia pivots more decisively and analytically on "variety." Coleridge may well be interested in "domestic affections," and if his life is taken into account, then especially those between a parent and child. However here, at least, he is thinking about craft, about what a play*wright* does. This is another "How is it done?" moment. How does Shakespeare produce dread and relief at the same time? Is variety an inevitable consequence of myriad-mindedness?

Something similar transpires when Coleridge comments on the discovery of Juliet, seemingly dead in her chamber (*CM*, 4.742). In fact, this is one instance when Coleridge comes close to quarreling with Shakespeare:

As the *Audience* knows that Juliet is not dead, this Scene is, perhaps, excusable—at all events, it is a strong Warning to minor Dramatists not to introduce at one time many different characters agitated by one and the same Circumstance. It is difficult to understand what *effect*, whether that of pity or laughter, Shakespear meant to produce/ The occasion & the characteristic Speeches are so little in harmony: ex. gratiâ, what the Nurse says, is excellently suited to the Nurse's Character, but grotesquely unsuited to the occasion—

Coleridge's "perhaps, excusable—at all events" is hardly aggressive; there is none of Dr. Johnson's massively self-confident ex cathedra determination here. But there is more than a hint of resistance. The sideways glance at minor dramatists (like Coleridge?) lasts one sentence only, and then Coleridge has Shakespeare back in focus when, again thinking about craft and effect, he wonders whether Shakespeare has lost his grip. The polarities endemic to Coleridge's thinking here are not hard to make out: "at one time many" is opposed to "by one and the same"; "harmony" is at odds with "grotesquely." Nor is it surprising that Coleridge should desire *an* effect, rather than simultaneous, contrary effect*s*. I think that we do too. It is difficult, maybe even embarrassing for us to manage both pity and laughter. But more embarrassing still for Coleridge is to have to excuse Shakespeare ("perhaps, excusable"). So much of what Coleridge writes in margins and what he says in lectures to audiences is built upon his confidence in Shakespeare's judgment. Indeed, so strong is this conviction that when he cannot figure out why Shakespeare writes what he writes, Coleridge usually defers to a time when he hopes he will be able to crack the nut. In the Ayscough edition, he refers to the "many instances I have ripened into a perception of Beauties where I had before descried faults" (*CM*, 4.807). Stymied by Oliver's speech about Orlando in *As You Like It*, he writes (in the Theobald edition margin): "[t]his has always *appeared* to me one of the most unshakespearian Speeches. . . . Yet I should be nothing surprised . . . to find it hereafter a fresh Beauty as has so often happened with me with the supposed Defects of the ανηρ μυριονουζ [myriad-minded man]" (*CM*, 4.697).[19]

Of course, in the *Romeo and Juliet* scene, the saving fact (face-saving for Shakespeare) is the Nurse. She, after all, is a grotesque. And Coleridge came back to her again and again, if for no other reason than that she was one of those characters that required him to adjust his thinking about Shakespearean meditation as opposed to observation. The commitment to a Shakespeare who was not merely "a child of nature . . . a Dutch painter copying exactly the object before him," depends on test cases like the Nurse. "In the meanest characters it was still Shakespeare, it was not the mere Nurse . . . but it was this great & mighty being changing himself into the Nurse . . . We know that no Nurse talked exactly in that way" (Dykes Campbell's transcription of Tomalin's notes [*CLect*, 1.224–25]). This version of the Nurse results in a "character of admirable generalization" (*CLect*, 1.308); she is the product of meditation. But "[t]he character of the Nurse," Coleridge later wrote in the Ayscough edition, is "the nearest of any thing in Shakespear to borrowing Observation" (*CM*, 4.829). This makes for a realist as opposed to an idealist version of the Nurse.[20] It is what we would expect from a Shakespeare whose plays are populated by "people who meet & speak to you as in real[i]ty life" (Carwardine lecture notes [*CLect*, 2.123]). Coleridge credited both versions of the Nurse because, at the end of the day, he regarded Shakespearean characters as "ideal realities" (via Collier [*CLect*, 2.514]), "at once nature & fragments of Shakespeare" (*CLect*, 1.289). Coleridge's "at once," which Seamus Perry equates with a recurrent Coleridgean "and yet" (or "muddle"), must be a consequence of Coleridge having to contend with Shakespeare's myriad-mindedness, the sign of his genius.[21] But what happens when Shakespeare fails to achieve "Harmonized Chaos" (*CLect*, 2.224)? When "occasion & . . . Speeches are so little in harmony," myriad-mindedness may produce an effect "unsuited to the occasion." In the margins of the text, Coleridge discovers that a theoretical commitment to a heterogeneous Shakespeare—a Shakespeare given to observation no less than meditation—cannot guarantee satisfaction in the event. Not harmony, but the grotesque may prevail.

Coleridge's Shakespeare marginalia often answered to his discursive, or what I have called his theoretical, claims about poetry (in *Biographia Literaria* and elsewhere). At other times, they served as lecture notes. Many, however, were generated largely within a zone of surprising discovery. It was all well and good to pronounce that "[t]he characters of Shakespeare are at once individual and general" (*New Times* report; *CLect*, 2.165). It was another thing, reading along in a play, to find oneself thoroughly perplexed: "[w]hat character does Sh. mean *his* Brutus to be?" (*CM*, 4.807). Here again, what disturbs Coleridge is what he finds "discordant"—the discrepancy between "our historical preconceptions of Brutus" and the Brutus of 2.1, who "would have no Objection to a King, or to Caesar, a Monarch in Rome." If lectures, especially Coleridge's early lectures, were the more appropriate venue for "illustrating great principles than for any minute examination" (Campbell's transcription of Tomalin's notes [*CLect*, 1.279]), margins were well suited to the "practical criticism" that Coleridge refers to in the *Biographia Literaria* and promised in his late lectures, "lectures of particular and practical Criticism" (*CLect*, 2.34). In the lectures, Coleridge tended to respond to the Shakespeare who was always "tell[ing] or explain[ing] some great & general truth inherent in human nature" (Collier's notes [*CLect*, 1.390]). In long notes on flyleaves, he might still focus on the Shakespeare who "brings forward no subject which he does not moralize or intellectualize" (*CM*, 4.810). But comments in the margins proper—commentary that feels like off the cuff response—are less given to grand statement. Or so it seems to me. The six Bollingen marginalia volumes, by virtue of their design matching each of Coleridge's comments to a particular "textus" (lines of text to which Coleridge is apparently responding) conjure a Coleridge whom H. J. Jackson imagines "moving along without stopping, or with only brief moments of hesitation, until he is arrested by something that makes him take notice, at which point he settles down to deal with it."[22] While this sounds accurate insofar as numerous apparent *aperçus* and passing arguments with the likes of Warburton are concerned, Elinor Shaffer has the much longer notes in mind and so demurs: "[a]nyone familiar with Coleridge's practice of reading a number of pages before expressing a marginal response, and writing comments on the entire work in the flyleaves, must feel some alarm at the arbitrariness of the [Bollingen] procedure." We beguile ourselves, Shaffer argues, if we imagine "an intimate dialogue between the author and Coleridge." Shaffer's Coleridge first "grasp[s] . . . the unity of an argument," then brings it to bear on an entire corpus, then "incorporate[s] gradually his own thoughts with others.'"[23] This would be the Coleridge who wrote at length to his son Hartley in defense of Shakespeare's Sonnets in his copy of Anderson's *The Works of the British Poets* (*CM*, 1.43). We again see this Coleridge at work on the Ayscough interleaves and, another example, on the fly-title to Jonathan Wordsworth's copy of Anderson's edition of the Sonnets (*CM*, 1.80–87). Hardly impromptu here, his elaborate ranking system classifies sonnets according to levels of "goodness" and entails placing sigla before, behind, and above the number of a sonnet to indicate whether it deserves praise for style, thought, or both. Across the length and breadth of his Shakespeare marginalia, both of these Coleridges are present.

To read Shakespeare is often to be reminded that particular words or phrases register with particular force for particular readers at particular moments. Coleridge is no exception. One of the small but lasting pleasures of reading his marginalia is to discover what attracts his attention. Thus, in the extant Shakespeare marginalia, Coleridge has nothing to say when Aufidius calls Coriolanus a "boy of tears" and Coriolanus three times repeats his "boy." However, when he reads Oliver's exclamation, "What, boy!" and Orlando's response, "Come, come elder brother, you are too young in this," Coleridge remarks: "There is a Beauty here. The word, *Boy*, naturally provokes and awakens in Orland [*sic*] the sense of his manly power . . . & makes him feel tha[t] he is no *Boy*" (*CM*, 4.697). Even less substantive but more aural is Coleridge's response to Theobald's certainty that Paulina would never be so "gross and blunt" as to call Leontes a fool; hence his suggestion that rather than speak of Leontes being "of a fool inconstant," Paulina must refer to his "soul inconstant" (*CM*, 4.707). Even though Coleridge accepts "fool," he has nothing at all to say about tact, or propriety, or decorum. He depends instead on his ear, and on his knowledge that late in his career, Shakespeare's "grammar" became more demanding: "1. My ear feels it Shakespearian—2. the involved grammar is Shakespearian . . . 3. the [Theobald's] alteration is most flat & *unshakespearian*" (*CM*, 4.707). In abbreviated commentary of this sort, there is the appearance of reasoning (1, 2, 3); but Coleridge relies almost entirely on sound and on intuition. An entirely auditory hunch is on display when Coleridge hears King Henry's "then happy low! Lie down; / Uneasy lies the head, that wears a crown." Argument dwindles to opinion which in turn fades into feeling: "I know no arguments by which to persuade any one of my opinion or rather of my feeling; but yet I cannot help *feeling* that Happy *low—lie—down!*—is either a proverbial expression or the burthen of some old Song" (*CM*, 4.714).

I mentioned Coleridge's eye. Reading *Antony and Cleopatra*, Coleridge saw something in his mind's eye that would not resolve itself. Caesar speaks of Octavia as a "piece of virtue," the "cement" that should keep his and Antony's love "builded," not the "ram to batter" their affection. Coleridge "suspect[s] both 'cement' and 'builded'. At least I recollect no instance in Shakespear of such an unrepresentable Eye-image, as—a *Piece* of—set betwixt—as *cement*—turned to a *Battering-ram*" (*CM*, 4.739). What is called for, what would better satisfy Coleridge's "eye-image" is "a Beam, or buttress-tree, or slant-column." As he protests, "Let not that which is the mortar of the wall, be turned to a ram!" Theobald was troubled by the "consonance of metaphor" here, but as Foakes points out, others have not batted an eye, so to speak (*CM*, 4.739, n. 135[1]). Still, it is difficult to get past Coleridge's objection. On such occasions, there is a compelling logic that is less Shakespeare's than Coleridge's own. For all that he may have fantasized a "convention of Antiquarians & Black Letter Commentators, to determine who should be appointed as the Editor of the Plays of Shakespear," complete with the "Ghost of Shakespeare . . . growl[ing] answers [to] their questions with a Let me alone! Let me alone" (*CM*, 6.6896), Coleridge himself was not a timid editor (nor anecdotist: Coleridge goes on to explain that, "recovering from their odorous Terrors," the conventioneers agreed that what they heard was "Let Malone"!).[24]

While grammar, syntax, logic, and etymology all contribute to Coleridge's practical criticism of the plays and poems, his local responses are themselves remarkable for their felicity. Consider, among his marginalia in the sixth volume of Rann's 1786–94 edition of the plays, Coleridge's astonishingly apt response to Lady Macbeth's "The raven himself is hoarse" soliloquy. "[C]haracter of L. M," he writes, "bullying her own feelings." There is a beauty here, so much so that it is hardly necessary for Coleridge to point out the "Bravado of Cowardice," much less to make the point about Lady Macbeth to which he is wedded, that "desperate reprobate Villains talk no such Language" (*CM*, 4.771). On its own, "bullying" captures the rhetorical, seemingly physical ("unsex me here"), task of self-persuasion that she sets herself. She gangs up on herself. That she knows she must do so tells us a good deal about her, and prospectively, about what she expects she will have to accomplish with Macbeth. Coleridge must have felt that he had hit upon the *mot juste* since two scenes later, he writes "[S]till [bu]llying" beside Lady Macbeth's lines about dashing out the brains of the babe that milks her (*CM*, 4.772). In what may have been the same month that Coleridge was reading from the Rann edition, it was reported in the *Bristol Gazette* that in his lecture, Coleridge confuted "the prejudiced idea of *Lady Macbeth* as a Monster." "[O]n the contrary, her constant effort throughout the play was, if the expression may be forgiven, to *bully* conscience" (*CLect*, 5.532). In the lecture at the White Lion, Coleridge modulates from "feelings" to "conscience." The accuracy of the *Gazette* report may be gauged by "if the expression may be forgiven" and by the fact that it is conscience—the cowardice of Macbeth's no less than Lady Macbeth's conscience—that is still Coleridge's theme in his *Macbeth* commentary in the Ayscough edition, where the word appears six times (*CM*, 4.786–94). "[B]ullying," however, does not reappear in the Ayscough interleaves. Instead, Coleridge finishes off a lengthy comment on the play's first scenes with "'Lady Macbeth = with the valor of my Tongue.' Day-dreamer's valiance" (*CM*, 4.789). "Valiance" obviously tallies with "valor," and etymologically (L. *valens*, strong), it may even contain a trace of bullying, but it is flaccid in comparison.

The editors of Coleridge's Shakespeare marginalia help us to see how often Coleridge had recourse to neologisms to say what he was trying to say. Does this have something to do with Shakespeare having exhausted readily available English, or with the rate at which Shakespeare himself begot new words? Is there a quiet contest with Shakespeare that Coleridge keeps reentering? Or is this simply Coleridgean intellecturition? Reaching for the apposite response must have made for one of the fine pleasures he took in construing Shakespeare. Midway through his commentary on the opening scenes of *Macbeth* that I have just quoted from, Coleridge notes in passing the "*unpossessedness* of Banquo's mind," then finds him "unintroitive" (*CM*, 4.787). The OED attributes both of these to Coleridge and both are marvelous. The effectiveness of the first must derive in some measure from the way it reminds us of the "possessedness" of Macbeth's mind. Because Banquo's mind, by contrast, is characterized by 'un-ness,' Coleridge goes on to describe it (once again word-coining) as an "unsullied un-scarified Mirror" for Macbeth. This suggests to me that it was Shakespeare's method to pair "'un'-characters," these thinned out interlocutors, with dense tragic protagonists. Thus Hamlet has his Horatio, Antony his Enobarbus, and Lear his Kent. They can be "wholly present to the present Object," as Coleridge writes of Banquo, because they are "unpossessed," without the plague of conscience, insinuating dreams, even the illusion of depth. About Banquo's response to the witches, then, Coleridge does not mince words. His is merely a "*natural* Curiosity" (*CM*, 4.788; my emphasis), natural in the way a fool is natural, is an idiot, not an artificial, cunning, or inquiring jester. Banquo's questions are the ones "a Girl would make after she had heard a Gypsey [*sic*] tell her School-fellow's Fortune—all perfectly general—or rather *planless*."

The simultaneous femininization and infantilization of Banquo, his diminution, enables Coleridge better to calibrate Macbeth. The standard is curiosity. On the one hand, there is Banquo's natural curiosity, the generalized, planless question-raising awakened by the unfamiliar. On the other hand, there is a borderline unhealthy *curiositas*, the sort of curiosity that makes Horatio—Hamlet's Banquo—feel uncomfortable. Hamlet aims to use his imagination to trace the dust of Alexander. Horatio, like us given over to what Coleridge calls "the common solution" (*CM*, 4.839), warns that "'Twere to consider too curiously, to consider so." Coleridge's Macbeth is similarly bent on "reasoning on a problem already discussed in his mind" (*CM*, 4.788). Like Hamlet, Macbeth is introitive ("enterable"; Coleridge also coined "extroitive"—*CM*, 4.688), and like Horatio, Banquo is "unintroitive" (not "enterable"; what we call impenetrable or unreflective). He only "addresses the appearances" (*CM*, 4.787) because his is the "easily satisfied mind of the self-uninterested" (*CM*, 4.788; again "un"). All of which makes Macbeth self-interested—"*self-concerning*" is Coleridge's way of putting it (*CM*, 4.788). Macbeth's self and his mind are full to the brim. Banquo's are "un." While some of us may want to attribute more depth to

Banquo (or to Horatio, or Enobarbus, or Kent), Coleridge continues to think in terms of how Shakespeare does what he does. Coleridge's unique marginal comment devoted to Kent reveals an "un-character" made up of allegorically "perfect goodness . . . and yet the most *individualized*." The point of Kent's hybridity is what it allows Shakespeare to do to us: it "acts on our feelings in Lear's own favor" (*CM*, 4.819). In *Macbeth*, dramaturgical technique requires a conspicuous distinction between "Banquo's mind" and "Macbeth's Mind" (*CM*, 4.787). Only the latter can be a repository for conscience, let alone possessed.

There are quite a few more neologisms to be found in Coleridge's Shakespeare marginalia. We already have seen "sympathists"; there are also "credibilizing," "featurely," "friendism,"and "accrescence," among others. These nonce words point us in another direction from the Coleridge who introduced us to Shakespeare the dramatic poet, from Coleridge the moral critic, and from the Coleridge I myself have been stressing, the analytical commentator on Shakespearean judgment, not genius. Poet that he was, he seems to have listened to Shakespeare the wordwright and to have responded in kind. That he found his way to what he took Banquo to be not simply via familiar terms but through coinages like "introitive" suggests that the process of Coleridgean character criticism may at times commence with an apt word, not with ethics or action or even psychology. Reading the earlier poet's coinages appears to have triggered the later's. In fact, not just his characters, but Shakespeare himself taxed Coleridge's word hoard. Struck by the intensity of Aufidius's hate for Coriolanus, Coleridge writes that only his "deep Faith in Shakespear's *Heart-Lore* (Herzlehre)" convinces him that Aufidius's fury "is in nature" (*CM*, 4.730). To get at what might be a "mere anomaly" on Shakespeare's part, Coleridge digresses through German back to English, striking a new English coinage off a common German compound in order to explicate character—Shakespeare's as well as Aufidius's.

Greek and Latin frequently helped Coleridge on his way to comprehension and interpretation (cf. *CM*, 4.736, 469, etc.), but German has its own curious relation to Coleridge's immersion in Shakespeare. While he lived in Germany, Coleridge composed German vocabulary lists in his notebooks. He read widely, sometimes turning to works in German that he knew well in English. Gottfried August Bürger's adaptation of *Macbeth* is a case in point. Part of what seems to have transpired when Coleridge read Bürger's *Macbeth* has to do with acoustics, with the way particular German words must have sounded in Coleridge's ears at the very moment that he would have been recalling Shakespeare's English. There is also evidence that Coleridge was struck by Bürger's choice of words. He seems to have experienced a kind of semantic or linguistic ricochet, with words from *Macbeth*, Coleridge's understanding of those words, Bürger's words, and Coleridge's translations of Bürger's words all simultaneously in play. At one point, Coleridge copied into his notebook Bürger's *"Wann sichs ausgetum-melt hat"* (*CN*, Text 1:354 *f*37ᵛ). Even as he would have savored and worked over *"ausgetummelt,"* perhaps hearing "tumult" or understanding "bustle" (or "romp"), he also would have been hearing the "hurly-burly" of "When the hurly-burly's done." Remarkably, he was also hearing or thinking in Latin, since on the same line he writes *"Cum desaeviit Temp,"* apparently hearing Senecan rage (*CN*, Notes 1:354 *f*37ᵛ). Julian Charles Young is not the only one to have noticed that Coleridge had a "defective ear" when it came to "his pronunciation of any language but his own." He was "unintelligible . . . when he tried to speak" German.[25] So while the sounds of these words must have registered after some fashion for Coleridge, I imagine that what intrigued him most were degrees of synonymy and felicity.

He certainly noticed the inventiveness of Bürger's versions of several other lines from the opening scene of *Macbeth*, along with what he may or may not have taken to be German neologisms. In the section of his vocabulary list that he charmingly and pseudoscientifically entitled "Names of Spirits, Men, Birds, Beasts, Fishes, and Reptiles, and of the constituent Parts of the Same," Coleridge copied down *"Wann die Krah am Aase kraht/*—Crow—Carrion—*dem beschmeissten Aase*—the fly-blown Carcase." The first phrase here ("when the crow croaks on the carrion") corresponds to Shakespeare's "When the battle's lost and won" (*CN*, Text and Notes 1:354 *f*7ᵛ). Under the rubric "Sensation, Passion, Touch, Taste, and Smell," Coleridge wrote *"Heiss in Kalt,"* no doubt noticing that to "Fair is foul and foul is fair," Bürger added "hot in cold [and cold in hot]" (*f*18). And under a heading which he first wrote but then crossed out ("Time & Space & their Relations"), Coleridge copied Bürger's *"Daumen-breit vor Eulenflug"* (*CN*, Text 1:354 *f*97ᵛ). While "a thumbsbreadth before owl-flight" stands for Shakespeare's "That will be ere set of sun," it was the typi-cally German compound noun that attracted Coleridge. Kathleen Coburn has noticed that Coleridge came back to *"Daumenbreit"* some five years later, in a notebook entry (*"thumbsbreadth from Sunset"*) written when he was in Scotland (*CN*, Notes 1:354 *f*97ᵛ; Text and Notes 1:1449 *f*4). Reading Bürger puts us at some remove from Coleridge reading and marking up Shakespeare's plays; still, each of these notations reminds us of the extent to which Coleridge met Shakespeare on the field of words. For all that he puzzled over images, motives, and meanings, Coleridge's desire to express his sense of a character, a scene, or an action in the most telling way is unmistakable and irrepressible. "The power of Poetry is by a single word to produce that energy in the mind as compells [*sic*] the imagination to produce the picture" (Collier's transcription of his own shorthand notes, taken in 1811 [*CLect*, 1.362]). Hence Coleridge zooms in on the "simple <happy> epithet *crying*" in Prospero's "Me and thy crying self," and on "young" ("the unobtrusive and yet fully adequate mode of introducing the main Character") in Horatio's "Let us impart what we have seen tonight / Unto young Hamlet" (*CLect*, 1.362 and 2.296). Hence another of Coleridge's splendid coinages. Having noticed the servingmen's "[w]it-combats and Quarreling with Weapons of sharper edge—all in humble imitation of their Masters" in *Romeo and Juliet*, Coleridge allows as how "there is a sort of unhired fidelity, an *our* ishness about it that makes it rest pleasant on one's feelings" (*CM*, 4.827). This sounds something like the relief due to the "real pleasures" of the "domestic" with which Coleridge says we respond to Lady Macduff's murder, but the compelling words here—"*our* ishness"—are entirely Coleridge's own. They dutifully acknowledge the servants' clan loyalty and perhaps our instinct to support this at the same time that they make it feel only skin deep, more a fashion than a conviction. Because Coleridge has invented a way to say what he thinks of an action and its motive, and because he appeals so shrewdly and so cleverly to our ears and to our imaginations, his words insinuate themselves into our settled sense of this familiar scene and leave there their tinct.

Indeed, Coleridge's effectiveness as a Shakespeare reader is apparent in a host of ways, save one. He listens closely to, even looks closely at, Shakespeare's words. Because he assumes that Shakespeare writes in accord with judgment, not instinct, he finds evidence of craft and calls it to our attention. He tutors us in the exigencies of dramatic poetry and in so doing, advances well beyond his eighteenth-century precursors' understanding of Shakespearean figures and conceits. He is responsive to the generic as well as the particular aspects of Shakespearean characters. And he is a shrewd, rarely sentimental critic of their conduct. Coleridge, then, must be our first professional reader of Shakespeare. His talk, lectures, and marginalia do show signs of connoisseurship and appreciation, but first and foremost, they consist of explanation. Coleridge the theorist explains method in Shakespeare. Coleridge the philosopher explains meaning in Shakespeare. Coleridge the moralist explains character and motive. Coleridge the poet explains metaphor. Coleridge the editor adjudicates cruxes. The constant, endless work of explanation is also his great pleasure. He models intellectual encounters with Shakespearean texts, imagining that we too will find such intellecturition pleasurable.

Only when Coleridge loses his analytical edge, when he sets aside the "How is it done" question and indulges in something like what follows, does he run the risk of disappointing us. In the Ayscough edition of *Romeo and Juliet*, Coleridge comments on 1.4, where Shakespeare "introduces Mercutio to us":

> O how shall I describe that exquisite ebullience and overflow of youthful Life, wafted on over the laughing Wavelets of Pleasure & Prosperity, Waves of the Sea like a wanton Beauty that distorted a face on which she saw her lover gazing enamraptured, had wrinkled her surface in the Triumph of its smoothness—Wit, <~~Fane~~ ever wakeful, Fancy (busy &) procreative as Insects,> Courage, an easy mind that without cares of its own was at once disposed to laugh ~~at~~ away those of others & yet be interested in them/ these and all congenial qualities, melting into the common copula of all, the man of quality and the Gentleman, with all its excellencies & all its foibles—/ (*CM*, 4.829–30)

We have every reason to expect that Coleridge will ask how he might best explain, not describe, Mercutio. This was what he did in an 1811 lecture, when he analyzed Mercutio as a type. Along with Berowne and Benedict, Mercutio springs from the class of characters known as gentlemen: "[t]hey were men who combined the politeness of the Courtier with the faculties of intellect; the powers of combination which only belong to an intellectual mind" (Collier's notes [*CLect*, 1.290]). Four days later, back in the Great Room of the London Philosophical Society, Coleridge once again essayed Mercutio, this time explaining that he "was a man possessing all the elements of a Poet: high fancy, rapid thoughts: the whole world was as it were subject to his law of association . . ." (Collier's notes [*CLect*, 1.307]). But in the Ayscough commentary, Coleridge's own fancy takes flight, and in the event, his language pales. Wending his way toward an acknowledgment of Mercutio's generic aspect—"the man of quality and the Gentleman"—Coleridge first elaborates an almost impenetrable sea metaphor neither the tenor nor the vehicle of which can be aligned confidently with Mercutio or Romeo (or Juliet?). He then unhappily mixes wit, fancy, procreative insects, and courage, of all things. The dull imprecision of every bit of this ("overflow," "wafted," "Wavelets," "wanton," "gazing," "smoothness," "melting," etc.) is made still more numbing when set alongside Mercutio's disquieting, high-wire facility. What seems to have happened is that for a moment only, Coleridge the professional reader has given himself up to inspiration. But Shakespeare at his best (with Mercutio, for example) sets the bar very high, and in the Ayscough remarks, at least, Coleridge makes an unusual error in judgment. Rather than make his opening salvo, his "O . . . exquisite," serve (as we have seen "O excellent" serve) as prelude to explication, Coleridge loses himself, and us, in vapid conceits.

Across the hundreds and hundreds of Bollingen pages that I mentioned at the start, there is mercifully little of Coleridge the inspired warbler. Instead, whether we pretend that we are peering over the shoulder of the reader or reconstituting what was said by the lecturer, we have to do with Coleridge thinking, thinking out loud, thinking about what explains the Shakespearean text, thinking about what we need to know. Coleridge might let himself get away with his own hackneyed waves and wavelets, but in one last example, we may observe him bearing down on no less a character than Lear with all of the marginal force of his high poetic and moral standards. Commenting in Ayscough on Lear's "Ingratitude! thou marble-hearted fiend, / More hideous, when thou shew'st thee in a child / Than the sea-monster," Coleridge zeroes in on "[t]he *one* general sentiment, as the main spring of his Feelings throughout, in Lear's first speeches—in the early stage the outward Object is the Pressure—not yet sufficiently familiarized with the anguish to for the imagination to work upon it" (*CM*, 4.820). This is to warn us that until Lear truly is bound upon a wheel of fire, the sources of his anguish will remain more generalized, more impersonal, more outward than inward. But Coleridge also has a literary critical point to make, that Lear's words themselves, his "marble-hearted fiend," spring from an imagination still untested. It being only the fourth scene of the play, our imaginations along with Lear's have a long way to go and so much anguish still to familiarize themselves with. Coleridge's ethical-literary point must be that early on in *King Lear*, Shakespeare is self-disciplined enough to rein in his own imagination. He is also self-assured enough, since with "marble-hearted fiend" Shakespeare risks our noticing his own flat footedness without our comprehending that it is tactical. This, I have been arguing, is where Coleridge explains how it is done.

II

JOHN KEATS ON
SITTING DOWN TO READ
SHAKESPEARE ONCE AGAIN

In a letter that he began on April 17, 1817, while lodging at Mrs. Cook's in Carisbrooke, on the Isle of Wight, twenty-one year old John Keats wrote to his "dear [John Hamilton] Reynolds" that he was "about to become settled."[1] Having explored the island, he had already "found several delightful wood-alleys, and copses, and quick freshes" (6; the latter is Caliban's phrase for freshwater springs). The nesting that now followed was for Keats both casual fussing and apotropaic ritual:

> I have unpacked my books, put them into a snug corner—pinned up [Benjamin] Haydon—Mary Queen of Scotts, and Milton with his daughters in a row. In the passage I found a head of Shakspeare [*sic*] which I had not before seen—It is most likely the same that George spoke so well of; for I like it extremely—Well—this head I have hung over my Books, just above the three in a row, having first discarded a french Ambassador— Now this alone is a good morning's work. (5)

Settling in to read and to write, hanging one portrait and demoting another, finding the right place for his editions of Spenser and Shakespeare—not just Keats's ambition but his humility and his humor are audible here. But what explains all of this stalling and puttering? Keats begins his letter by telling Reynolds that, "Ever since [two days earlier] I wrote to my brothers from Southampton I have been in a taking" (5). At the end of the portion of the letter that he wrote on the 17th, just before he writes out a sonnet entitled "On the Sea," Keats seems to circle back to his having been agitated: "From want of regular rest, I have been rather *narvus*—and the passage in Lear—"Do you not hear the sea?"—has haunted me intensely" (6).

In a taking and *narvus*: the causes of Keats's distress were twofold. He was not making much headway with *Endymion*. Having agreed to Shelley's flattering if sly proposal that each of them try his hand at a long poem, Keats was getting nowhere fast. As it turned out, holing up on the Isle of Wight was no help to him. He probably is being self-deprecating when he calls unpacking a "good morning's work"—in a letter to his brother George (it is now missing but Keats transcribed some of it in an October 8, 1817, letter to Benjamin Bailey) that also dates from the spring, he compared reading a short poem—"a Morning [*sic*] work at most"—unfavorably with the pleasures of working through "4000 Lines" that have tested a poet's "Powers of Imagination" (27). Keats was also reading Shakespeare's plays intensively throughout 1817, and both Shakespeare and his reputation were continuously on his mind. He began a letter on May 10 to Haydon by quoting seven lines on "Fame" from *Love's Labor's Lost* and wondering whether he had the "right to couple" himself with Haydon in response to the King of Navarre's speech about bating death's "keen edge" with endeavors that will make men "heirs of all eternity" (11). Keats's mood swings are evident in another letter written on the same day to Leigh Hunt: "I vow that I have been down in the Mouth lately at this Work. These last two day [*sic*] however I have felt more confident—I have asked myself so often why I should be a Poet more than other Men. . . . What a thing to be in the Mouth of Fame" (10). In the missing letter to his brother, Keats acknowledges that even if he completes *Endymion*, he will be but "a dozen paces towards the Temple of Fame" (27). Staving off a Shakespeare-induced bout of Gloucester-like despondency with "On the Sea," Keats nonetheless begins the sestet of his sonnet by invoking "ye who have your eyeballs vext and tir'd." He seems to be hanging on by his fingernails when he writes to Haydon that "I never quite despair when I read Shakespeare" (14).[2]

What with his "horrid Morbidity of Temperament" (13), Keats was susceptible to being shut down by Shakespeare. "He has left nothing to say about nothing or any thing," Keats wrote to Reynolds. "He overwhelms a genuine Lover of Poesy with all manner of abuse" (40). In November, Keats was reading Shakespeare's Sonnets and marveling that "they seem to be full of fine things said unintentionally." Stunned by the Shakespearean "intensity of working out conceits," Keats asks, "Is this to be borne?" (40). In April, he tried to recoup by turning reading Shakespeare into a parlor game. He suggested that Reynolds and Keats's brothers celebrate Shakespeare's upcoming birthday by sending him "a Word or two on some Passage in Shakespeare that may have come rather new to you; which must be continually happening, notwithstand^g that we read the same Play forty times" (7). Keats gets the ball rolling with lines from *The Tempest* that never "struck me so forcibly as at present": "Urchins / *Shall, for that vast of Night that they may work*, All exercise on thee—" (7). This was but one of many lines that Keats both underlined and marked in the margin in his copy of *The Tempest*, so why single it out here? Has Shakespeare been exercising on Caliban-Keats throughout the vast of night? And what about "*forty* times"? Cleopatra, who overwhelms her lover with all manner of abuse, "hop[s] forty paces through the public street" (2.3.239).

Keats was the first to admit that reading Shakespeare could nonplus him. "I shall I think never read any other Book much," he told Haydon. "I am very near agreeing with Hazlit [*sic*] that Shakspeare is enough for us" (14).[3] But the possibility of depletion or preemption is diminished in these lines when Keats inserts telling words of qualification. "I think," "much," "very near": these monosyllabic demurrals preserve a margin of creative breathing space. In fact, reading Shakespeare could also fortify Keats. Just when he had become "all in a Tremble from not having written any thing of late," Shakespeare's haunting line gave rise to his sonnet "On the Sea." Writing the poem did him "some good. I slept the better last night for it." But "this Morning . . . I am nearly as bad again." Striking Keats forcibly puts his "nerves . . . in their infancy again" (*The Tempest*, 1.2.485), so he must find a way to convert "*narvus*" into reinvigorated "nerve": "I must think that difficulties nerve the Spirit of Man—they make our Prime Objects a Refuge as well as a Passion" (11–12). If Shakespeare unnerves Keats, he also nerves him. Keats's diction—haunt, tremble, strike, nerve, abuse—is susceptible to de-metaphorizing because Keats reads and writes Shakespeare psychosomatically. Like the subsequent writers discussed in this volume (Woolf, Olson, Berryman, Ginsberg, Hughes), his was a thoroughgoing mind-body reaction to Shakespeare.

In his letter to Haydon, Keats weaves Shakespeare deeply into the fabric of his self-conception, coupling acute self-doubt with lofty aspiration. He has been reading—evidently Shakespeare, among others—"about eight hours a day" and "truth is I have been in such a state of Mind as to read over my Lines and hate them. I am 'one that gathers Samphire dreadful trade' the Cliff of Poesy Towers above me" (12). Child Keats, on the march with *Endymion*, has come to the "dread summit" (4.6.57) of *King Lear*; but like Shakespeare's samphire gatherer, he is at only the half-way point (4.6.14–15). And as he himself acknowledges, "There is an old saying well begun is half done'—'t is a bad one. I would use instead—Not begun at all 'till half done'" (12). Viewed from atop the cliff that Edgar conjures for Gloucester, the "fishermen that walk upon the beach / Appear like mice" (4.6.17–18). When Keats reports that his brother Tom has been reading Pope's Homer to him, he says with confidence that the verses "seem like Mice to mine" (12). Keats's vertiginous play of perspectives is as confusing as Edgar's and it, too, relies on distortions of the mind and body. He is on top and he is half way up, he is the precariously perched samphire gatherer, he is Edgar the illusionist, Poor Tom fleeing Flibbertigibbet (Shakespeare?), and he is tormented Gloucester. He tries to steel himself, contending that "the Trumpet of Fame is as a tower of Strength the ambitious bloweth" (12), but his flagrantly mixed metaphor betrays doubt and awkwardness. "Is it too daring to Fancy Shakespeare" his "Presider," he asks Haydon? "I hope for the support of a High Power while I clime this little eminence and especially in my Years of more momentous Labor" (12). Even here, Shakespeare's professional success bears down on Keats—the also ambitious Shakespeare who promised the Earl of Southampton "some graver labor" than *Venus and Adonis* (Dedication, 6).[4] Having dared to claim Shakespeare as his "good Genius presiding over" (12) him, Keats recurs to the portrait that he was traveling with: "When in the Isle of Wight I met with a Shakespeare in the Passage of the House at which I lodged—it comes nearer to my idea of him than any I have seen—I was but there a Week yet the old Woman made me take it with me though I went off in a hurry—Do you not think this is ominous of good? (12) "Ominous" may mean favorable or Keats may mean it neutrally, but its familiar, sinister connotation makes "ominous of good" a parapraxis that captures Keats's hopes and fears.[5]

The Carisbrooke Shakespeare, which traveled extensively with the peripatetic Keats, usually found a place near his books or writing desk. In 1819, he was again "sitting opposite the Shakspeare I brought from the Isle of wight," its frame now draped with the "silk tassels" with which Georgiana, his sister-in-law, had decorated it, maybe affectionately mocked it (214).[6] For all that Keats kept reinstalling himself beneath the presider's gaze, he also indicated a need for mental and physical distance from it. In a March 1819 letter to his sister Fanny, he fantasized about a huge, "handsome Globe of goldfish" that he would set before a "handsome painted window" shaded "round with myrtles and Japonicas": "I should like the window to open onto the Lake of Geneva—and there I'd sit and read all day like the picture of somebody reading" (203).[7] Having imaginatively constituted an ideal reading space, Keats frames it, then glides quietly in an out-of-body moment from subject to object. As for Shakespeare, he makes a cameo appearance early in this letter, but Keats deftly absents all authors from his ekphrastic scene of reading (unless, that is, Keats's Globe intimates Shakespeare's).

The still life with reader that Keats composes bears comparison with lines written by thirty-four year old, pre-"Combray" Marcel Proust in "On Reading" ("*Sur la lecture*"), his preface to his translation of Ruskin's *Sesame and Lilies* (*Sésame et les Lys*, Paris 1906).[8] As Keats admired Shakespeare, so Proust admired Ruskin; as Keats's Shakespeare reading was part and parcel of his emergence as a writer, so reading Ruskin (in this instance, Ruskin writing about reading) was for Proust; and as reading could nerve Keats or make him "rather *narvus*," so Proust warned that, although reading could be "the initiator whose magic keys open to our innermost selves the doors of abodes into which we would not have known how to penetrate," it could also, like "nervous ailments" ("affections du système nerveux"), substitute for rather than wake us to "the personal life of the spirit" (43). In his preface, Proust reminisces about the times in his youth when he gave himself over to what he calls the "spell" ("*sortilège* [27]) of reading—if not amidst "myrtles and Japonicas" then "under the hazels and hawthorns of the park" (33). Only later did he begin to find paths of resistance, just as in this preface he acknowledges that he finds himself at odds with Ruskin. Moreover, for Proust as for Keats, reading is embodied, a physical as well as a metaphysical activity. Proust writes not of what he read but where he read ("the dwellings and the ponds" [3]), and he writes about settling into (*Je m'installais*) a chair perfectly positioned for reading:

> Who does not remember, as I do, those books read during vacation time, that one used to take and hide, one after another, in those hours of the day that were peaceful enough and inviolable enough to be able to give them refuge. . . . (I settled on a chair near the little wood fire) where I would have as companions, very respectful of reading, only the painted plates hung on the wall, the calendar whose sheet of the previous day had been freshly pulled, the clock and the fire which speak without asking you to answer them, and whose peaceful talk devoid of meaning does not come, like the words of men, to substitute a different sense from that of the words you are reading. (3 and 5)

Proust remembers the thrill of being *caché* and *inviolable* while everyone else is on promenade. The abandon and solace of reading, "*un plaisir divin*," are impatient with any "*obstacle vulgaire*." A space is found and a spell is cast; then, how dismaying it is to have them interrupted by "lunch, which, alas!, would put an end to reading." "Unfortunately the cook used to come long in advance to set the table; if only she had done it without speaking!" (5). Like Keats, Proust is half in earnest and half self-mocking. He both acknowledges and hyperbolizes the human comedy: "alas! [*hélas!*] . . . desolation . . . the fatal words: 'Come, shut your book'" (5 and 7).

However, to the privacy and solipsism of reading by and to himself, Proust contrasts a room and a method which vacates the self: "I feel myself living and thinking in a room where everything is the creation and the language of lives profoundly different from mine, of a taste opposite to mine, where I find nothing of my conscious thought, where my imagination is excited by feeling itself plunged into the depths of the non-ego" (17).[9] While for Proust, as for Keats, the "*non-moi*" was a source of receptiveness (of Proustian negative capability), it was not the same as wholesale self-surrender. Proust argued that the reader's wisdom begins precisely where the author's leaves off ("*notre sagesse commence où celle de l'auteur finit*" [34]). As we have seen, Keats, who had been reading the Sonnets, may have told Reynolds that Shakespeare "has left nothing to say about nothing or any thing" (40), but he wrote to Benjamin Bailey that he is "not old enough or magnanimous enough to anihilate [*sic*] self" (99). To reject the "wordsworthian egotistical sublime" in favor of the "camelion Poet" (157) was not to equate a chameleon with a cipher.[10]

Such distinctions clarify the way Keats conceived of himself as a reader and a writer in relation to Shakespeare. "Nothing is finer for the purposes of great productions," wrote Keats to his brothers George and Tom, "than a very gradual ripening of the intellectual powers—As an instance of this—observe—I sat down yesterday to read King Lear" (57). Keats was again calibrating his fitness for "more momentous labor" by comparison with Shakespeare, whose great tragedy led to Keats's "intellectual break with the Romance mode."[11] But their bond was more subtle than straightforward. "I have an idea," he wrote to Reynolds almost a month later, in February 1818,

> [t]hat a Man might pass a very pleasant life in this manner—let him on any certain day read a certain Page of full Poesy or distilled Prose and let him wander with it, and muse upon it, and reflect from it, and bring home to it, and prophesy upon it, and dream upon it—untill it becomes stale—but when will it do so? Never—When Man has arrived at a certain ripeness in intellect any one grand and spiritual passage serves him as a starting post towards all "the two-and-thirty Pallaces" How happy is such a "voyage of conception," what delicious diligent Indolence! (65)

If this time the conjunction of ripening intellect and Shakespeare is not explicit, the "Page of full Poesy" is still distinctly Shakespearean. Edgar's "ripeness is all" (5.2.11) may be audible, but Cleopatra's lineaments—her "habiliments" (3.6.17)—are unmistakable. "Stale—but when will it do so? Never" echoes Enobarbus's certainty that "custom" cannot "stale / Her infinite variety." "Never" is Enobarbus's curt response to Maecenas's supposition that "Now Antony must leave her utterly" (2.2.243–46). Keats recommends confining oneself to but "a *certain Page* of full Poesy." He then writes that such a "*sparing touch* of noble Books" will be no "irreverence [*sic*] to their Writers." "The Benefit done by great Works" may derive from "their mere *passive* existence" (65–66; my emphasis). Thinking out loud, Keats is gauging his proximity to and distance from "great Works" like Shakespeare's. His calculations lead him to distinguish knowledge from memory, or "Custom," by which "Many [who] have original Minds . . . are led away" (66). But if custom does not stale Shakespeare's infinite variety, how does one confine oneself to a sparing touch of merely a certain page of his poesy?

Given Keats's desire not to be irreverent toward "great Works," the temporary solution to the independence (knowledge) versus indebtedness (memory) conundrum is for a "Man . . . like the Spider [to] spin from his own inwards his own airy Citadel" (66), conveniently comforted by the expectation that minds which "leave each other in contrary directions, traverse each other in Numberless points, and all [*for* at] last greet each other at the Journeys end" (66). On a morning when he wrote to Reynolds that he has "not read any Books," Keats nonetheless would have it that the giver (Shakespeare) and the "receiver" (Keats) "are equal in their benefits" (66–67). On the one hand, it is better to "sit like Jove" than "to fly like Mercury"; on the other hand, "I will not deceive myself that Man should be equal with jove—but think himself very well off as a sort of scullion-Mercury" (66–67). Once again, Keats inserts a stanza of his own poetry into his letter, asking Reynolds to "give your vote, pro or con" (41).

The push and pull of reading Shakespeare was for Keats both pleasurable and provoking. Charles Cowden Clarke remembered that when Keats was "reading the 'Cymbeline' aloud, I saw his eyes fill with tears, and his voice faltered when he came to the departure of Posthumus."[12] In Oxford, Keats read aloud from *Troilus and Cressida* to Benjamin Bailey; he often discussed and read Shakespeare with Haydon in the latter's studio. He reminded Reynolds that the two of them used to "feast upon" Shakespeare (89). They would hike through Hampstead Heath taking turns with what Keats called "my folio Shakespeare," the edition of the plays in which he put his own stamp on Shakespeare by inserting "the first few stanzas of my [Isabella; or, The] 'Pot of Basil'" (90) as well as his sonnet on reading *King Lear*.[13] To John Taylor he wrote, "I have great reason to be content, for thank God I can read and perhaps understand Shakespeare to his depths" (70).[14] And when his friends were absent, when he felt "rather lonely . . . at breakfast," Keats "unbox'd a Shakespeare—There's my Comfort" (4). If this makes Keats out to be Stephano ("Here's my comfort" [*The Tempest*, 2.2.44 and 54]), imbibing at breakfast, in his own defense we find this note in his copy of Hazlitt's *Characters*: "the poet by one cup should know the scope of any particular wine without getting intoxicated—this is the highest exertion of Power, and the next step is to paint from memory of gone self storm."[15] "Gone self storm"? "Gone self" chimes with negative capability, but "gone self storm" sounds like, "when the self that Shakespeare temporarily intoxicated (or caught up in a storm or "consumed in fire," see below) reasserts itself—when I recollect Shakespeare in tranquility—I can commence writing."[16]

Keats's reading often induced writing. There is "On first looking into Chapman's Homer" and there are his sonnets to Homer, Chatterton, Byron, and Burns. Having sat up all night in Clerkenwell, reading a 1616 Folio of Chapman's Homer with Cowden Clarke, Keats was already composing his sonnet as he made his way home early the next morning.[17] Cowden Clarke reports that he "had the reward of one of his [Keats's] delighted stares" when Clarke read of Ulysses's shipwreck."[18] Hours later, these stares were transmuted into those of "stout Cortez, when with eagle eyes / He star'd at the Pacific."[19] Nearly a year and a half later, Keats "sat down to read King Lear . . . and felt the greatness of the thing up to the writing of a Sonnet preparatory thereto" (55). So Keats wrote to Bailey even as brother Tom's "Spitting of blood continues" (55). On the same day (January 23, 1818), he began a letter to George and Tom in which he wrote that "the thing [*King Lear*] appeared to demand the prologue of a Sonnet, I wrote it & began to read" (57). What does Keats mean by "demand," and who is making this demand? What does "up to" mean?—"welling up in me to the point that I was moved to write a sonnet," or "I felt the greatness but only up until I began a sonnet of my own"? Keats, who imagined himself sitting and reading "like the picture of somebody reading" (203) and who thought "it would be a great delight . . . to know in what position Shakspeare sat when he began 'To be or not to be'" (223), sits down in order to brace himself against the "greatness of the thing." Again, the embodied reader: Keats *felt* the greatness of *King Lear*, of the *thing*. Both readerly and writerly posture and deportment always count for Keats. Even though his brother and sister were in America, he wrote in December 1818 that he knew the manner of their "walking, standing, sauntering, sitting down. . . . You will rember me in the same manner—and the more when I tell you that I shall read a passage of Shakspeare every Sunday at ten o Clock—you read one <a>t the same time and we shall be as near each other as blind bodies can be in the same room" (176).

When we, in turn, "sit to read Keats' sonnet in Shakespeare's folio," writes Randall McLeod, "we sense the immediacy of his body, the position in which he sat, conveyed by the writing, the literal and literary posture in one coherent body which *is* his text (and *their* text)."[20] In the sonnet, Keats recalls the play's "fierce dispute" and anticipates reliving it. He hopes to be "consumed with the Fire" of the play and then, phoenix-like, to emerge from it. After he copied out the sonnet in his letter to his brothers, his confidence was still in contention with doubt. He tentatively asserts himself ("So you see I am getting at it, with a sort of determination & strength"), then he retreats ("though verily I do not feel it at this moment") (57). The version of the sonnet that he penned in the approximately five inches of blank page beneath the "Finis" at the end of his Folio *Hamlet* and opposite to the first page of its *Lear*—a space on a page McLeod judges one of the more "charged emptiness[es] in English literature" (32)—he entitled, "On sitting down to read King Lear once again"; the version he transcribed in his letter, he entitled, "On sitting down to King Lear once Again" (57). Here is the version that appears in the Gittings edition of Keats's letters from which I have been quoting (we have this entire letter in John Jeffrey's transcription only):

"On sitting down to King Lear once Again"
O golden tongued Romance with serene Lute!
Fair plumed syren! Queen! if far away!
Leave melodizing on this wintry day,
Shut up thine olden volume & be mute.
Adieu! for once again the fierce dispute,
Betwixt Hell torment & impassioned Clay
Must I burn through; once more assay
The bitter sweet of this Shakespeareian fruit
Cheif Poet! & ye clouds of Albion.
Begettors of our deep eternal theme,
When I am through the old oak forest gone
Let me not wander in a barren dream
But when I am consumed with the Fire
Give me new Pheonix-wings to fly at my desire

And here is Keats's Folio version:

On sitting down to read King Lear once again.
O golden tongued Romance, with serene Lute!

Fair plumed syren! Queen of far-away!
Leave melodizing on this wintry day,
Shut up thine olden Pages, and be mute.
Adieu! for, once again, the fierce dispute,
Betwixt Damnation and impassion'd clay
Must I burn through; once more humbly assay
The bitter-sweet of this Shakspearean fruit.
Chief Poet! and ye Clouds of Albion,
Begettors of ~~this~~ our deep eternal theme!
When through the old oak forest I am gone,
Let me not wander in a barren dream:
But when I am consumed in the fire,
Give me new Phoenix-wings to fly to [revised to "at"] my desire.

Jan^ry.22.1818[21]

Although Keats writes that his sonnet was composed "preparatory" to (re)reading the play, he appears to be spurring himself to "burn through" and "assay" it so that it will propel him beyond the "melodizing" of romance. If it is meant to function as a "prologue," then perhaps it can safeguard Keats on his passage "through the old oak [Shakespearean] forest . . . consumed with the Fire." Oscillating like Keats at the Cliff of Poesy, the sonnet pertains to matters both precedent and subsequent to the play. It confirms that the relationship between a writer and a reader—in this instance, Shakespeare and Keats—is as Proust imagines it: the reader looks to the author for answers (for wings), but "all he can do is give us desires" (35). McLeod argues that the Keats-Shakespeare relationship is neither anticipatory nor behindhand; it is, as he nicely puts it, "Keatspearian" (33). And on the Folio page, Keats appears to corroborate McLeod's argument; for example, he strikes out "this" in the phrase "this eternal theme" and substitutes "our." But who is it, if not Shakespeare, who will give Keats his wings—Shakespeare, who is to Keats more of a sponsor than a partner, or Keats, who heretofore has been begotten and not a begetter? With the poem's variant titles in mind, McLeod imagines that if Keats is sitting down not "*to read* King Lear once again" but "*to* King Lear once Again," and if his sonnet is the "prologue" that the play demanded, then Keats has "entered into collaboration with Shakespeare . . . the new Phoenix Wings . . . [are] given even *before* they were entreated" (33; my emphasis).[22] If Keats is *re*reading the play, then perhaps not. Potent though the desire for, or fantasy of, collaboration may be, the fact of belatedness is inexpugnable. No wonder writing four letters and this sonnet, not to mention the prospect of working through *King Lear* again, temporarily saps Keats's "determination & strength": I "feel rather tired & my head rather swimming—so I will leave it [the letter but perhaps the sonnet and the play, too] open till tomorrow's post" (57).

The frontispiece to Caroline Spurgeon's *Keats's Shakespeare: A Descriptive Study* provides us with another way to imagine Keats reading Shakespeare.[23] Spurgeon reproduces a copy of a watercolor drawing of Keats attributed to Joseph Severn (to whom, shortly before he died in Rome, Keats bequeathed his copy of *The Poetical Works of William Shakespeare* as well as his seven-volume Whittingham edition of Shakespeare). Keats is bundled up in an overcoat and leaning back into a deck chair, apparently on the *Maria Crowther* on his way to Naples in 1820. A folio-sized volume gripped in Keats's left hand rests on his left thigh, which is crossed over his right leg. Keats's head is tucked in to his chest, tilted over the book. According to Spurgeon, "it is noticeable how ill and hollow-cheeked he looks" (vii). At the end of her foreword, she reproduces a pencil drawing, this time of a fully recumbent Keats, apparently reading in a berth (Marianne Hunt's 1820 silhouette of the poet, semi-recumbent and again reading something folio-sized, depicts Keats in a posture somewhere between that of the drawing and that of the watercolor).[24] This drawing is Arthur Severn's recollection of a sketch executed by his father—the younger Severn informed Spurgeon that the original was "removed" from a scrap-book in his possession (viii). Keats's Shakespeare Folio, the edition from which he read with Reynolds and which he eventually gave to Fanny Brawne, would have required both of his hands for support and so would not have lent itself to just any reading posture (the pages are 8.75 by 14.25 inches). But Keats's duodecimo Johnson-Steevens edition of Shakespeare (the edition we know he had with him on the Isle of Wight and with which he was still traveling when he sailed to Europe) was pocket-sized (4.75" x 3") and so it would have been manageable in almost any position. Each of these seven volumes weighs approximately seven ounces and the entire set weighs a mere three pounds, one and one-half ounces. Each book fits nicely in one hand and can be held open rather easily with a thumb in the gutter and an index and middle finger providing support from behind. Keats appears to have been right-handed, so he could have held one of the Whittingham volumes comfortably in his left hand and kept a pen or pencil at the ready in his right hand (Severn's posthumous portrait of Keats, sitting reading in Wentworth Place, depicts the poet seemingly oblivious to the painter, leaning his left arm on the back of a bentwood chair with his left hand resting open on his head, his right hand on the recto of an open book, now supported by his right thigh crossed over his left leg).[25]

Whether seated, slouching, or lying on his back, whether reading *King Lear* for the first time or reading it once again, we know that Keats "read . . . with his pen, not just his eyes" (McLeod, 34). He marked up five plays in his facsimile of the 1623 Folio (possibly with Fanny as his intended reader), extensively underlining and five times annotating *Troilus and Cressida*, underlining much of *King Lear* and adding notes in addition to his sonnet, underlining and annotating a portion of *A Midsummer Night's Dream*, and underlining in *Romeo and Juliet* and *1 Henry 4*. Keats's markings in his modern edition of the plays are extensive—most noticeably in *The Tempest* and *A Midsummer Night's Dream*, but they may be found in *Measure for Measure*, *Antony and Cleopatra*, and other plays.[26] At times Keats had recourse to a broken or dotted line down the side of a page; at other times he used a solid line; and in either case, he might underline as well. Occasionally we find two solid lines drawn down a margin. When he asked Reynolds to respond to *Hyperion*, Keats advised him to "put a mark X to the false beauty proceeding from art, and one ‖ to the true voice of feeling" (292). Spurgeon believes that Keats's markings correspond with "significant" passages, places where Keats "admires an image or expression for its poetical and imaginative value, for vividness or beauty of phrase" (24). McLeod suspects that the mid-line breaks in Keats's underlinings indicate his "sensitivity to metre (especially caesura) and to rhetorical pauses": his "pauses may represent something of his actual intonation" (43–44). White speculates judiciously about Keats's underlining in his Shakespeare editions but frankly acknowledges that Keats's "precise intention[s]" are irrecoverable and that his "interest is dispersed and opportunistic, and it would be misleading to suggest any consistency."[27]

Perusing Keats's Shakespeares gives us a limited measure of access to his "original psychological act called *reading*," as Proust puts it (27). It also tells us something about what *we* do when we write in *our* books, our Shakespeares in particular. If a heavily marked up page is not a sign of co-authorship, it may point to the ways we make a text more our own. It is evidence of our participation. The profusion of Keats's lineations tells us that he could not have meant for all of them to operate merely as mnemonics. They are his real-time responses to what he read, regardless of whether he expected to return to the pages in which he made them. Keats was remarking and elaborating on what he was reading. He may have been signaling his temperament of the moment—White argues that Keats was sucking the melancholy out of *As You Like It*.[28] But he also was decorating and tagging (as he and Bailey did when they, like so many others before them, wrote their names on "that truly honored wall" at the Shakespeare birthplace in Stratford-upon-Avon).[29] When we read Shakespeare's plays, we often feel as though we simply have to underscore a word or a phrase, or insert a bullet or an asterisk in the margin. How else, when alone, shy of breaking into song, do we register our visceral delight, our astonishment or *jouissance*? Most of us experience some degree of amusement or embarrassment or surprise when we come upon comments we have written in margins during prior readings. We have second thoughts about loaning out books littered with our uncensored annotations.[30] But we know that Keats left his Shakespeare editions to those who were closest to him. And now we can pore over his markings online, without regard for his privacy. There are facing pages in his Johnson-Steevens edition of *A Midsummer Night's Dream* on which every single line of text is marked after one fashion or another. In some instances, a dotted line around the margins partially frames or encages the Shakespearean text. In *Measure for Measure*, Keats underscores the Duke's "And liberty plucks justice by the nose," then he adds an exclamation mark to the left of the line. On other pages, entire lives come painfully, if momentarily, into view. While looking after his gravely ill brother Tom, who would die in less than two months, Keats underlined (and marked with an *x*) the words "poore Tom" in his Folio *Lear*. In between two, short vertical lines in the adjoining margin, he wrote "x Sunday Evening Oct. 4. 1818." As we scan through play after play, we inevitably find ourselves wondering why Keats has failed or refused to put his imprint on particular passages. To read his Shakespeare editions is to notice even their unremarked passages as unremarked.

The 1814 Whittingham edition does not offer a reader much room for marginalia. It is a serviceable traveling companion, but as a consequence, its margins are scant. A typical page left Keats perhaps one-quarter to three-eighths of an inch at the top, one quarter of an inch at the bottom, perhaps five-sixteenths of an inch at the left of each verso, and anywhere from one-quarter of an inch to one and one-quarter inches (in the event of a short line) along the right of each recto. This edition entertained Keats with "Two hundred and Thirty Embellishments"—engravings on each volume's title page (one of the seven ages of man for each of the seven volumes), at the start of each play, and at the start of each act of each play. Keats stood his best chance of getting in his own two pence worth at the end of a play, where there is generally an extended note of either Johnson's or Steevens's, and then often some blank page.

One finds that Keats regularly upbraided Dr. Johnson in saucy handwritten responses to his remarks. He defaced large swatches of these comments with curling, swirling, looping lining-out and cross-hatching. These energetic lines further testify to the healthy, even aggressive physicality of Keats's Shakespeare reading. Spurgeon calls attention to Keats's own marginal comments' "humorous impatience and scorn of Dr. Johnson's measured and matter of fact criticism of the plays."[31] But Keats's anger comes through in his slashes before we even get to his discursive commentary. At the end of *A Midsummer Night's Dream*, the Whittingham edition appends the following:

> Wild and fantastical as this play is, all the parts in their various modes are well written, and give the kind of pleasure which the author designed. Fairies in his time were much in fashion; common tradition had made them familiar, and Spencer's [*sic*] poem had made them great.
>
> JOHNSON

Keats unfurls two broad spiraling lines that seem to run from left to right across the whole of this comment, set mid-way down the page. Just to the left of "JOHNSON" Keats writes "Fie," and just to the right, he inserts an exclamation mark. He fills up the bottom half of the page with his versions of four passages from the play separated from one another by short horizontal lines:

"Such tricks hath <u>weak</u> [for Shakespeare's "strong"] imagination."

"To kill Cankers in the Musk rose buds."

"The clamorous owl that hoots at our

quaint Spirits"

"Newts and blind worms do no wrong

Come not near our faery queene"

Page 64 of Keats's edition of *Dream*, then, consists of Puck's unmarked "If we shadows have offended" speech in italics down to almost the middle of the page, then a simple horizontal ornament, next Johnson's roughed up comment followed by Keats's one-word rejection, and finally, at least a third of a page of Keatsian refutation in the form of citational graffiti. With Shakespeare's own verse, Keats dispatches Johnson (see fig. 2.1).

This is by no means the only time that Keats first cancels out Dr. Johnson and then turns the Bard against him. He lets loose on the comment at the end

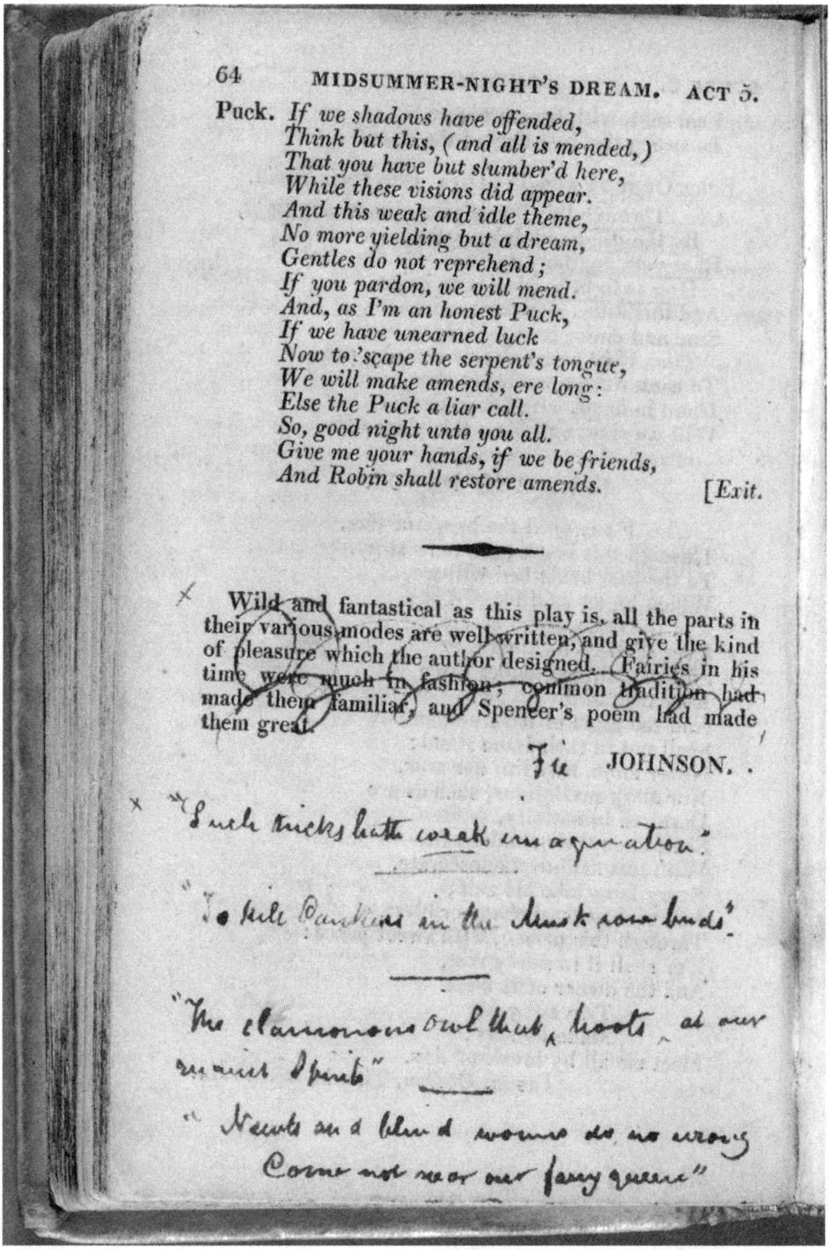

64 MIDSUMMER-NIGHT'S DREAM. ACT 5.

Puck. *If we shadows have offended,*
Think but this, (and all is mended,)
That you have but slumber'd here,
While these visions did appear.
And this weak and idle theme,
No more yielding but a dream,
Gentles do not reprehend;
If you pardon, we will mend.
And, as I'm an honest Puck,
If we have unearned luck
Now to 'scape the serpent's tongue,
We will make amends, ere long:
Else the Puck a liar call.
So, good night unto you all.
Give me your hands, if we be friends,
And Robin shall restore amends. [*Exit.*

Wild and fantastical as this play is, all the parts in their various modes are well written, and give the kind of pleasure which the author designed. Fairies in his time were much in fashion; common tradition had made them familiar, and Spencer's poem had made them great.

Fie JOHNSON.

"Such tricks hath weak imagination"

"To kill cankers in the musk rose buds"

"The clamorous owl that hoots at our quaint spirits"

"Newts and blind worms do no wrong
Come not near our fairy queene"

Figure 2.1: John Keats's Whittingham edition of *A Midsummer Night's Dream*. Photograph courtesy of Houghton Library, Harvard University.

of *Antony and Cleopatra* with intersecting slashes and concentric circles. Then he turns a fragment of Charmian's into a comical riposte to Johnson, writing "Your crown's awry I'll mend it." Keats foregoes the swirl and instead lines through and then crosses out separate parts of the final paragraph of Johnson's long comment at the end of *Measure for Measure*. In Act 2, Scene 2 of the play itself, Keats had underlined Isabella's lines about "proud man." Now these same lines (in Keats's adaptation: "But Man! Proud Man! / Drest in a little brief authority / Plays such fantastic tricks before high Heaven / As makes the Angels weep.'"!!!) are copied out by Keats in pitying and caustic response to Johnson's reservations about Shakespeare's art and plotting. Keats is terse but still laughing after he has scrolled through a few lines of Johnson's at the end of *The Winter's Tale*. Just below and to the left of "JOHNSON" he writes, simply, "lo fool again"! The helical, corkscrewing lines that he scratches through Johnson's words following *As You Like It* seem to be especially agitated. Spurgeon imagines an "exasperated" Keats pointedly asking JOHNSON, "Is <u>Criticism</u> a true thing?"[32] At the bottom of the page, Keats enlists Touchstone to make his point: "When a man's verses cannot be understood, nor a man's good wit seconded by the forward child, understanding, it strikes a man more dead than a great reckoning in a . . ." ["little room" is indecipherable at the bottom of the page].

After Keats vigorously crosses out every single line of Johnson's comment at the end of *Macbeth*, he turns the play on him, filling the bottom of the page with two curt quotes: "Thou losest Labour" and "As the Hare the Lion" ("or the hare the lion" [1.2.35]). To the comment at the end of *Titus Andronicus* in which Johnson sees no reason to differ from "all the editors and critics" who suppose "this play is spurious," Keats responds with lines fetched from *Julius Caesar*: "Ye Blocks Ye stones! Ye worse than senseless things Knew ye not Pompey." And where the final comment on a play is Steevens's, Keats is no less brusque. At the end of *The Comedy of Errors*, Keats writes "No Mr. [STEEVENS] Sir You are too wise." The last words on the final page of each of these plays, then, are no longer Johnson's or Steevens's, but they are not quite Keatspeare's, nor are they precisely Shakespeare's. Instead, Keats ventriloquizes Shakespeare in gestures of witty self-assurance (putting down the editors) and Borgesian self-effacement (damning them in Shakespeare's own words). He speaks on Shakespeare's behalf, and even when he infuses Shakespeare's words with his own tone and meaning, it is as if he has Shakespeare's approval. Thinking about *Hamlet* in particular, Keats wrote to Reynolds that "we read fine———things but never feel them to thee [*sic*] full until we have gone the same step as the Author" (93). If marginal Keats does not try to fill Shakespeare's shoes, still he seems to match steps with him. At one point, when Keats was reading *King Lear,* he responded to what he calls "bye-writing" in a note in his Folio edition. Four rather undistinguished lines from Regan, Gloucester, and Edmund elicit from Keats a small burst of professional admiration: "This bye-writing is more marvellous than the whole ripped up contents of Pernambuca—or any buca whatever—on the earth or in the waters under the earth." For whom is Keats writing the phrase "or any buca whatever"? Is this his sense of humor or his self-consciousness, his intimation that we will one day come upon his commentary on Shakespeare? He suspects that his letters will endure, so why not his annotations? Maybe Shakespeare himself would take an interest in them. "What would Rousseau have said at seeing our little correspondence!" he asked Fanny Brawne. "I don't care much—I would sooner have Shakspeare's opinion about the matter" (362). Surely there is some bravado here. It may not cost Keats anything when he turns Shakespeare's words against Johnson but, as his letters attest, it is another thing to enlist Shakespeare in one's own self-assessment.

Keats's Folio markings range from precise textual notes and emendations to marginal commentary. In a number of instances he apparently compared the Folio text with what appeared in his Whittingham edition of *Troilus and Cressida.* Sometimes he lost patience with prior editors. Responding to Troilus's "the Sunne doth light a-scorne," he dismisses "Commentators [who] have contrived to twist many beautiful passages into commonplaces" and so to have "hocus pocus'd" Shakespeare's "a scorn" into "a storm" thereby "destroying the depth of the simile." He underlines, double underlines, and rules down the margin alongside Ulysses's strictures on Achilles, he asterisks "<u>blowne up</u>" ("<u>The seeded Pride</u> / <u>That hath to this maturity blowne up</u> / <u>In rank *Achilles* . . .</u>"), and then he observes: "'Blowne up' &c. One's very breath while leaning over these Pages is held for fear of blowing this line away—as easily as the gentlest breeze ~~despoils a~~ Robs dandelions of their fleecy Crowns." Is it too fanciful to picture Keats himself leaning over his large-format text? Who or what is holding his breath? Keats wrote to George and Georgiana, "I throw [*corrected from* through] my whole being into Triolus [*sic*] . . . 'I wander, like a lost soul upon the stygian Banks staying for waftage'" (170).[33] No doubt this is mostly figurative, as is Keats "with Achilles shouting in the Trenches" or Keats "repeating" Shakespeare's lines only to "melt into the air with a voluptuousness so delicate that I am content to be alone" (170). But the conjunction of plausible behavior (held breath, shouting, repeating a line, being alone) and metaphorical behavior (blowing away a line, melting into the air) lessens the distinction between the two even as it reconfirms for us the bodily dimensions of Keats's reading. "Prostrate," in Keats's note to a Folio passage from *Troilus and Cressida*, positions Keats every bit as much as it does the achievements of "human intellect": "The Genius of Shakspeare was an inate [*sic*] universality—wherefore he had the utmost atchievement [*sic*] of human intellect prostrate beneath his indolent and kingly gaze—He could do easily Man's utmost." Glimpses of Keats sitting, settling, leaning, wafting, and prostrate (also underlining, asterisking, and cross-hatching) help us to imagine both a more or less literal physiology of reading and a variety of metaphorical stances toward Shakespeare, any one of which may be our own. Keats pelts Johnson and Steevens, but prostration best comprehends the Keatsian psychosomatics of reading Shakespeare: it is a posture and a form of address, a sign of his devotion and depletion, his possession and forfeiture.[34]

Virginia Woolf, whose one criticism of Harley Granville-Barker's "de-Luxe" edition of the 1623 Folio *Midsummer Night's Dream* was that it was "a trifle too broad for the ordinary size of human hands," inventories the expense of energy it takes to read Shakespeare:[35]

> Anyone who is left alone in a tumultuous frame of mind is quite likely to <sit up> read<ing> Shakespeare, ~~choosing that~~ one of the plays <It ~~is an effort. It is~~ One must make the plunge; it is an effort> which most agrees or most contrasts with his mood. ~~However~~ <but> in ten minutes or so the personal cobwebs are *blown* clean away. The vigour of the language is too *overwhelming* <to be missed> . . . *Every ounce of energy is used up* in realising the perpetual succession of images which coin even the thinnest pencilled thoughts on the borderlands of our consciousness into robust highly coloured shapes. <bodies> Merely to *throw* ourselves this way and that with the emotions of the different speakers gives the illusion of *violent physical exercise*. To seize the first phrases of each character . . . requires the utmost agility of imagination. The vitality, the intensity, the compression and pressure of ~~each~~ <every> page keep one on the stretch *almost to the exclusion of comment* . . . (3.496; my emphasis)

Woolf's self-preserving "almost" accomplishes much the same thing as Keats's "quite" in "I never quite despair and I read Shakspeare" (14). But Woolf also uncannily echoes Keats's "overwhelms," his sense of "highest exertion," even the Shakespeare who has left "nothing to say about nothing or any thing." "Every ounce" of her "energy is used up realizing" Shakespeare's "perpetual succession of images." "O Shakespeare," Keats wrote in response to a passage in his Folio *Midsummer Night's Dream*, "thy ways are but just searchable!" Keats threw his "whole being into" Troilus. Woolf writes that she "become[s] absorbed" in the plays. . . . The exercise has been continuous without interruption and always at ~~full~~ <high> pitch" (3.497). Several years later, she corralled Shakespeare and Keats in a single sentence, writing about the "intoxication and intensity" of the body when reading their poetry (4.396). Sounding like Keats (and Coleridge and Berryman), Woolf gives us no sign that she is exaggerating when she insists that "it is clear that reading is one of the most arduous and exhausting of occupations" (4.393).

But this, too, can happen: "<reading great books> it is always an effort, often a disappointment, and sometimes <a> drudgery ~~of a repulsive nature~~" (3.488). "Suddenly the book becomes dull as ditchwater and heavy as lead. We yawn and stretch and cannot attend. The highest flights of Shakespeare and Milton become intolerable" (4.393). The reader Virginia Woolf toggles between intoxication and boredom. For his part, the reader Roland Barthes is both self-possessed and lost to himself, "split twice over, doubly perverse" (14).[36] According to Barthes, there is a text of pleasure: "it manages to make itself heard indirectly; if, reading it, I am led to look up often, to listen to something else. I am not necessarily *captivated* by the text" (24). It "contents, fills, grants euphoria." Then there is the "text of bliss: the text that imposes a state of loss, the text that discomforts (perhaps to the point of a certain boredom)" (14). The reader who keeps "in his hands the reins of pleasure and bliss . . . simultaneously and contradictorily . . . enjoys the consistency of his selfhood . . . and seeks its loss" (14). Barthes's "consistency of his selfhood" corresponds with the self which Keats told Bailey he was not ready to annihilate. His "state of loss" tallies with Proust's "*non-moi*" and with "negative capability." Keats imagined our most searching thoughts prostrate beneath Shakespeare's "indolent and kingly gaze." If in his letters, Keats sometimes wittily, sometimes inconspicuously, appropriated dozens and dozens of lines from the plays, when he was reading Shakespeare, even if he was underlining and annotating, he felt pliant. What he was subjected to he also subjected himself to. Recall Keats telling Reynolds that Shakespeare "overwhelms a genuine Lover of Poesy with all manner of abuse" (40).

The "state of loss" imposed on Keats the reader of Shakespeare, he recuperated by writing. As he read but before he wrote, he marked up the plays. Writing in the text is something that Shakespeare provokes in Keats, and it is something that Keats does to Shakespeare. What Barthes "enjoy[s] in a narrative is not directly its content or even its structure, but rather the abrasions [*éraflures*] I impose upon the fine surface: I run on, I skip, I look up, I plunge in again" (11–12).[37] When Keats marked up his Shakespeares, he, too, was abrading text. He was seizing what he heard characters say not with what Woolf called the "utmost agility of [his] imagination" but with his pen. Most of us do this. We (re)encounter the word *chat* when indignant, self-righteous, slightly defensive Hotspur describes a certain lord's "bald unjointed chat" (1.3.65), and we underline it. We asterisk "chuck" when Antony calls the queen of Egypt his "chuck" (4.4.2). The hard "t" in "chat" catches us up short even though "unjoin*t*ed" warns us that it is coming. Antony's "chuck" is disarmingly informal, playful, and tender.[38] Shakespeare is "writing aloud," as Barthes puts it, exploiting "the *grain* of the voice, which is an erotic mixture of timbre and language." He "searches for . . . the language lined with flesh . . . the patina of consonants, the voluptuousness of vowels . . . the articulation of the body, of the tongue, not that of meaning." Antony's "chuck" "crackles" (67; "*ça grésille*" [105]) when Shakespeare's "vocal writing" throws the "body of the actor into my ear" (66–67). The bliss of the text is to (over)hear, to repeat to ourselves, and to underscore these sounds.

Keats responded to "passages of Shakespeare" with "the ardour of the pursuer" (73). He wrote to Bailey that he looked "upon fine Phrases like a Lover" (277). This was undoubtedly true, and it bolsters the often-repeated claim that Keats responded to "discrete, isolated passages" in Shakespeare's works, to what he called the Sonnets' "beauties" (40). But Keats's Folio Shakespeare and his Whittingham edition of Shakespeare, in which he underscored not just words, phrases, and lines but many extended passages, provide evidence of a reader responding to much more than "striking phrases and images."[39] Almost at random in *The Tempest* (Keats marked approximately one-third of the lines in this play), we find the following underlined verses:

> A rotten carcass of a boat, not rigg'd,
> Nor tackle, sail, nor mast; the very rats
> Instinctively have quit it: there they hoist us,
> To cry to the sea that roar'd to us, to sigh
> To the winds whose pity, sighing back again,
> Did us but loving wrong.

First an image (carcass), then wit (rat instinct), then an apt verb (roared), then lyrical affect (sighs) expressed by *synaeceosis* (loving wrong). There is the sound of "Rotten . . . rigged," "not . . . Nor . . . nor," "cry . . . sigh," the rhythm of enjambment ("rats / Instinctively"), and the compressed construction of "Did us but." Too many things are going on here, things that Keats may or may not be acknowledging, for us to guess why all of Prospero's explanation to Miranda in this passage and the next, but not all of the one after that, or the one after that, is marked. In the next passage, Keats underlines "<u>When I have deck'd the sea with drops full salt</u>," then he pens a little vertical line in the margin to its left, but not beside the lines before or after it. For some reason he interrupts his underline then cuts it off altogether: "<u>Under my burthen groan'd</u>; <u>which rais'd in me</u> / An undergoing stomach." Perhaps Barthes's "I run on, I skip, I look up, I plunge in again" explains Keats's failure to mark the last phrase.

Even when we triangulate Keats's letters, his discursive annotations, and his markings on the page to encapsulate his response to, say, Cleopatra, a gap opens up between Keats recruiting Shakespeare to help him make a point in a letter and Keats sitting down to read Shakespeare. The route to Cleopatra in an October 1818 letter to his brother and sister-in-law turns gossipy ("Now I am becoming the Richardson" is Keats's humorous and self-conscious excuse) as it passes from an unnamed "east indian" niece of Mrs. Reynolds's to Charmian and so to Cleopatra. Keats initially reports that the fickle "Miss Reynoldses" have gone from praising to hating their cousin, even as he himself has to acknowledge that "she is not without fault—of a real kind:"

> but she has othe[r]s which are more apt to make women of inferior charms
> hate her. She is not a Cleopatra; but she is at least a Charmian. She has
> a rich eastern look; she has fine eyes and fine manners. When she comes
> into a room she makes an impression the same as the Beauty of a Leopard-
> ess. She is too fine and too conscious of her Self to repulse any Man who
> may address her—from habit she thinks that nothing *particular*. I always
> find myself more at ease with such a woman; the picture before me always
> gives me a life and animation which I cannot possibly feel with anything
> inferior—I am at such times too much occupied in admiring to be awk-
> ward or in a tremble. I forget myself entirely because I live in her. You will
> by this time think I am in love with her; so before I go any further I will
> tell you I am not—she kept me awake one Night as a tune of Mozart's
> might do—I speak of the thing as a passtime and an amuzement . . . I
> dont cry to take the moon home with me in my Pocket not [*for* nor] do
> I fret to leave her behind me. (162–63)

Although he is already protesting quite a bit, Keats is not yet done with his appraisal:

They call her a flirt to me—What a want of knowledge? she walks across
a room in such a manner that a Man is drawn towards her with a mag-
netic Power. This they call flirting! they do not know things. They do
not know what a Woman is. I believe tho' she has faults—the same as
Charmian and Cleopatra might have had—Yet she is a fine thing speaking in a worldly way: for there are two distinct tempers of mind in which
we judge of things—the worldly, theatrical and pantomimical; and the
unearthly, spiritual and etherial . . . As a Man in the world I love the
rich talk of a Charmian; as an eternal Being I love the thought of you
[Georgiana Keats]. I should like her to ruin me, and I should like you to
save me. (163)

There is an unmistakable have it both ways quality to these lines. George and
Georgiana are asked to believe that Keats can forget himself entirely and keep
his ethical compass, too. If not in the moment then in retrospect, he maturely
distinguishes between erotic ruin and eternal salvation. For the normally "awk-
ward" Keats, there is confirmation that he can be a "Man in the world." The
lover of "fine Phrases" is "worldly" enough to admire a "fine thing speaking."
But "theatrical and pantomimical" is a suspiciously clinical and aloof way to
describe the aroused mental temperament of an ambitious Cockney in the presence of an "imperial woman" (162). Not wanting to sound like the Romans
in *Antony and Cleopatra*, Keats nonetheless betrays understandable stress—he
wants to express his connoisseurship and discrimination, but he is afraid that he
will appear immature or foolish. This helps to explain his "Man in the world"
posturing and his need to repeat that "she has faults."

In his Whittingham edition of the play, beside the "Fie" in Antony's "Fie
wrangling queen! / Whom everything becomes" (1.2.48–49), Keats pens an
"x" and then, at the bottom of the page, glosses it as follows: "How much more
Shakespeare delights in dwelling upon the romantic and wildly natural than
upon the monumental—see Winter's Tale, 'When you do dance, &c.'" Keats
is still discriminating: even if the meaning of "monumental" is obscure, it is
as at odds with romantic and natural as ruination is with salvation. Moreover,
Keats is also attributing a comparable degree of discrimination to Shakespeare.
When he explained what he meant by *"Negative Capability,"* Keats described
"a man [who] is capable of being in uncertainties, Mysteries, doubts, without
any irritable reaching after fact & reason." This thought, he told his brothers,
"pursued through Volumes would perhaps take us no further than this, that
with a great poet the sense of Beauty overcomes every other consideration, *or*

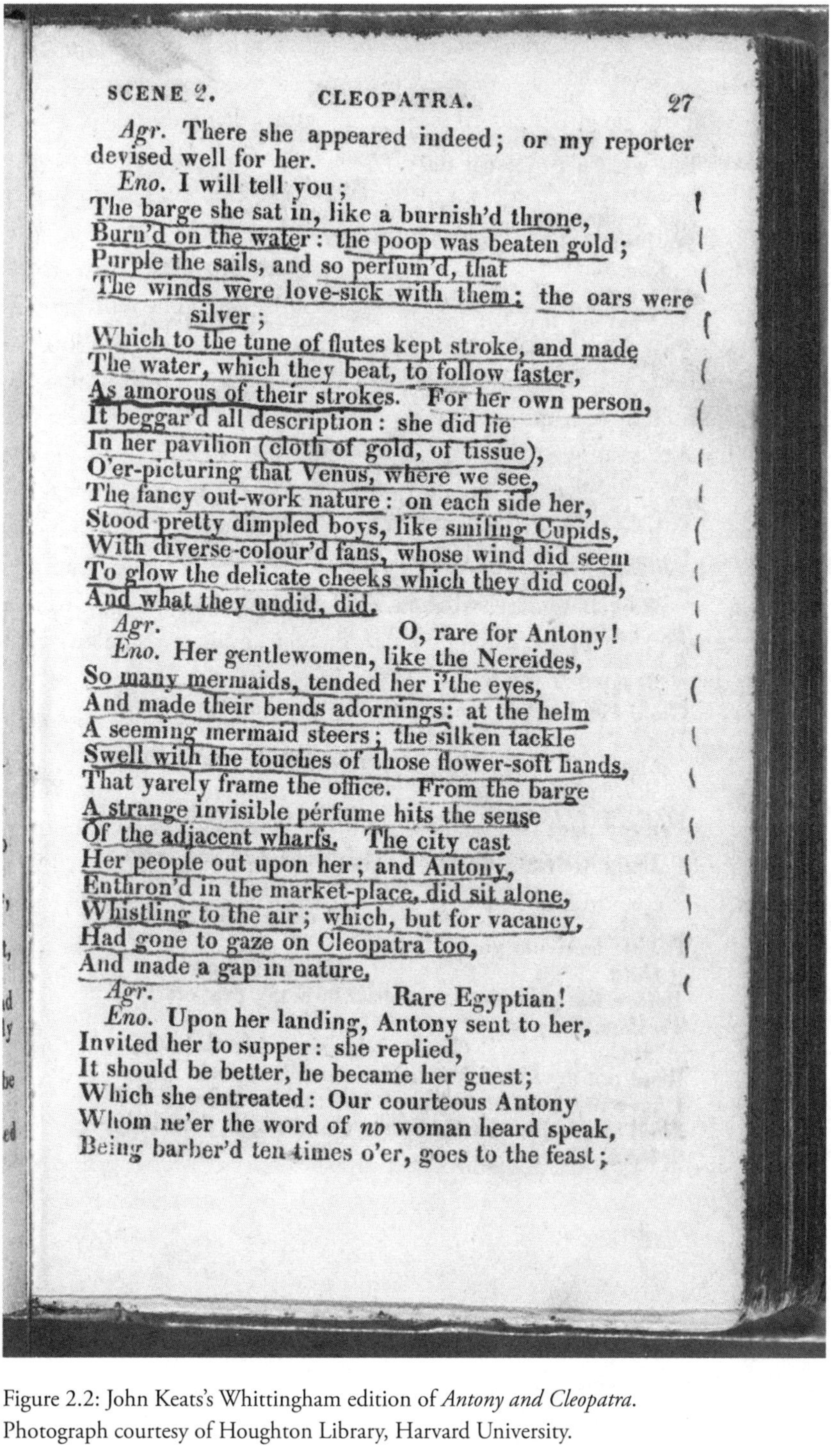

Agr. There she appeared indeed; or my reporter
devised well for her.

Eno. I will tell you;
The barge she sat in, like a burnish'd throne,
Burn'd on the water: the poop was beaten gold;
Purple the sails, and so perfum'd, that
The winds were love-sick with them: the oars were
　　　silver;
Which to the tune of flutes kept stroke, and made
The water, which they beat, to follow faster,
As amorous of their strokes. For her own person,
It beggar'd all description: she did lie
In her pavilion (cloth of gold, of tissue),
O'er-picturing that Venus, where we see,
The fancy out-work nature: on each side her,
Stood pretty dimpled boys, like smiling Cupids,
With diverse-colour'd fans, whose wind did seem
To glow the delicate cheeks which they did cool,
And what they undid, did.

Agr.　　　　　　　　O, rare for Antony!

Eno. Her gentlewomen, like the Nereides,
So many mermaids, tended her i'the eyes,
And made their bends adornings: at the helm
A seeming mermaid steers; the silken tackle
Swell with the touches of those flower-soft hands,
That yarely frame the office. From the barge
A strange invisible perfume hits the sense
Of the adjacent wharfs. The city cast
Her people out upon her; and Antony,
Enthron'd in the market-place, did sit alone,
Whistling to the air; which, but for vacancy,
Had gone to gaze on Cleopatra too,
And made a gap in nature.

Agr.　　　　　　　Rare Egyptian!

Eno. Upon her landing, Antony sent to her,
Invited her to supper: she replied,
It should be better, he became her guest;
Which she entreated: Our courteous Antony
Whom ne'er the word of *no* woman heard speak,
Being barber'd ten times o'er, goes to the feast;

Figure 2.2: John Keats's Whittingham edition of *Antony and Cleopatra*.
Photograph courtesy of Houghton Library, Harvard University.

rather obliterates all consideration" (43; my emphasis). In his gloss on "wrangling queen," however, consideration has been obliterated neither for Keats nor for Shakespeare. Everything may become Cleopatra, but Keats's Shakespeare, and apparently Keats himself, dwells on some things rather than others.

Reflection, whether in a letter or a marginal gloss, subjects beauty to consideration. In the moment, however, as he reads along, Keats responds to beauty inconsiderately or, as Woolf puts it, "almost to the exclusion of comment." Unlike Coleridge, who filled his Shakespeare margins with discursive glosses, Keats did not often add glosses in his own words. Instead, the sign of his apprehension and wonder is his underlining and marking thousands of phrases and lines. It is as if consideration yields to admiration and astonishment; as if Keats makes a physical connection with the "vitality, the intensity, the compression and pressure" (Woolf) of Shakespeare's words by running a pen beneath and alongside them; as if, insofar as self-consciousness is concerned, the Shakespearean text has imposed on Keats a "state of loss" (Barthes, 14). All of this underlining in the bliss, the indolence or languor, of reading *Antony and Cleopatra* gives us no sign of Keatsian ethics in contention with aesthetics, of a leopardess as opposed to a flirt, of the natural versus the monumental—there is simply the omnibus thrill of going the "same step as the Author" (93). "Pleasure," according to Barthes, "can be expressed in words, bliss cannot . . . *criticism* [like Coleridge's?] *always deals with the texts of pleasure, never with the texts of bliss*" (21). Page 27 of Keats's Whittingham edition of *Antony and Cleopatra* is a text of bliss (see fig. 2.2). Inarticulate though this page may be, it—and many others like it—is expressive. As well as but differently from his *King Lear* sonnet, it reveals not what Keats did after he "[re]boxed a Shakespeare" (4) but what he so often did when he held it open in his hands.

III

VIRGINIA WOOLF READS
"THE GREAT WILLIAM"

Virginia Woolf was by turns a passionate common reader and an intensely self-conscious professional reader. Reading was for her pleasurable, but it was strenuous; both second nature and hard work, it imposed corporal as well as psychological rigors. A designer, binder, and publisher, Woolf had a thoroughgoing physical relation to books: their heft, their appearance, even their smell got her attention. An accomplished novelist, essayist, and reviewer, she also read analytically.[1] But Virginia Woolf the invigorated reader was often out of phase with Woolf the calculating, programmatic reader. The sometimes embodied, sometimes disembodied reader that she imagined herself in her diaries shadowed one another. Throughout her life—not just in her diaries, but in her letters, notebooks, essays, and novels—Woolf took stabs at making sense of reading, of herself as a reader, and of herself as someone who was read. There are essays entitled "Reading" and "The Reader"; "On Re-reading Novels" and "How Should One Read a Book?"; there was *The Common Reader*, *The Common Reader: Second Series*, and the planned *Reading at Random* or *Turning the Page*. There are also her reading notebooks—sixty-seven volumes now divided between the New York Public Library and the University of Sussex Library.[2] Amidst all of this, Shakespeare has a very significant place. As he is for Keats, so for Woolf, Shakespeare is a pleasure-giving taskmaster. We can learn something about how we read Shakespeare from how Woolf read Shakespeare; but, to borrow from Coleridge, Woolf will not carry us on her shoulders: "we must strain our own sinews, as [s]he has strained [hers]."[3]

The insistently physical, the tactile, sensual, oral aspects of reading were noted by Woolf early on. In 1903, at the age of 21, she wrote in her journal of the "delight" she took in planning her summer reading: "I get the volumes together—lay them out on my table & think exultingly that all that thickness of paper will be passed through my mind."[4] Merely to contemplate a syllabus is not enough. Woolf gathers the books and sets them out on a table for inspection and for massing, something to do with volume, density, and weight. There is an active, willed component (the mental filing, "putting aside books in my mind," and the actual book retrieval); but curiously, there is also a passive, hands-off or incorporeal quality to Woolf's version of "intellecturition": the paper "will be passed through my mind." "I think I could go on," she writes a sentence later, "browsing & munching steadily through all kinds of books as long as I lived." If triumph and self-esteem ("exultingly," "*my* mind") are tempered by a compensatory modesty ("I wish I felt sure it [the "thickness of paper"] would leave any impression"), the keynote is a barely metaphorical voracity.

Late in 1940, Woolf was still using what otherwise might have seemed a juvenile locution: "I would like to pack my day rather fuller: most reading must be munching" (*Diary*, October 12; 5.328).[5] And a month later she again playfully depicts herself as the proverbial voracious reader who devours books. To her friend Ethel Smyth she wrote, "I am almost—what d'you call a voracious cheese mite which has gnawed its way into a vast Stilton & is intoxicated with eating—as I am with reading history, & writing fiction & planning."[6] Browsing hands lead to a munching, voracious mouth, the conduit to a swelling brain. Still back in 1903: "I read a great deal, I say: all the big books I have I have read in the country. . . . I feel sometimes for hours together as though the physical stuff of my brain were expanding, larger & larger, throbbing quicker & quicker with new blood—& there is no more delicious sensation than this."[7] The paper does not now pass into her mind so much as it distends her brain; but reading could also calm and solace Woolf. At age fifteen, she wrote that "books are the greatest help and comfort." She "[r]ead Mr. [Henry] James to quiet me" (*Early Journals*, May 1 and 2, 1897, 79–80). In addition to the somatic androgyny of reading, books themselves were deeply pleasurable to Woolf in a synesthetic manner ("What a vast fertility of pleasure books hold for me!" [*Diary*, August 24, 1933; 5.173]). In the diary entry from which I have been quoting, seeing, smelling, tasting, and touching all come into play. "I went in & found the table laden with books. I looked in & sniffed them all. I could not resist carrying this one off & broaching it" (173). Years later, Woolf wrote that she read "with a pen—following the scent" (*Diary*, April 11 1939; 5. 214). Penetrative and receptive, phallic and oral, reading a book by turns quieted her and caused her to throb.

While Virginia Woolf's earliest exposure to Shakespeare dated back to Leslie Stephen reading out loud to the family, self-consciousness about the plays and poems seems to have arisen for her in relation to her brother, not her father. From her teenage years through *A Room of One's Own* right up to *A Sketch of the Past* near the end of her life, Woolf associated Shakespeare with sibling relations as well as with formal schooling and its lack. It was Thoby Stephen, who was a year and a half older than his sister and who, of course, got a Cambridge education, with whom Woolf first worked out her sense of Shakespeare. In one of her 1901 letters to Thoby, the "goat," as Woolf signed herself and was known in the family, first mentions reading Plato. Then she trains her sights on "the great William":

> My real object in writing is to make a confession—which is to take back a whole cartload of *goatisms* which I used at Fritham and elsewhere in speaking of a certain great English writer—the greatest: I have been reading Marlow, and I was so much more impressed by him than I thought I should be, that I read Cymbeline just to see if there mightnt be more in the great William than I supposed. And I was quite upset! Really and truly I am now let in to [the] company of worshippers—though I still feel a little oppressed by his—greatness I suppose (*Letters*, November 5, 1901, 1.45).[8]

Thoby is off at school ("Oh dear oh dear—just as I feel in the mood to talk about these things, you go and plant yourself in Cambridge" [46]), having left nineteen-year-old Virginia at home to fend for herself with Shakespeare. She apologizes to him for her "*goatisms*"; she finds characters in *Cymbeline* "beyond me—Is this my feminine weakness in the upper region?"; and she worries about what "a dotard you will think me!" (45–46). And yet there is plenty of assuredness here. Woolf has, after all, just been reading Plato and Jonson and Marlowe and Shakespeare. She is confident that she has "spotted the best lines in the play" (45), and she warns Thoby that if they do not "send a shiver down your spine, even if you are in the middle of cold grouse and coffee—you are no true Shakespearian!" (46). Woolf's two steps forward one step back approach to her brother begins with her asking for a "lecture" on Shakespeare when she next sees him, yet *she* wants to "talk about these things." Although "weak in the upper region," she does not hesitate to distinguish between the way Imogen, Posthumous, and Cymbeline "talk divinely" and their absence of "humanity" ("But really they might have been cut out with a pair of scissors" [45]). The assertive "But really" and the certainty that she knows who is a "true Shakespearian" offset the meekness of "[j]ust explain this to me" and the worshiper's submission. From start to finish, Woolf's sense of humor leavens her confidence no less than her humility, and her precocious if untutored penchant for analysis makes itself felt. A paragraph after she has worried the humanity of Shakespeare's characters, she circles back to the topic, acknowledging that "Shakespeare's smaller characters are human; what I say is that superhuman ones *are* superhuman" (46).

Years later, in her diary, recollecting her reading at the time of this letter, Woolf came close to mixing up Thoby and Shakespeare. In the letter, she wrote that she still felt "a little oppressed by his [Shakespeare's]—greatness I suppose." The diary entry has her remembering that "[w]hen I was 20, in spite of Thoby who used to be so pressing & exacting, I could not for the life of me read Shakespeare for pleasure " (*Diary*, August 15, 1924, 2.310). The "great William" oppressed and Thoby pressed. But how? In *A Sketch of the Past*, Woolf writes that while she "*listened* passively to the story of the Greeks on the stairs outside the water closet," her "first *arguments*" with Thoby "were about Shakespeare."[9]

> He would sweep down upon me, with his assertion that everything was in Shakespeare. He let the whole mass that he held in his grasp descend in an avalanche on me. I revolted. But how could I oppose all that? Rather feebly; getting red and agitated. Still it was then my genuine feeling that a play was antipathetic to me. . . . And he was ruthless; exasperating; downing me, overwhelming me; with enough passion to make us both heated. So that my opposition cannot have been quite ineffectual. He made me feel his pride . . . (138)

The "whole mass that he held in his grasp" sounds like a huge complete works of Shakespeare and like all of Thoby's schoolboy knowledge of Shakespeare, too. Together, Shakespeare and Thoby were downing Virginia. And she, the object of this overwhelming, antipathetic, fraternal, bardic avalanche (ruthless, passionate, red, heated, prideful), feebly revolted. Or not so feebly, since the older brother had to do with an "ingenuous," "sheltered," younger sister who was also "bubbling, inquisitive, restless, contradicting" (138). By 1939–1940, Woolf had read a fair amount of Freud. To the suggestiveness of the language I have been citing (note not only the mass, the agitation, the downing, the passion, the heat and pride, but also the "candle grease smelling landing" outside the water closet), and to the force of phrases in this same paragraph like "[t]he unspoken thought . . . when he came into my room. . . . We were, of course, naturally attracted to each other. Besides his brother's feeling" (138), she can hardly have been oblivious. Shakespeare, no less than Thoby, is at once unnaturally attractive and instinctively to be resisted.

Thoby may have come by his Shakespeare in school, but for Virginia there was something crude, physical, and manly about the way he "took" Shakespeare. "He had consumed Shakespeare, somehow or other, by himself. He had possessed himself of it, in his large clumsy way . . ." (138). Thoby's approach to Shakespeare was "casual, rough and ready and comprehensive" (138). Thoby, she knew, was not a (would-be) writer reading Shakespeare; he was not, as she was, "a breaker off of single words, or sentences, . . . a note taker" (138). "That large natural inhumanity in Shakespeare delighted him. It was a tree's way of shedding its leaves" (138). What she munched, he consumed. But for him, it was equipment for living, not writing: Shakespeare was "the place where he got the measure of the daily world. He took his bearings there; and sized us up from that standard" (138–39). Because of Shakespeare, Thoby was "unperturbed; equipped; . . . he knew his own place; and relished his inheritance, ... [was] proud of his station as a man; ready to play his part among men" (139). As girl and then as a woman—a "shell-less little creature, I think he thought me; so sheltered, in my room, compared with him" (138)—Woolf must have sensed early, and would later assert, that Thoby's inheritance bore little relation to her own.

Woolf's status as legatee (five hundred pounds and a room of one's own) and its consequences are worked out most famously in *A Room of One's Own*. There, the "extraordinarily gifted" sister Judith Shakespeare was not yet seventeen when she gathered up her inheritance—"a small parcel of her belongings"—and "took the road to London."[10] This conjuration of Judith follows hard on the heels of Woolf's catching sight of "the works of Shakespeare on the shelf" (46). This, I take it, refers to the shelf filled with the works of Shakespeare in Leonard and Virginia Woolf's library, although one wonders whether or not it entails a penumbral memory of Leslie Stephen's library.[11] In any case, the core of Woolf's narrative at this point in her lecture is neither domestic nor filial—it is sororal. When Judith "picked up a book now and then," it was "one of her brother's perhaps" (47). The siblings shared still more than this: "[s]he had the quickest fancy, a gift like her brother's, for the tune of words. Like him, she had a taste for the theatre" (48). While there is a father in this story, one who beats, scolds, and begs his daughter, the genealogical fantasy that Woolf is tracing really starts with the brother and sister. They share "the same grey eyes and rounded brows" and the same "gift," which each of them brings to London "to feed abundantly" and to disseminate (48). In the end, the "great William" bequeathed us his works. Judith, the pregnant, potential progenitor of a line of her own, "killed herself one winter's night and lies buried at some cross-roads" (48).

This is not, however, the story's only chiasmus. Woolf's own brother, Thoby, had been dead for more than twenty years when she spoke to the women students at Newnham and Girton, and by 1929 she herself had successfully broadcast her "genius for fiction" (*A Room*, 48). Thoby may have "relished his inheritance" from William Shakespeare, but whatever it was, typhoid snuffed it out. Virginia's inheritance from Shakespeare was patent yet equivocal, not unlike the sentence Hermione Lee quotes from Woolf's holograph draft of *To the Lighthouse*: "Lily Briscoe remembered that [everyone] man has Shakespeare [behind him]; & women have not."[12] Woolf's inheritance from Judith was also mixed, no less disturbing than it was encouraging. In her peroration, Woolf inspired her audience with her conviction that Judith "lives in you and me" (113). Judith "never wrote a word" (113) but Woolf and many others have and will. Readers of *A Room of One's Own* now know that the Judith who "killed herself" (whose "nervous stress . . . might well have killed her" [50]) also left Woolf the darker legacy of suicide. If Shakespeare left Thoby "unperturbed" (*Sketch*, 139), was it Judith who left Virginia perturbed ("I feel certain that I am going mad again," wrote Virginia to Leonard Woolf)?[13] Oddly enough, it is William Shakespeare who figures for Woolf in a fantasy of easeful, if not necessarily self-inflicted, death. Two months before her suicide, she wrote to Ethel Smyth, "Did I tell you I'm reading the whole of English literature? By the time I've reached Shakespeare the bombs will be falling. So I've arranged a very nice last scene: reading Shakespeare, having forgotten my gas mask, I shall fade far away, and quite forget" (*Letters*, February 1, 1941, 6.466; "Fade far away, dissolve, and quite forget" is from Keats's "Ode to a Nightingale").

Perhaps, then, it is neither coincidental nor surprising that Woolf believed that the scene of reading also *began* with Shakespeare. In her reading notes on Allardyce Nicoll's survey of British drama and in drafts and fragments of "The Reader" (her last, unfinished, essay), Woolf asks several times, "When is the reader born?" and each time, she more or less concludes, "With Sh^{re} of course" (Silver, 1979/80, 431). This is Woolf as historian of reading in a mostly figurative mode; she was, after all, perfectly capable of wondering whether "Shakespeare read Chaucer" and so imagining Shakespeare himself with a readerly, "literary past." Woolf also commented now phenomenologically, now cognitively, on reading Shakespeare. As if she were writing about Cleopatra, Woolf explains that "every critic finds his own features in Shakespeare" because of his "variety," "his perpetual vitality . . . [which] excites perpetual curiosity. He does not as

so many writers feed momentary appetites. . . . His styles are too innumerable"
(Silver, 1979/80, 431–32).[14] In the absence of a definitive reading—be it the
"Johnson S. the Coleridge S. [or] the Bradley S."—with "[o]ne reading always
superced[ing] another," Woolf concludes that the "truest account of reading
Shakespeare would be not to write a book . . . but to collect notes, without trying to make them consistent" (Silver, 1979/80, 431–32). And this is just what
she did. But before turning to these notes, I want to consider Woolf's affective
responses as a Shakespeare reader.

Throughout her notebooks one finds studied responses to Shakespeare, but
the hallmark of her diary and essay accounts of reading his verse is physicality. His words have velocity and weight; they shock and they tire, startle, and
astound:

> I was reading Othello last night, & was impressed by the volley & vol-
> ume & tumble of his words: too many I should say, were I reviewing for
> the Times. He put them in when tension was slack. In the great scenes,
> everything fits like a glove. The mind tumbles & splashes among words
> when it is not being urged on: I mean, the mind of a very great master
> of words who is writing with one hand. He abounds. The lesser writers
> stint. As usual, impressed by Shre. But my mind is very bare to words—
> English words—at the moment: they hit me, hard, I watch them bounce
> & spring. (*Diary*, April 24, 1928, 3.182)

> I read Shakespeare *directly* I have finished writing, when my mind is agape
> & red & hot. Then it is astonishing. I never yet knew how amazing his
> stretch & speed & word coining power is, until I felt it utterly outpace
> & outrace my own, seeming to start equal & then I see him draw ahead
> & do things I could not in my wildest tumult & utmost press of mind
> imagine. Even the less known & worser plays are written at a speed that
> is quicker than anybody else's quickest; & the words drop so fast one can't
> pick them up. . . . Evidently the pliancy of his mind was so complete that
> he could furbish out any train of thought; &, relaxing lets fall a shower of
> such unregarded flowers. Why then should anyone else attempt to write.
> This is not 'writing' at all. Indeed, I could say that Shre surpasses literature
> altogether, if I knew what I meant. (*Diary*, April 13, 1930, 3.300–301)

> The vigour of the language is too overwhelming. . . . Every ounce of en-
> ergy is used up in realising the perpetual succession of images which coin

even the thinnest pencilled thoughts on the borderlands of consciousness into robust highly coloured shapes. . . . The vitality, the intensity, the compression and pressure . . . keep one on the stretch almost to the exclusion of comment . . . ("Byron & Mr Briggs")[15]

Woolf consistently responds to Shakespeare's verbal kinetics. The rush and tumble, the pace and speed, push and pressure of his language register with intensity. Like Keats, who writes a sonnet as a way of revving up, readying himself to burn through *King Lear*, Woolf describes coming at Shakespeare when she herself has already gathered up a full head of steam, as if the only chance she stands of holding her own in her race with him is if she gets a head start. Speed is preeminent, but Woolf also admires rhythm and modulation, not just pace but pacing. Shakespeare can tell when "tension was slack," when "relaxing" was more to the purpose than stretching.

There are a host of gradations that we can identify in these three passages. "Writing with one hand" and "worser plays" point tacitly to writing the best plays with two. Tumbling and splashing speak to something different from being urged on. "Stretch" and "speed" sound like they have to do with pace, but then they are joined to "word coining" by Woolf's recurring ampersands. In this case, as often, Woolf fuses the agility of Shakespeare's mind with his language. "Everything fits like a glove." Woolf herself will momentarily merge with Shakespeare only to acknowledge distinction and defeat. At first glance the splashing mind seems to be Woolf's. She notices this and so momentarily pauses ("I mean") in order to make clear (to herself?) that it is "the very great master of words," not the reader (Woolf), whose mind is tumbling. She is his "equal"— for a moment—and then she is surpassed.

In each of these passages, Woolf's own rush of words, her attempt to keep pace, is stymied but never entirely foiled. It appears that each passage ends in linguistic breakdown or despair. Like Coleridge ("Feeble ~~would every~~ will my voice be ~~that would~~ to my own ears, while I speak of SHAKESPEAR") and Keats (Shakespeare "has left nothing to say about nothing or any thing"), she finds that her mind is "bare to words"; there is no further reason to "attempt to write"; one is excluded from comment. In each case, this is a matter of physical as well as mental exhaustion, akin to everything we mean when we speak of being run down (recall Thoby and Shakespeare "downing" Woolf). Yet, as if by instinct, out of a compelling writerly drive toward self-preservation in the face of what Berryman called "that multiform & encyclopedic bastard," Woolf safeguards a bit of turf for herself.[16] In the first passage, her mind is bare to English words, but she goes on to allow that she has been reading "French for 4 weeks. An idea comes to me for an article on French." Hit hard by (Shakespeare's) English, she can outflank his assault in another language. In the second passage Woolf's characteristic sense of humor keeps her going. She suggests the futility of writing after Shakespeare, but she manages to preserve the category of literature for others by positioning Shakespeare somewhere else altogether. Even this *o altitudo* has to be read in the context of her wry self-deprecation ("if I knew what I meant"). It is not quite fair to equate the end of my third citation with the preceding two because I have cut off Woolf mid-sentence. Nevertheless, the "almost" antecedent to the last words I cite betrays Woolf's probably unselfconscious devotion to her own voice.

Woolf identified one other way to hold one's own when pressured by Shakespeare. Since when we are "fully conscious and aware his fame intimidates us," Woolf commends reading Shakespeare when we are ill. "Illness in its kingly sublimity sweeps all . . . aside, leaves nothing but Shakespeare and oneself . . . the barriers go down, the knots run smooth, the brain rings and resounds with *Lear* and *Macbeth*, and even Coleridge himself squeaks like a distant mouse." Committed to preserving the "pleasure" of reading Shakespeare, Woolf champions illness because it is with illness that she associates "rashness," both "one of the properties of illness" and what we "chiefly need in reading Shakespeare" ("On Being Ill").[17]

Illness and rashness. Woolf was ill quite a lot. She spent a significant part of her life laid up, depressed, feverish, head-achy, back-achy, exhausted, nervous, comatose, manic, euphoric. Take this representative diary entry from March 1, 1937: "very cold: impotent: & terrified. As if I were exposed on a high ledge in full light. Very lonely. . . . Very useless. . . . No words. Very apprehensive" (5.63). Illness, however, lowered the barriers not only between Woolf and Shakespeare but within Woolf herself. Entitlement might supplant intimidation; the license granted by illness that Woolf does not seem to have insisted on with friends and family may have emboldened her with Shakespeare. Yet boldness, or rashness ("praised be rashness," declares Hamlet; "Our indiscretion sometimes serves us well"), was never self-indulgent or a cover for "doff[ing] the intelligence in reading him." Instead, it was another way of leveling the playing field and allowing Woolf simply to catch up with the sprinting Bard. Even if bedridden, impotent and terrified, Woolf could take advantage of her amateur status. Unlike public, professional readers, acutely conscious of "the buzz of [Shakespeare] criticism," the sick and the amateur have unmediated (or at least less mediated) access to the plays, to "nothing but Shakespeare." Like the notebook, the sick-bed was an asylum, a privileged locus of security where one could "hazard one's conjectures privately" ("On Being Ill," 325).

In a brief piece entitled "*Twelfth Night* at the Old Vic" (1933), Woolf writes that there are "those who prefer to read Shakespeare in the book; those who prefer to see him acted on the stage; and those who run perpetually from book to stage gathering plunder." The advantage to reading is that "[t]here is time . . . to make a note in the margin; time to wonder at queer jingles."[18] This is somewhat odd since Virginia Woolf tended not to write in margins. With the exception of her Latin and Greek books, the volumes in her library contained almost no annotations by her. While Woolf did write with a pen in her hand, she used it to write in notebooks, not in margins. Indeed, among her papers, there is a rather carefully worked out three-page squib in which she mocks those who write in books (MSS Sussex, A23c 1–3). Woolf begins by conceding that "in the big affairs of life," like love, we are all pretty much alike. On "trivial occasions" and insofar as "trifles" are concerned, however, the "student of character" will find a great deal of distinction. Such a trifle is the penchant for "writing observations in the margins of books." To illustrate her point, Woolf sketches the lineaments of a trio of fatuous annotators. One "anonymous commentator," a gentleman, "old Colonel Ta[l]llboys," cannot help but "scrawl his O, or his Pooh, or his Beautiful upon the unresisting sheet as though the author received this mark upon his flesh."[19] The Colonel "wishes to nudge you as it were, to admire this beauty" or to set you against "the lies you are told in the text." Woolf's only half-comic resentment stems from her sense of herself as a reader and as a writer. The annotator who "wreaks his vengeance on the margin" and so "assault[s]" or "violate[s] margin[s]" is also having his unfettered way with the author and subsequent readers. Avidly occupying both positions, Woolf chides by turns hectoring and "pedantic" annotators. For their designs on future readers, such commentators are subjected to the Woolf's lampooning, but so too are those who hardly seem to notice what they are doing. Their "lachrymose lines," indicative of a "half conscious sigh of tearful satisfaction," are just as intolerable. Will not such self-absorbed readers later be ashamed of their "handiwork"? Is there nothing that can extirpate "one of the most permanent and vigourous instincts in the human mind"?

The obvious overkill of this last question, and of much of what precedes it, answers nicely to Woolf's clever satire. She, for one, would not be guilty of such a "serious infringement of the rules." Or of such self-exposure. But when she wrote this, she already had published most of her best-known work, work that was received internationally, and she was more than twice Keats's age when he was writing in his Shakespeare editions and commenting on Shakespeare in his letters. So anyone who sits reading this exercise in Woolf's notebooks has to wonder what she imagined would become of her carefully preserved reading notebooks, not to mention her letters and diaries. They may not be marginalia, but her notes are still chock full of commentary, nudges, and expressions of "likes or dislikes." The notebooks certainly feel like they have future readers in mind. Having read *Romeo and Juliet*, Woolf began her notebook entry, probably in 1909, asking "Who shall say anything of Romeo & Juliet? Do I dare?" (MSS New York, 29.3). Yes, she is posing these questions to herself, writing out loud, so to speak. But is she anticipating future readers? The notebook entry continues with what would appear to be an unnecessary caution: "in private: it seems to me very immature work." Like illness, Woolf's notebook afforded her enough privacy and confidence to criticize "the great William." *Romeo and Juliet* is not just "immature" but "very immature; weak joinings, & no care of individualism in hero & heroine." In other words, much the same thing that she wrote to Thoby back in 1901, when she was wondering about Shakespeare's characters' lack of humanity. In her notebook, as in her youthful letter, she feels the need to backtrack, to acknowledge that "[i]t is not true, of course, that Romeo & Juliet are without character; I mean that in their relations with each other they have very little that is individual. . . . But in their relations with other people, they have a great deal of character." This distinction curiously mirrors Woolf's belief (expressed in her remarks on annotators) that one finds "a great family likeness among all people who are in love. But you cannot in anyway forecast the temper in which Brown will meet the loss of his umbrella." With Romeo, Juliet is characterless; but "[t]ake the scene in which Juliet tests the nurse," and you will find real "character."

For Woolf, as for most readers of Shakespeare, character and language command attention. In her letter to Thoby, she explained that Shakespeare's superhuman characters are superhuman, that only the "smaller characters" are "human." But in just over a half of a page of notes on *Macbeth*, also dating from 1909, she is certain that "Macbeth is the most human of the villains" (MSS New York, 29.9). Because Woolf's memory of reading *Macbeth* (as opposed to her memory of the play itself) is so specific, we get a very precise scene of reading. She does not mention that she was reading Shakespeare on the heels of an unsuccessful visit in Florence with her sister Vanessa and her husband, Clive Bell; instead, she records that she read *Macbeth* "in the train, wedged between Germans, by the light of sunset in Switzerland (the mountains raised like Titan women making supplications) & by the steady glare of midday in France." Now back in London, Woolf explains that, "reading it thus, I read it simply for the story." Perhaps she is excusing herself to herself. She "hesitate[s] to write of this play" because of the "[i]nnumerable subtleties of character & beauties that I missed of course & even find [not "found"] it difficult to get a complete impression."[20] The play "moved in all its parts"; but she, "wedged" in, let herself be "drawn on [by the play], without making any effort." No pen in hand, no reading notebook at the ready, she had to acknowledge that it was (and apparently remains) not she but Macbeth who is best equipped to form "a complete impression." As she writes at the end of this note, "[i]t is always these twisted characters, like Macbeth, who have the great illuminations—seem to get some queer view of the whole. His speech about tomorrow. They see everything." Not Woolf the common reader, for whom "fragments are unendurable," but the "twisted" Macbeth is endowed with the "whole in one's mind" on which she believed her very comfort as a reader depended (I quote from "Byron & Mr Briggs," written some dozen years after this notebook entry). On the one hand, Woolf attributes to Macbeth a "view of the whole" that she still cannot achieve and that she must know he famously lacks, given all of the moving parts of the play that Macbeth cannot see but that Woolf, reading for the story, could not miss. On the other hand, his "queer" view, as his "Tomorrow" soliloquy indicates, puts him in touch with "everything." Where it counts, Woolf seems to be saying, Shakespeare's and Macbeth's powers of perception are well in excess of the common reader's. If reading "simply for the story" while she was in Europe made for a kind of holiday reading, back in London, there was a discernible awareness of insufficiency, even dereliction of duty.

The set of Shakespeare notes that begins with *Romeo and Juliet* and ends with *Macbeth* also includes three pages on *Hamlet*, two on *King Lear*, and two on *Othello* (MSS New York, 29.3–9). While a goodly portion of what Woolf jotted down about *Hamlet* pertains to A. C. Bradley's lecture, in her own estimation, Hamlet, like Macbeth, "sees around everything" and "perceives all possibilities" (years later, she still imagined Hamlet to be "the complete character" [Silver, 1979/80, 422]). Commenting very briefly on each of the first four acts, Woolf mentions Polonius and Laertes "careful of the honour of their name"; Hamlet justifying his "antic disposition" to Horatio; Hamlet with the players and Gertrude's impatience with Polonius; the "strength—almost brutality—of Hamlet"; and finally, in Act 4, Claudius's character and the way "Ophelia makes one pity old Polonius." Some of these notations, perhaps the surprising last among them most of all, have been thought by Alice Foxe to "correlate remarkably" with Woolf's perception of her own familial circumstances.[21] This may be so, but for Virginia Woolf the Shakespeare reader, identification often has more of a phenomenological than a psychological cast. Despite her own conviction, noted by Foxe, that "to write down one's impressions of *Hamlet* as one reads it year after year, would be virtually to record one's own autobiography," the 1909 *Hamlet* notes, whether in terms of what Woolf pauses to remark upon or her own remarks, never quite coalesce around her life beyond the moment of reading. When Woolf begins her summary comment, at the top of the second page of her notes—a point at which her successive, act-by-act comments ought to have led us to expect observations about Act 5—we find ten lines that begin, "The impression left is of one of dream." At first glance, this dream(iness) appears to be Woolf's; hence the random quality of the first page of her notes. But just as at precisely the same interval in her *Othello* notes—coincidentally, at the top of the second page—Woolf writes of Desdemona, "Seems as though everything were a dream round her," so it is Hamlet whom Woolf imagines dreaming and for whom "the unknown seems to press at all points. overwhelmingly. Immense size & grandeur of the thing." Woolf has correlated her version of Hamlet's method ("He works through different states in his imagination.") with her own experiences as a *reader* (as opposed to a daughter or sister or even a writer). Woolf the reader and Hamlet the revenger are overwhelmed ("he cant do anything of what is expected of him") by the "size and grandeur of the thing."

In her *Macbeth* notes, Woolf implicitly acknowledges the relief she felt reading "simply for the story." I suspect that the relatively lengthy synopsis of Bradley in her *Hamlet* notes has a similar effect. Critics appear infrequently in Woolf's Shakespeare notes. In the "Byron and Mr Briggs" typescript, she wrote that "[i]t is all very well, when the impression has spent itself, to take down Coleridge and Coleridge will delight ~~astound~~ and instruct, but only in the margin of the mind. It is I who have read the play. I hold it in my mind. . . . No third person can explain or alter or even throw much light" (478).[22] Nonetheless, for a few moments at least, Bradley would have been easier to read and to comment on than Shakespeare. The giveaway is Woolf's last notebook response to *Hamlet*—"I think there is something deeper." This comes hard on the heels of a page and a half of notes based on Bradley and it intimates future engagements with the play, for example some twenty years later in *The Waves*, when Woolf is less stunned by the immensity "of the thing."

Woolf's commentary on *King Lear* reads more like one long summary gloss than moment by moment reader's responses, and it is tempting to read her first lines autobiographically: "One realises that Lear has always been stormy. His daughters have suffered from it. . . . an arbitrary imperious old man." However neither Leslie Stephen nor his daughter's tribulations governs this set of notes. The page and a half that Woolf writes on *King Lear* is a mix of qualified assertion, uncertainty, quotation, and query typical in her reading notebooks. Woolf is consistently alert to the rhythm and density of Shakespeare's verse. "The writing seems to me tumultuous, sometimes absolutely turgid with meaning." She finds that the "language is often difficult and very many latin words are used." But then there are those breathtaking moments of almost monosyllabic Shakespearean simplicity. When Woolf copies out "And to deal plainly, I fear I am not in my perfect mind," she first explains that Lear's "language, & thought, is simple as a childs." Then explanation quickly gives way to sheer admiration: the "scene seems to me as great as any."

The play as a whole speaks to Woolf of our vulnerability ("all human kind exposed on the heath") and to our impotence. Misfortune in *King Lear* is "not so much the result of human ill doing, but from the vengeance of the gods." Parenthetically, she herself registers something of the confusion that she attributes to the play: "I should judge it a much later, & somehow more confused work than Hamlet, the characters (if I can explain myself) seem less definite." "Should . . . somehow . . . confusion . . . if": this tentative reading of Shakespeare at his most daunting is itself, I think, the gist of Woolf's response to a play in which "profound doubts" come "again & again." Woolf seems confident that Cordelia has a "simple, honest mind, somewhat stubborn; without imagination. perfectly transparent," and that Goneril and Regan, who "scold like fishwives," are "passionate women"; but her *Lear* notes, studded with "I suppose," "seems," questions and hesitations, reveal Woolf in her late twenties to be no more able to form a "complete impression" of *King Lear* than of *Macbeth*. In 1926, Woolf imagined that were she to read precisely these two plays when she was ill, she could counter Shakespeare's "overweening power" with her own "overweening arrogance," causing the "barriers [to] go down, the knots [to] run smooth." In her notebook, however, she settles for "hazard[ing her] conjectures privately." Not arrogance but hazard, in this formulation from her essay "On Being Ill," answers to what Woolf felt as the "intensity" of reading *King Lear*. And "conjectures" picks up on the interrogative quality of her reading. "Why is there a fool?" she asks. "What does his gibberish mean?" These unanswered notebook questions comport with the play's own "doubts" and with those that are raised "again & again" in the novels Woolf would soon begin to write, novels whose stylistic achievements include their own bevy of incomplete impressions.

In 1921, more than ten years after her first series of Shakespeare reading notes, Woolf wrote what appear to be three separate notebook entries in response to *Measure for Measure*, a play she had already read twice. Formal, writerly preoccupations are on her mind when she compares plays with novels: "In a play there is no background of the contriver. It starts straight off from the character. ~~Who~~ The comment, the motive, one must supply for oneself: making it up, I suppose, from hints in what is said. In this plays differ from novels" (MSS Sussex, 38.16). The character Woolf seems to be thinking most about is Isabella, and here, as elsewhere in her Shakespeare notes, she copies out several lines, then conjectures in an extremely compressed fashion about the sort of character who would speak such lines, about their quality, and about their relation to the unfolding plot. Isabella's famous "More than our brother is our chastity" strikes her as "unreal." Shakespeare has "put it in like a block at the end of the speech, for the sake of the story." Her "coldness" and "sanctimonious hardness" are "odious." But then there is the "fiery & quick witted" Isabella, and the Isabella whose disquieting erotic fantasy of wearing the "impression of keen whips" and stripping herself to death Woolf also copies down—"Now that's vehement," she writes. "Would she not have kept at that heat?—then possibly swung round"? Several disparate comments (touching on, among other things, Shakespeare's fondness for malapropisms in his clowns and beadles) intervene before Woolf finds her way back to Isabella at the very end of this set of notes, at which point Woolf decides that Isabella is "consistent" after all. She is "a <u>religious</u> woman all through," and her "clearheaded coldness" explains how she can hold her brother to a higher standard than Angelo. Curiously, it is that brother, Claudio, not "quick witted," vehement," "clearheaded" Isabella, who triggers Woolf's unique generalization in this series of notes about Shakespearean method—in this instance, about the relationship between character and plotting. Probably thinking also of Hamlet, she writes that "Claudio's speech about death is in line with the other Shakespeare speeches—It has that expansion of the imagination wh[ich] seems to paralyse action." While this has all of the apothegmatic acuity of Coleridge's marginalia, its pertinence to Woolf's own characters and plotting is hard to miss.

Not just Isabella's motives, but Shakespeare's, too, occupy Woolf. She fills most of a page with a series of "points made by [Georg Morris Cohen] Brandes" in his two-volume *William Shakespeare: A Critical Study* (1898) that she must have had to hand. For example, Shakespeare "had no interest whatsoever in ecclesiastical movements [Woolf occasionally quotes from but mostly paraphrases Brandes]. But the Puritans hated art & sexual frailties. The interest of the theatre demanded that he should write comedy. It would have been unwise, politically, to carry out the punishment of the puritanical hypocrisy to the extreme. We have therefore the unsatisfactory end." Woolf also copies out Brandes's assertion that Shakespeare "was earnestly bent on proving his own standpoint to be the moral one." But there is reason to doubt that Woolf was persuaded by Brandes's reading of the play or its playwright. Elsewhere in these *Measure for Measure* notes, Woolf imagines a more deliberative than dogmatic Shakespeare: he "wished to *argue* the *question* of chastity himself. I mean there is a *brooding & question*[ing] behind it all" (my emphasis). Brandes may imagine Shakespeare currying favor with King James in the person of the Duke, especially when Vincentio's authority is criticized by Lucio; but Woolf finds Lucio's position "odd": "I suspect that S^he meant to poke fun at the Duke, only didn't take the trouble to work this out." Once again, what Woolf notices about character, even politics, hinges on the sort of Coleridgean surmise about Shakespeare's craftsmanship that only a writer might make. Moreover, in the tiny phrase "didn't trouble to work this out," we get another tiny glimpse of Woolf's self-confidence in relation to the "great William." Here is something Shakespeare failed to work out (only) because he did not "take the trouble" to work it out. Shakespeare has not nodded off; his lapse, though not inconsequential, is apparently intentional.

Woolf's reflections on *Troilus and Cressida* (MSS Sussex, 49.23; probably 1922) begin with a stupefied or even exasperated, "The words—the words—the words—" (hence a touch of the Hamlet in Woolf). The page and a half of notes appear hectic, with lines from the play and abbreviated responses ricocheting off one another as Woolf was reading, pen in hand. There are staccato bursts, fragments of explanation and astonishment: "Everything realised[?]: brought out with violent metaphor"; "tumbles over knots"; "such quickness—so many changes of mood"; "What about form? art?"; "this the dramatic form not the poetic form"; "up & down in & out—conflict, always taking sides for & against." Then Woolf seems to slow down, and the notes themselves momentarily expand. She mentions the "Alms for oblivion speech" and comments, "we do get a general point of view also something lofty & noble & confronting life & time. a kind of melancholy always?" We may even begin to hear a hint of self-consciousness. The Woolf who would later write in her diary that Shakespeare "abounds. The lesser writers stint" remarks in her notebook that he is "able to coin full blooded images where we have only the ghosts of ideas." Then Woolf is back to her admiring fragments: "woven together—all at the highest pitch," "concentrates an argument into 10 words," and so on.

Toward the end of the *Troilus* notes, we come upon two connected phrases: "being the character—shocked to imagine an actors [*sic*] voice—." This seems to adumbrate an old argument about reading versus watching a Shakespeare play, but in light of this particular set of notes, it may be evidence of the intensity of Woolf's reading. With all those words, words, words resounding silently but still "at the highest pitch" in her ears, she suddenly catches herself up short and imagines an actor, a body, a voice not her own. There is a shock of abrupt disengagement, of pulling back not from a page of a novel, from which, after all, we have no intended alternative, but from a page of a play, which inevitably suggests a production—in our mind's ear or on stage. So what does Woolf mean when she writes, "being the character"? Something like, "Given the stand-on-its-own full-bloodedness of a Shakespeare character, it is shocking still further to imagine an actor giving voice to that character"? Or, "Given that to this point I have been (and still am) this character, it is shocking . . ."? Perhaps it is only fanciful to posit an unintended transposition in this notebook entry when, three lines after the shock of imagining an actor's voice, Woolf (apropos of nothing obvious) copies out Cressida's line: "And mighty states characterless are grated to dusty nothing" (3.2.183). First there is a moment of identification, "being the character," then there are ghostly "characterless" states. By "characterless," Cressida means "having or leaving no record"; however, Woolf may be registering a reader's shock at passing not merely from absorption in, to distance from, a character but to her own momentary absence: it is as if she knows that she is no longer "being the character" but is not yet again herself.

Antony and Cleopatra "is the most extravagantly languaged of the plays but extremely difficult" (MSS Sussex, 47.3). Woolf's notes on this play run to only five or six lines, but we feel something of her experience of reading it when she writes of its "pelt of ideas & words." This is consistent with the experience of being hit hard by words that we already have heard Woolf describe—the "volley & volume & tumble" of words in *Othello* that "hit me, hard." It is evidence of the kind of corporal- or sense-reading that Shakespeare apparently provokes and, as such, it may clarify what an opening gambit at the top of a notebook page like "The words—the words—the words—" denotes. I do not mean to suggest that Woolf felt the least bit sorry for herself as a reader of Shakespeare. Rather, she records gratifying stress. In her diary, sounding a bit like Keats readying himself to "burn through" *King Lear*, she asked herself, "Shall I read King Lear? Do I want such a strain on the emotions? I think I do" (November 16, 1921).[23] In the case of being pelted by *Antony and Cleopatra*, then, Woolf seems to call to mind the play's cultivated masochistic pleasures, whether those of the Cydnus, its water beaten by oars but "amorous of their strokes," or of Cleopatra, nursed asleep by the asp biting her breast.

Woolf's *Antony and Cleopatra* notes, which seem to date from 1924, appear in the same notebook in which she comments on *King John*, *Richard 2*, and *Richard 3* (MSS Sussex, 45.25, 27, and 29). Reading these history plays, Woolf continued to hear the press of their language, their "rant," "mouthing," and "rhetoric." She found the plays a sometimes unsettling mixture of "country speech" and "out of place evanescent poetry"; of patriotic "full mouthed rhetoric" and "outbreaks of meditation[,] comment" (*King John*); of "gallery speech" and "psychological subtlety—the peculiar pondering hesitation of Sh$^{re.}$ analysis" (*Richard 2*). Once again, Woolf is impressed by Shakespeare the wordsmith, the Shakespeare who in *Richard 2* "moulds" words "on his tongue" and can "coin everything into words—make brilliant what cd. have been left dim." But like many readers before her, from Ben Jonson to Samuel Johnson, Woolf is not quite sure what to make of either the "flood of poetry trying to burst through in these early plays" or "the prodigality of Sh^{re} genius" (reading *Richard 3*, she notes the "bottomless store of words rushing out"). The *copia* in *Richard 2* seems to surprise her, as does the "absolutely unreal language of [the] gardener," and still more so, Shakespeare's apparent "lik[ing] it to be so." Meanwhile, running beneath her comments on language and character, Woolf's notes disclose an affective undertow. Her recourse to phrases like "gallery speech" and "gallery play" is evidently more understanding and empathetic than it is judgmental. Indeed, just before the end of her *Richard 2* notes (and her comments about the gardener's language), Woolf sketches out a fleeting but poignant picture of "the audience pulling" at Shakespeare. "[H]e can't get away alone to think." Many constraints with which Woolf was or would be familiar crowd in here: having to please an audience, having to write for a living, the risks of stylistic innovation, the appeal and the bad faith of what she calls "patriotic" fictions, respect for and disappointment in "common readers," even the need for a room of one's own.[24] One professional writer, Woolf, is thinking about the best interests of another, Shakespeare. There may even be a hint of Judith Shakespeare looking out for her brother.

In 1934, Woolf either read or reread *Troilus and Cressida*, *The Taming of the Shrew*, *Pericles*, *Titus Andronicus*, *Coriolanus*, *Timon of Athens*, and *Cymbeline*. The most sustained set of notes at this time pertains to *Coriolanus*, which Woolf first read in July 1934 (MSS New York, 26.25) and then reread, and took one more page of notes on, in 1940 (MSS Sussex, 37.7). Woolf clearly liked reading the play, but since it was not "easy to read," it was not easy "to enjoy." In 1934, she notes its "close-packed elliptical style" and "the difficulty from the hurry of action." In 1940, she notices the play's "rugged, turbid: broken: violent" language and wonders whether it was employed to dramatize "the physical effect of fighting on speech." All of its insistently masculine words and rhythms, coupled with Coriolanus's "breathlessness," his "turgid[ity]," his "pent up energy," the play's "contortions" and its "obscur[ity]—too few words for the meaning," seem to have left Woolf much as she describes Shakespeare (and perhaps Coriolanus): "[c]aught up—impatient." At one point she cites several lines ("fortune's blows, / When most struck home, being gentle, wounded, craves / A noble cunning") then half exasperated, half astonished, asks, "how translate that"? Since this "seems to be what he wrote, not corrupt," Shakespeare must have "chopped up for pleasure."

But whose pleasure—his or ours? And what sort of pleasure?[25] When she read *Coriolanus*, Woolf does not seem to have experienced the "strain on the emotions" that she associated with *King Lear*, or "difficulty in the thought as in the [great] tragedies." If anything, in *Coriolanus* there is "very little contemplation." Still, the language of the play proved vexing. On the final page of her 1934 notes on *Coriolanus*, she copies down three and a half lines spoken by Menenius, then takes five lines of her own to paraphrase and explain them. Not surprisingly, the word "difficulty" appears four times in this three page set of notes ("difficult" appears once at the bottom of the single 1940 page). Woolf writes that she rates the play "very high for vigour"; but she keeps remarking its thorniness. All of the "stir & chop & change of action wh. cant be seen in reading" makes for hard going. Add to this her sense that the playwright is doing this "intentionally" and it must be Shakespeare, not Coriolanus, about whom she is writing in 1940 when she imagines him "very crabbed, as if irked by the necessity of telling a plain story." Of course Woolf, who spent years experimenting with prose style, might well have identified with the Shakespeare whose "magnificent story" was told, not in glib "gallery speech," but in language that makes substantial demands on listeners and readers. Indeed, she herself knew something about chopped-up language. "Few books have interested me more to write than The Waves," she wrote. "No glibness, no assurance; you see . . . I'm chopping & tacking all the time" (*Diary*, January 7, 1931, 4.4). As early as 1908, Woolf wrote that "as for writing, . . . I attain a different kind of beauty, achieve a symmetry by means of infinite discords, . . . achieve in the end, some kind of whole made of shivering fragments."[26] In 1923, she credited Dorothy Richardson with developing a sentence "which we might call the psychological sentence of the feminine gender.

It is of a more elastic fibre than the old, capable of stretching to the extreme, of suspending the frailest particles, of enveloping the vaguest shapes."[27] And two years later, in *Mrs. Dalloway*, Woolf composed "a frail quivering sound, a voice bubbling up without direction, vigour, beginning or end, running weakly and shrilly and with an absence of all human meaning into

eee um fah um so

foo swee too eem oo——"

Of this "voice of no age or sex . . . an ancient spring spouting from the earth"—of this example of what Roland Barthes called "vocal writing"—we, too, might well ask, "how translate that"?[28]

In one of the fragments of "The Reader," Woolf writes that Shakespeare "is the most read of all writers. And every reader has a dozen methods of catching him." In another fragment, she explains that "[o]ne reason why Shakespeare is still read is simply the inadequacy of Shakespearean criticism" (Silver, 1979/80, 431). Given how much time Woolf gave over to reading, thinking, and writing about Shakespeare, it is worth recalling that, as Brenda R. Silver reminds us, she never did collect her thoughts about him in one essay or place. According to Woolf, any "reader-writer" would recognize that Shakespeare's "styles are too innumerable" to permit summary comment. "Perhaps then he is chiefly used for more general purposes—when the ink has gone dry upon the pen to revive the sense of language; or to testify, when words seem motionless, to the enormous possibilities of speed" (432). Just as "speed" is the mainspring of Charles Olson's "Projective Verse" manifesto, and motion is what he responds to in *Antony and Cleopatra*, so speed is the heart of what we might call the "Woolf S." Nor should this surprise us, given Woolf's desire to get her own prose moving. Witness the same diary entry in which she reflects on writing *The Waves*: "I could perhaps do B[ernard]'s soliloquy in such a way as to break up, dig deep, make prose move— yes I swear—as prose has never moved before: from the chuckle & the babble to the rhapsody" (*Diary*, January 7, 1931, 4.4).

The flood, the burst, the tumble, the bounce, the chopping, the tacking, the stretch, the shower, the pressure, the pelt, the pitch, the quickness, and always the speed of the words, the words, the words are what Woolf felt, literally, as a reader of Shakespeare. The "reader-writer" is left behind, labors to catch up, races alongside, or simply watches from the sidelines. She feels "the friction of reading and the emotion."[29] She is exhausted, exhilarated, exasperated, overwhelmed. "Reading classics is generally hard going."[30] None of this speaks precisely to enjoyment, or for that matter, to work; reading Shakespeare is more like "exercise": when Woolf writes to Vita Sackville-West that "[l]ove is so physical; and so's reading—the exercise of the wits," she captures the psychology, physiology, and phenomenology, even a touch of the ethics, of reading Shakespeare, but she spares us all of these "ologies" (*Letters*, December 29, 1928, 3.570). Her notebooks, too, are shot through with evidence of "the exercise of the wits," although she hardly ever engages in anything like (academic) Shakespeare criticism. One thing Woolf very often does instead—something I have failed to indicate sufficiently—is copy out lines from the plays. This, too, is a kind of exercise. When she copies down lines that she does not comment on and that do not appear to have any great import for her, it is as if she foregoes underlining or asterisking these passages so that she can better register her presence to Shakespeare by replicating them in her own handwriting. This conspicuous and seemingly nonjudgmental portion of her Shakespeare notes has the feel of a commonplace book in which Woolf practices verbatim mimesis. She responds with pen in hand in a purely physical way to the words speeding by her. One could say that this is how she slows them down and then, like Shakespeare, chops them up for pleasure.

IV

CHARLES OLSON'S
"OBJECTIST SHAKESPEARE"

Over the course of a decade that started in the mid-1940s, the ornery, imposing American poet Charles Olson came into his own as a writer. In 1945, he wrote *Call Me Ishmael*—his "assault" prose essay-poem on Herman Melville by way of Noah, Moses, and Shakespeare.[1] A year later, he began a long series of visits with Ezra Pound, then incarcerated in St. Elizabeths Hospital in Washington, DC, and he published poems in *Harper's*, *Atlantic Monthly*, and *Harper's Bazaar*. Reynal and Hitchcock published *Call Me Ishmael* in 1947. Black Sun Press published Olson's first collection of poems, *y & x*, in 1948. He had begun to lecture at various writers' conferences and universities, and to meet other poets (Robert Duncan, Kenneth Rexroth, and Muriel Rukeyser, among them); now he was asked by Josef Albers to give three lectures at Black Mountain College in North Carolina. Through the spring of 1949, he was in residence at the college for roughly a week each month. His ambitious, "archaic postmodern" poem "The Kingfishers," which took pride of place at the beginning of Donald Allen's benchmark *The New American Poetry, 1945–1960*, also dates from 1949.[2] The following year, Olson wrote his first Maximus poem ("I, Maximus of Gloucester, to You") and began a voluminous correspondence with Robert Creeley. Then *Poetry New York* published "Projective Verse," the challenging *ars poetica* that Olson had been hashing out in letters to Creeley. Between 1951 and 1956, he was either teaching at or rector of Black Mountain College, where beside Duncan and Creeley, Olson collaborated and argued with, hectored and inspired, the likes of Robert Motherwell, Franz Kline, Robert Rauschenberg, Ben Shahn, Cy Twombly, John Cage, and Merce Cunningham. With the publication of *Maximus Poems 1–10* in 1953 and *Maximus Poems 11–22* in 1956, the lifelong project that was still ongoing at Olson's death in 1970 was well launched.

Call Me Ishmael provides us with some of the first published evidence for Olson's disposition toward Shakespeare. He had been granted an MA from Wesleyan University for his 1933 thesis, "The Growth of Herman Melville, Prose Writer and Poetic Thinker." At the end of that year, the friendship that he had struck up with Eleanor Metcalf, Melville's granddaughter, led to a December meeting with her sister, Mrs. Frances Osborne. Olson suddenly found himself entrusted with ninety-five volumes that had once been Herman Melville's own. Among these was the seven-volume Shakespeare edition that Melville read from and marked up just before he began *Moby-Dick*. Olson's comprehensive, source-tracking Melville scholarship was on display in a long seminar paper that he would write for F. O. Matthiessen, when he was a graduate student at Harvard in 1936. Later, prodded and scolded by Edward Dahlberg, Olson reworked his paper into "*Lear* and *Moby-Dick*," a twenty-five page essay that appeared in 1938, in the inaugural issue of *Twice A Year*. "What was solvent within Melville," Olson wrote, "Shakespeare, in the manner of a catalytic agent, precipitated."[3] In *Call Me Ishmael*, Olson repeats his conviction that the "rough notes for *Moby-Dick*" appear "in the Shakespeare set itself. They are written in Melville's hand, in pencil, upon the last fly-leaf of the last volume, the one containing *Lear*, *Othello* and *Hamlet*."[4]

Traces of Melville's Shakespeare reading provided Olson with fresh genetic evidence for the transformation in Melville's writing that occurred with *Moby-Dick* ("the ferment, Shakespeare, the cause" [*Call Me Ishmael*, 39]).[5] We know that reading Shakespeare had occupied Olson, too. When he first met Dahlberg, he made it clear that he "knew pages of Shakespeare's *Measure for Measure*, *Lear*, *Troilus and Cressida*, *Timon of Athens* by rote."[6] A folded sheet of paper (now at Simon Fraser University) that Olson covered with notes about *Coriolanus* ("it is the tragedy of the impolitic, not even of the idealist, but of the insolent egoist") appears also to date from 1936. In a letter to Matthiessen written some three years later, we get a glimpse of a fledgling Olson who wants to believe that Shakespeare could have a "catalytic" effect on his own writing: "[y]our book's been in my mind. . . . My own's a slow thing, and I strive to give it wings. I find my method, and lose it again. Shakespeare usually recovers my prose: I found him again this summer. . . . But myself is still to be discovered."[7] The recuperative powers that Shakespeare had for Melville, Olson seems to have sought on his own behalf; but he also believed from early on that for neither of them was Shakespeare motive enough. Yes, Melville's writing career, which began in the Pacific (whence came myth, anti-Christ, and Ahab [*Call Me Ishmael*, 102]) and ended in the Mediterranean (whence came Christ, "contracted . . . vision," and "decline" [102–4]), pivoted on Shakespeare. Indeed, in Melville's Shakespeare marginalia, Olson had found the moment precisely antecedent to *Moby-Dick* when the playwright "emerged from the first rush of Melville's reading a Messiah" (41). Now, suddenly, Melville "studied Shakespeare's craft" (66). *Lear* in particular "had deep creative impact" on *Moby-Dick*: for "an Ahab, a Fedallah and the White, lovely, monstrous Whale," Melville "found answers in the darkness of *Lear* (47 and 49). "Ahab speaks Lear's phrases" (60) and in his rhythms; his "tense and nervous speech" are Macbeth's (54). Ahab's suffering and his "humanities" (61) are Lear's, his "isolation from humanity" is Macbeth's (54), his "disillusion" Timon's (44); he is the "American Timon" (73).

So yes, Shakespeare was necessary—"As the strongest literary force Shakespeare caused Melville to approach tragedy in terms of drama" (*Call Me Ishmael*, 69)—but he was not sufficient. One discrepancy was temperamental. For example, Olson seems to subscribe to Keats's argument about Shakespearean "negative capability." In his marginalia in his copy of Wyndham Lewis's *The Lion and the Fox: The Rôle of Hero in the Plays of Shakespeare* (in the Olson archive at the University of Connecticut in Storrs), Olson applauds Lewis for doing the "best job on the feminine, accomodatory [*sic*], responsive negative capability of Shks." But when Olson cites Hawthorne's journal entry on Melville—"[h]e can neither believe, nor be comfortable in his unbelief; and he is too honest and courageous not to try to do one or the other" (*Call Me Ishmael*, 91)—and when he does not demur, one senses Olson's, no less than Melville's, intellectual irritability as opposed to Shakespearean detachment. Another divergence was of a more metaphysical sort. According to Olson, and to Olson's Melville, even if Shakespeare mastered "the ancient magnitudes of TRAGEDY" (71), he was less bountiful when it came to the two other, requisite "forces [which] operated to bring about the dimensions of *Moby-Dick*": "MYTH" and "SPACE" (71; *mutatis mutandis*, the dimensions of what would become *The Maximus Poems*). Shakespeare at best adumbrates these in *Antony and Cleopatra*, "the play Melville pencilled [*sic*] most heavily" (71). "There is space here," writes Olson; the eponymous characters "live life large" and the "stage [is] as wide as ocean" (72). But Shakespeare lacks the "'American' advantage" (41). His myth is insufficiently "antemosaic" (71), and his ocean is merely the Mediterranean, not the Pacific. It would be some time before Americans, and only Americans, could comprehend "*an experience of SPACE*" that derived from the Pacific. For space, as Olson comprehends it, "has a stubborn way of sticking to Americans, penetrating them all the way in" (114). "SPACE, its price and power, American" (71) would have to await Melville's (and Whitman's) articulation, and then Olson's. If "[t]he substitution of the Atlantic for the Mediterranean . . . worked a revolution for England," "the Pacific opens the NEW HISTORY" and "Melville felt th[at] move-

ment as American" (117). In time, Olson himself would call out from Gloucester, invoking "Okeanos," god of all of the seas (*Maximus*, 2:70, "Maximus, at
the Harbor").[8] This would be to "find in him [Melville] prophecies, lessons he
himself would not have spelled out" (*Call Me Ishmael*, 13). "A hundred years
gives us an advantage" (13) which enables Olson to reach beyond the Atlantic
and the Pacific, to surpass Homer, Shakespeare, and Melville, to undertake an
American epic for all SPACE and TIME.[9]

But this is to get ahead of things. And it is too soon to cashier Shakespeare,
for whom Olson maps out a writing career very different from the trajectory
of decline and diminishment that he scrupulously, if dishearteningly, attributes
to Melville. We can pick up on young Olson's earliest responses to Shakespeare not only by watching him read Melville reading Shakespeare, but starting around 1936, when Olson purchased and began to annotate his copy of
George Lyman Kittredge's *The Complete Works of Shakespeare* (also at the University of Connecticut in Storrs). Some of what Olson writes in this volume
unsurprisingly dwells on Melville. In notes on the page facing the inside back
cover, for example, Olson links *The Tempest*'s "Full fathom five thy father lies"
with "Father murder—incest in Melville." When Olson goes on to write of
Melville that "his use of crime [is] mythic not modern—Cain's murder," he
seems to recall "Cain's jawbone" in *Hamlet*. Responding to Macbeth's speech
at the start of 5.3 ("Bring me no more reports"), Olson writes "Ahab, here."
And in *King Lear*, 4.2, he comments, "Same shift in Melville's language as in
Shakespeare—but without the reasonable bounds of verse." But for the most
part, when Olson annotates particular plays, for example *The Tempest*, Melville fades from view. It is Faustus, not Ahab, whom Prospero calls to mind.
Pausing over Ceres's "turfy mountains" and her "pioned and twilled brims" in
The Tempest, Olson underlines the adjectives and wonders, "amazing pastoral
stuff—is it not possible this play is very early?" When Prospero tells Ariel to
release everyone who is under his spell, Olson again underlines ("And they shall
be themselves"), comments "how horrible!," and then at the top of the page
adds, "What a lax S.—even in his line." The "tone" of *Measure for Measure*, "or
rather its color[,] is dun." Lucio and Pompey are "night grotesques." Shakespeare's "consideration of death is singularly medieval & Christian"; the "play
is in a sense an exemplum on lust & justice." Hindsight reveals that something
central to Olson's understanding of Shakespeare is percolating here. The linch-
pins of his comprehensive, 1954 account of the late plays will turn out to be
another line from *The Tempest*'s masque along with the conflict between lust and
innocence.

Of course, some of what appears in the Olson's Kittredge margins comports with what one would expect from spur-of-the-moment responses by a twenty-something Harvard graduate student. Young Keats did not hesitate to express his impatience with Dr. Johnson in his duodecimo Shakespeare edition, and Olson occasionally lays into Kittredge on the more spacious pages from which he read. Half-way through *Measure for Measure*, he has decided that "[t]o depend on critics is a form of masturbation." The looser handwriting in the margins of Olson's Kittredge, for example in the *Troilus and Cressida, Macbeth, The Winter's Tale*, and *The Two Noble Kinsmen* pages, may derive from a later date. Alongside Kittredge's introduction to *Troilus and Cressida*, we still find the likes of "read the play professor"; but such testiness is now exceptional. Atop the list of characters in *The Winter's Tale*, Olson writes that "the tones of A&C [are] now dried," "dryness" being another keyword in Olson's later analysis of late Shakespearean verse. *Troilus* has extensive markings and annotations. Throughout the volume, Olson underlines and copies down words that strike him and here, right from the start, "orgillous," "fraughtage," and "Sperr" get his attention. Later, "Tortive" catches his eye, and then, toward the end of the play, "orts" is underlined, even defined in the margin at the top of the page. His impatience, not just with Kittredge but with Shakespeare, is still on display. Act 1 of *Troilus and Cressida* is "weak." Act 2 "is stronger, but still in language and concept lax: if S meant to make fools of heroes, especially the Greeks, by his own Thersites, then he has not done it well, but as his own Dick Tarleton might." In the margin of 3.3, he complains that "[t]here is something phoney [*sic*] in this play. . . . Shks makes his characters play like an advertisement; . . . each of the characters are their Homeric epithets made single." In response to the soldier talk in *Macbeth*, 5.4, Olson writes, "The war speech of S.—dull and pontifical—stuffed warriors." On the same page, apparently thinking of "Tomorrow, and tomorrow, and tomorrow," a more appreciative Olson writes, "All is time—the pressure & peace—in terror of it he murders, and in horror of murder, he embraces time."

His *The Two Noble Kinsmen* marginalia also anticipate the later turn in and notable concentration of Olson's thinking about Shakespeare's development, a line of thought that eventually would become a thesis and then an argument. It all begins with what Olson hears in the "the last plays!": "wow—note inner rhymes"; "dotty verse! Crazy . . . telescoping"; "the celerity now, of the verse . . . crazy!" Late in 1949, he writes to Frances Boldereff about "The Dryness, of 'The Tempest.'" "Prospero, and the verse, are an odd mark of Shakespeare's play, and for a common reason: they back and halt as though they bridle at what life is, and spring their act, or burden, out, in despite of it, that is, in despite of life."[10]

Like Prospero, the verse in *The Tempest* feels "cool" to Olson. He explains—somewhat obscurely—that *The Tempest* shows us that Shakespeare "knows verse shall be as sharp and sweet as wood is made, of its grain, and use."[11] In "Projective Verse," it becomes clearer that when Olson writes that, for a poet, the "relation of man to experience" is "as the necessity of a line or a work to be as wood is," he is speaking on behalf of objects and what he calls "objectism."[12] Wanting to offer Boldereff an example of objective, "fresh" and "clean" verse, Olson begins by citing the line that recurs again and again when he writes about Shakespeare over the next half a dozen years. "Of wheat, rye, barley, fetches, oats, and pease," spoken by Iris at the start of Prospero's epithalamic masque, serves here and will continue to serve as Olson's touchstone. Later, he will call this verse "dried and flatted" ("THE HUMAN TITLE" in Olson's Shakespeare MS); but for connotation, he might have called it wooden. In 1949, he can only telegraph to Boldereff what will become his closely argued explanation for what he, like many before him, recognizes as the strangeness of late Shakespeare's verse and themes. The abbreviated essay on *The Tempest* in the Boldereff letter, the poem "The Kingfishers" of the same year, his "Projective Verse" mandate published one year later, and dozens of sorties in his 1951–52 letters to Creeley all feed into ten unpublished Shakespeare chapters from 1954 (archived at the University of Connecticut) as well as into Olson's unique, published distillation of this work, his 1956 essay, "Quantity in Verse, and Shakespeare's Late Plays." As he will begin to argue, *The Tempest*, *Henry 8*, and *The Two Noble Kinsmen* are more "knot[ted] up" than "running on" in their verse ("THE NEW MORRIS"), more choric than dramatic in their method. In other words, Olson's late Shakespeare chimes felicitously with Olson's own developing poetics.

If at first blush Shakespeare's late plays seem distant from "The Kingfishers," it bears remarking that in a 1951 letter to Creeley, Olson writes of "the only man who, properly, taught me, I wanted to write, & what it was, William Shakespeare" (CO/RC, 7.119).[13] More particularly, late in "The Kingfishers" itself, Olson returns to *Timon of Athens*, a play that figures importantly in *Call Me Ishmael*, when he decries how in a Poundian "pejorocracy . . . awe, night-rest and neighborhood can rot" (in *Timon*: "Domestic awe, night-rest and neighborhood" [4.1.17]).[14] For Olson, however, the connection between Shakespeare's verse and his own first major poem was predominantly methodological; the point of intersection was what Olson understood to be "objects." In "The Kingfishers," the motivating object is unmistakably the bird. It inaugurates the "kinetic of the poem" ("PV," 243) and then yields to successive objects, be they citations from prior texts or the *E* on the stone at Delphi. The poem may be *about* change or progress ("What does not change / is the will to change"; "not accumulation but change"), but it is its "Objectism" ("PV," 247) that activates our response. Easy enough to understand about objectism is the way it speaks to Olson's aspiration to get "rid of the lyrical interference of the individual as ego, of the 'subject' and his soul, that particular presumption by which western man has interposed himself between what he is as a creature of nature . . . and those other creations of nature which we may, with no derogation, call objects" ("PV," 247). Less easy to specify is the sort of poetics this mandates. Olson insists that poetry "is a matter, finally, of OBJECTS, what they are, what they are inside a poem, how they got there, and, once there, how they are to be used" ("PV," 243). Hence *poiesis* ought to proceed as follows: "objects which occur at every given moment of composition (of recognition, we can call it) are, can be, must be treated exactly as they do occur therein and not by any ideas or preconceptions from outside the poem, must be handled as a series of objects in field in such a way that a series of tensions . . . are made to *hold*, and to hold exactly inside the content and the context of the poem which has forced itself, through the poet and them, into being" ("PV," 243–44). Not preconceptions (in "The Kingfishers," about Mao or Heraclitus), not abstractions (ruin, change), neither observation nor description (which "sap the going energy of the content toward its form" ["PV," 243]), but objects (the poet among them, they through the poet) in the field that is the poem ring the changes that are the experience of the poem. Passing like a projectile through the poet toward the reader, verse is "energy transferred from where the poet got it . . . by way of the poem itself to, all the way over to, the reader" ("PV," 240). Succeeding syllables that resonate with what the poet hears, and succeeding lines that enact the poet's breath, bring a poem to the reader "now," "immediately, bang," like a "passage of force" ("PV," 244).

Rereading Shakespeare late in 1951, Olson found confirmation of these dicta. "Apparently," Olson wrote to Creeley on November 15, "I'm in one of those returns, to Mister William Shaksper. They happen every so often, he being the man who opened *language* for me" (CO/RC, 8.137; my emphasis). Certainly it is a happy circumstance that Shakespeare abides by projective versification's ban on self-expression. Following on Coleridge, Keats, and Hazlitt, Olson appreciates that Shakespeare was a master of shutting down his ego and sidestepping preconceptions: "how this man put his thought away *behind* the act of his story . . . how cool & clear he did his work . . . how definitely he dealt with each thing under hand in its terms" (CO/RC, 8.173). Is it fortuitous that Shakespeare's language also corroborates projective verse's "dogma" (the word is Olson's ["PV," 240])? Reading *Antony and Cleopatra* intensively ("still obsessed by this play"), Olson found that its "verse itself is not mere skin & voice but is, rather, the energy & the action, the PRESENT" (CO/RC, 8.179 and 177). This neatly encapsulates the "Projective Verse" campaign: in Olson's essay, "get on with it, keep moving, . . . speed" ("PV," 240); in Shakespeare's play, "energy & the action" or "*motion & solidity*." Olson worries for a moment that he is merely telling Creeley that "the dramatic is dramatic." But no, that is not his point. Rather, Olson's "increasing interest in drama as such is due to . . . presentness and sequence." Hence "what, in A & C is illuminated . . . I wld, of course, tab OBJECTISM" (CO/RC, 8.174 and 178).[15]

Among the bogeymen in "Projective Verse" are argument, description, and abstraction—all of which, because they produce drag, impede motion. In *Antony and Cleopatra*, Olson can find "no abstraction or extra-informing . . . any more than any forcing of meaning." The "whole play" militates against the "tendence [*sic*] . . . to become abstract" (CO/RC, 8.181). In his fourth Shakespeare letter from Black Mountain to Creeley in four days, Olson exults ("has me wild") that he has found the "SINGLE ACT" through which Shakespeare "enters plot, character, & the other characteristic of the cloth of it, the verse." He now sees "how goddamn PARTICULAR such a perception forces each play (at least fr 1601 on) to be & to stay." "[*I*]*nstead* of the exterior measurements it strikes me he has, fr him to now, been altogether measured by: dramaturgy—characterization—plot—big scenes—soliloquies—etc etc [instead of] ALL THIS SHIT, leading like, the biggest turd of all: universe-all VERSE, ALL, & ONLY: my god, wild." "At last" Olson has found a way to "talk abt the formal force of this man, can start to examine it, can speak of him COMPOSITIONALLY" (CO/RC, 8.201).

This last formulation applies in several precise ways to Olson's developing understanding of Shakespeare's verse and of his own. One: in "Projective Verse," Olson cleaves to "the *act* of composition" ("PV," 239; my emphasis); reading Shakespeare, Olson aims to capture him in "the act of his language," in "the rip and tear" of versification (CO/RC, 8.189 and 180). Two: "Projective Verse" does not seize on form *per se*, but on form's force ("formal force"). Shakespeare's verse in *Antony and Cleopatra* is "all like a hoop, a fine steel band, so porous, flexible, yet firm" (CO/RC, 8.201). Three: such force derives from content in motion. In "Projective Verse," when Olson cites Creeley's dictum that "FORM IS NEVER MORE THAN AN EXTENSION OF CONTENT" ("PV," 240), he leans hard on "extension." The extension of content, which persists throughout the duration of composition and then carries over into reading, takes shape or form according to the weight and proportion of each syllable, the breath of each line, and the expanse of the whole poem, the "FIELD" ("PV," 242). For Creeley, form is never *more* than this extension because it must be, as Creeley puts it, "intimate" with content—with "what's being stated as it is being stated."[16] But for Olson, the relation between form and content has more to do with physics than with eros. Inert content forfeits its trans*act*ion with form. When Olson cites from *Antony and Cleopatra*, he "mark[s] the *process*" (CO/RC, 8.181; my emphasis) wherein the poet "stretch[es] the very conventions on which communication by language rests" and "kick[s] around anew" the time and "space–tensions of a poem" ("PV," 244). "Communication" is the process word that Olson wields in his contention with the lethargy of argument, description, and abstraction. It stands for getting content moving toward us. And it aptly describes Olson's extension and our reception of the content—the objects—in a poem like "The Kingfishers": its birds, *E*, and priests; Fernand, Mao, and Rimbaud; honey, maggots, and stones.

So when on November 29, 1951, Olson writes that "NATURE" is in *Antony and Cleopatra* "all OBJECT" and in *King Lear* "all MOTION" (CO/RC, 8.202), Creeley would have recognized Olson's objectivist diction. But would he have understood what Olson meant? Even though Olson still marvels at the "*composition* this man [Shakespeare] was exerting," and even though he still says that "verse is where his plays arose, not the verse as, the result of, his play" (CO/RC, 8.204 and 199), verse is now unexpectedly compounded of an *un*-projective-sounding "image system" or "metaphorical system" (CO/RC, 8.200 and 203). In *King Lear*, this system incorporates eyes, bleeding rings, zero, wheel, nothing, and never (CO/RC, 8.201). On December 4, Olson condenses these to "hollows & huts, hovels, hearts," then still further to "*the inside* of a round thing" (CO/RC, 8.226). One day later there is no more than the binary "IN & OUT." An "OBJECTIST SHAKESPEARE," predicated on *King Lear* and *Antony and Cleopatra*, arises from Shakespeare's "counterpoise of IN & OUT" (CO/RC, 8.228). Although Creeley may have found this interpretation obscure, a more and more excited Olson is convinced that it stems first and last from Shakespeare's verse. "Just crazy today, wild, crazy, excited by a whole series of sights, breaking" (CO/RC, 8.198). "[H]as me wild" (CO/RC, 8.201). "[G]od, jesus," the in and out of the two plays "is something so known we know nothing, is what it is, & no goddamned interpretation, is the thing [Lear's "thing itself"?] and gets that way by, is the Verse" (CO/RC, 8.202). "I get giddy, that i can't say this, that, these outlines [Olson's remarks about motion and object, in and out] will destroy *where they came from*—for I got them in in IN the play, in IN, the verse, no where else" (CO/RC, 8.203). "[O]h, god, I am either crazy, or in the presence of something very fine" (CO/RC, 8.204). In this fine frenzy, Olson dissolves the

IN-ness of *King Lear* into the "IN, the verse" of the play and (if you will) vice versa. When, initially, Olson dwells on eyes, and rings, and wheels in *King Lear*, he appears to retreat to an analysis of the *content* of Shakespeare's metaphors that recalls nothing so much as Caroline Spurgeon's *Shakespeare's Imagery and What It Tells Us* (a book that Olson first read within a year of its publication in 1936). However, when he zeroes in on the "in IN . . . the verse" and so strips the play of its humanist content, he suddenly apprehends within it the urgent "energy-construct . . . energy discharge" poetics of projective verse ("PV," 240). Now he is well on his way toward nailing down an objectist, as opposed to an imagist, Shakespeare.

Olson proceeds by finding in Shakespeare what he demanded of himself: particularity not abstraction, objectism not subjectivity. His exasperation with "dramaturgy—characterization—plot—big scenes—soliloquies," with the "universe-all" as opposed to the objective particularity of "VERSE, ALL" correlates with what he has to say in another essay—"Human Universe" (also 1951)—in which "universe" is opposed to "particularism."[17] This essay may also gloss the IN and OUT of the Shakespeare plays when Olson opposes the skin, "the meeting edge of man and external reality" that happily makes each of us one object among others, to the humanist's soul, "which has softly stood as a word to cover man as a selecting internal reality posed dangerously in the midst of . . . externals" ("HU," 161). "If man is active, it is exactly here [at the skin] where experience comes in that it is delivered back, and if he stays fresh at the coming *in* he will be fresh at his going *out*" ("HU," 162; my emphasis). This activity, Olson insists, "[a]rt does not seek to describe but to enact" ("HU," 162). No surprise, then, that Olson is encouraged by what he makes out to be Shakespeare's "movement *away fr* soliloquy (in A & C, & L)": "Wld figure S as catching on—just in these years between H & Lear—that the lyric & psychological both dead" (CO/RC, 8.227). From Olson's point of view, the literary trappings of humanism were and again are happily on their way out, along with them such insufficiently textured (these are Olson's words) characters as Edgar and Gloucester (CO/RC, 8.204). "[A]t this latter day," Olson "can't . . . take this play [*King Lear*] by a handle of evil or innate depravity whatsoever" (CO/RC, 8.226). Edgar's and Gloucester's is less a "moral position" than a "passive humanistic one" wholly impertinent to Lear and Edmund, characters who display an Olsonian affinity for action and for verse that moves (CO/RC, 8.204). The latter pair "know NATURE is more than gods" and that "the act of to howl or the act of to kill is the action—the only action—men can oppose" (CO/RC, 8.205).

At the end of his long, November 29 letter, Olson tells/asks Creeley, "[T]he point ultimately is, VERSE: eh?" (CO/RC, 8.205). But for a few days, at least, image, not verse had been the focus of Olson's attention. In his December 4 and 5 letters, verse—projective verse—returns to the fore. It so happens that the warrants for what Olson goes on to write—about punctuation in the Shakespeare quartos and First Folio, about Elizabethan and so Shakespeare's pronunciation and graphology—are by turns misinformed and wishful thinking; nevertheless, his new plan to "restore texts of A & C, Lear, and the romances" wells up unmistakably from his desire to get closer to Shakespeare's breath, to recover "Shk's verse as it got itself writ" (CO/RC, 8.221 and 227). Olson proposes to use the second quarto of *Hamlet* as an exemplar that will install him beside Shakespeare punctuating his lines of verse (although "got itself writ" really does make it sound as though the verse passes through its amanuensis poet). By clearing away the debris of "stupid capitals, semi-colons, exclamation points" supposedly introduced in the printing house, Olson will restore the "limpid[ity]" of Shakespeare's line (CO/RC, 8.221). Freed of "rhetoric and declamation," the force of the verse would now emerge. A worthy "restoration" project, it would also entail the "translation" and re-composition of what Olson called "A CAREFUL 'FREE' TEXT" (CO/RC, 8.227 and 228). The right man to do the job "wld have to be (1) himself a poet, and, I'd guess, a contemporary one; (2), somewhat knowing in how the language was *pronounced* in Shk's time; and (3), acquaint himself with . . . S's graphology" (CO/RC, 8.228). There is no "likelihood any of the scholars will do it out of piousness" (CO/RC, 8.228).

The right contemporary poet would thus affiliate his or her poetry with the Shakespearean verse to which this recovered punctuation and pronunciation had given rise. This prescription reemerges in Olson's unpublished Shakespeare manuscript, where a gap in time is said to open up following Shakespeare's late plays, only to be closed in the twentieth century by Ezra Pound, William Carlos Williams, and then Charles Olson. At the tail end of the December 5 letter, he frankly admits that his "whole idea is a cheap substitute for a better one i haven't yet had the guts to tackle." Again, an alignment of Shakespeare's with his own verse is what he has in mind: Olson wants to do "a GLOSS of any play which catches me at the time—that is, to let his verse be the provocation for passages of my own *alongside*" (CO/RC, 8.229; my emphasis). Thus would Olson enter the realm in which Keats's sonnet appears, directly after the "FINIS" in his copy of the First Folio's *Hamlet* and just before its *King Lear*. Olson's gambit may also recall a wry comment of his in the margin of his Kittredge edition of *Hamlet*, a comment that is reminiscent of Coleridge's "I have a smack of Hamlet myself, if I may say so." Pre-empting Hamlet *and* Shakespeare, Olson writes that "the trouble with Hamlet [is that] he could never add any thing to me, for I was he." For better or worse, the gutsy project never materialized; but a day after writing to Creeley, Olson did in fact pitch his "OBJECTIST" edition of *Antony and Cleopatra* and *King Lear* to Robert Giroux, then at Harcourt Brace.[18] The letter, written from Black Mountain, recaps the proposal that Olson had mooted to Creeley as well as his consideration that "maybe i could float myself an advance, on such a proposition"—"maybe i cld stick up one of the houses in NY" (CO/RC, 8.228–29). This may sound opportunistic; but money, which Olson never had much of, was hardly ever his primary goal. He unembarrassedly tells Giroux that, "frankly, I shld like to get some stake to proceed on such a job immediately"; but just before he signs off, he restates the felt exigency of his proposal. "THE OBJECTIST'S SHAKESPEARE" would be a genuine "departure in (1) Shks scholarship (2) critique and (3) influence the practice of verse now." If an edition that could give the world "a new grasp of his [Shakespeare's] processes as a poet," and poems like "The Kingfishers," and a manual like "Projective Verse" were opportunistic, then Olson's was a principled opportunism, and what he was setting out to do was, as he writes to Giroux, "impossible until this date of time." The goal was to "influence the practice of verse *now*."

To take the measure of Charles Olson the reader of Shakespeare by emphasizing *poiesis* is fairly to assess what engaged him deeply, but unfairly to downplay what he calls "critique." In his letters to Creeley, Olson has many more—more maverick and more complex—thoughts about the plays than his Kittredge marginalia or *Call Me Ishmael* portend. Having just listened to the Robeson, Hagen, Ferrer recording of *Othello*, he writes to Creeley that "it gave me again the chance to dislike that play, to look upon it as the most offensive act of Shakespeare's. I cannot tolerate his pitching love-lust-&-jealousy in such a low pulp plot as this one." "Gullibility," he goes on to say, "works where money, say, is the matter— Jonson's VOLPONE, e.g., has much more dimension than OTHELLO simply because Jonson had the accuracy to place it there" (CO/RC, 8.124). When Olson writes that "Shakespeare was sick of the infidelity of woman from 1601 on—and I'd guess until he found the content of A & C, he could not free his horror from the only known measure, the Christian system" (CO/RC, 8.125), he leagues himself with Ted Hughes and John Berryman, who also were struck by what in one of his notebooks Berryman calls Shakespeare's "sex nausea." At other times, Olson's blend of playfulness and earnestness must have charmed

Creeley. In "A & C," he fancies, "all things, including that gypsy or the rule of the world, are as perfect as candy, and put in the mouth, candy—melts" (CO/RC, 8.237; Olson previously had done a riff on the "wonderful verb 'discandy'" and "the image of CANDY"—CO/RC, 8.175). This sort of "Shks scholarship" calls to mind Hughes's at once zany and zealous readings of Shakespeare, not to mention his tremendous impatience with academic Shakespeare. In the letter to Giroux, Olson (like Hughes) writes that scholars are too "timid" to "risk" an edition like the one he has in mind. Several of his letters to Creeley make it clear that Olson's "critique" of *King Lear* is nothing if it is not intrepid. Edmund "IS, actually, LEAR'S SON (this is the craziest thing of all, that, the intrication is so exact—and the play's plotting as a result so careful and clear . . ." "[F]or Edmund is the thing Lear is only the previous generation of, in this sense that they are the two creatures in the play who understand that they issue from nature . . ." (CO/RC, 8.204). Five days later he hits upon "another way of posing E as 'son of' L . . . that both of em [*sic*] appeal for sanction to Nature as Procreative Goddess . . . with this huge difference, that E does it *as generated . . .* and L *as generator*" (CO/RC, 8.225). (In this instance, Olson, who would eventually come to own four copies of *The White Goddess*, anticipated *Shakespeare and the Goddess of Complete Being*, Ted Hughes's own Gravesian tome.) Still another six days after this and just beginning to see that "Mr S's distinction is his clarity that there is no hierarchy [among characters], that there is only difference of capability," Olson writes that "one can throw the scales between Edmund & Lear" but this will do no "more than disclose that Edmund is one man and Lear is such another" (CO/RC, 8.237). Olson calls Shakespeare's disposition of "living things" his "human phenomenology": "no plugging, not a damned thing added to the facts than the most wonderful thing of all, the motion of same facts & things in their relevance to each other." At this point, remarkably, he circles back to "the out & the in," which he now sees "as one" (CO/RC, 8.238). No plugging (hence no preconceptions), nothing added to the facts, nature, living things, phenomenology, motion: in a critical-poetic tour de force, Olson knits "critique" and the "practice of verse" seamlessly together. The disposition of Edmund and Lear is both a metaphor for and the message of the "distributed" (CO/RC, 8.239)—hence differential not hierarchical—relations among objects in projective verse. Having construed Lear and Edmund as vectors, as signs of verse in motion, Olson once again asserts his post-humanism, insisting that "the *ordering of motion* is the only morality" (CO/RC, 8.239; Olson's emphasis).

So by 1954 Olson apparently was ready to draft a book—an introduction plus ten chapters, approximately 117 pages—largely devoted to Shakespeare's late plays. Unweeded and unpruned, these pages are sometimes repetitive, ingrown, or digressive. But from start to finish, Olson continues to argue that form (practice) and content (critique), even biography, now dovetail, now egg each other on. "Quantity in Verse, and Shakespeare's Late Plays" (1956; first published in 1966), a synopsis of Olson's argument, is the only published form that the manuscript ever took.[19] Weighing in at just over twelve pages in the *Collected Prose*, the essay provides a fairly taut summation, but it inevitably cuts scores of the manuscript's many felicities, both large and small.

In the first chapter of the manuscript ("THE DIFFERENCE OF MEN"), Olson launches into a remarkable story that is based on what he *hears* in Shakespeare's verse. Even if Olson is by no means the first to chart the development of Shakespeare's writing, his account of Shakespeare's "three successive poetries" is replete with memorable surprises. The novelty of what Olson argues is due in good measure to his desire to advance beyond a mere description of Shakespeare's "development." His ambition (reminiscent of what he essayed with *Moby-Dick*) is to get past the usual diachronic review in order to arrive at a genetic analysis, at an answer to the Coleridgean question, "*How* did he get from one to the other?" (my emphasis). Olson begins by identifying the "First Verse of Shakespeare," the one "Projective Verse" accurately predicts that Olson will be least interested in. Shakespeare inherited this first style—"lyric, erotic, and some comic song"—from Wyatt, Surrey, and Marlowe. To its detriment, it is "the mean of" what "passed as poetic pretty much" not only then but "down to just a short while ago." This is the Shakespeare of *A Midsummer Night's Dream, Romeo and Juliet, Venus and Adonis*, and *The Rape of Lucrece*. "In some quarters . . . [this] is the most some people can experience of him, still what's taken to be pleasure." Past this verse Olson moves along even more quickly than Shakespeare "quickly moved along into a verse which has absorbed his name." This is the "Second Verse," the "verse of 'character,' of—though it is all inside the iambic pentameter, and blank verse at that—of speeches individualized to the voice & nature of each person's speaking." Cue John of Gaunt, Hamlet's soliloquies, and "the miseries of Mrs Macbeth"!

The genesis of the Second Verse, the form that enabled him to "move off his earlier poetry as method," was Shakespeare's "cut back" to the "vernacular" by means of Falstaff's prose. (By the by, notes Olson, some three hundred years later, Americans finally would adopt Shakespeare's course change.) Falstaff heralds Shakespeare's discovery of "flexible individual speech loaded with narrative and based on insight"—the kind of insight that makes possible an Iago or an Edmund. To hear Falstaff's speech, "seized where it issues from any of our mouths . . . presiding over things done," is to hear the first intimations of Shakespeare's "final exploitation" of his discovery: Lear "running that trial scene in the hovel." As for vernacular, it is city speech. If the First Verse was sponsored by Erato (erotic poetry) and Euterpe (lyric song), the Second Verse became possible when Thalia (comedy and idyllic poetry) "moved in town." Ben Jonson may have understood this, but if so, he was not equipped to compete with *Hamlet*, by means of which Shakespeare engineered "this tumbling comedy in upon Melpomene [tragedy]." Only Shakespeare could manage "this chiasma," this crossing of the masks of Thalia and Melpomene. Marrying the speech of Falstaff's prose with, Olson now adds, the "'tragedy' coming from the person" of Richard II, Shakespeare delivered Hamlet, their "issue." Genetics, indeed.

After passing briskly from the lyric First Verse to the dramatic Second Verse, Olson pauses at 1608, twice asking a question first raised during the Restoration, a question upon which the rest of Olson's manuscript turns: "What went on, to move this fellow further on this road? What brought it about that he should take another step" toward the Third Verse, the verse that Olson finds more "pertinent to verse now than either of the previous Shakespeare 'poetries'"? From the start, Olson dismisses the "tendence [*sic*] to look lightly on the last p[l]ays as 'tragi-comedies' or 'romances,' those terms of description which are usually used as classifications to keep attention away from what's really going on." Instead, he points to the 1609 publication of the Sonnets—which "include in their midst all the poetries" Shakespeare had written to date—as a sign that Shakespeare (like Hamlet "wip[ing] away" the "records" in his "tables"—1.5.99 and 107) was "wiping the slate clean." Olson then returns to the Muses: Shakespeare had "arrogated to himself" Erato, Euterpe, Thalia (had even renewed "the oldest of Thalia's powers, the saturos," with *Troilus and Cressida*), and then Melpomene; but what about Calliope, Polyhymnia, and Terpsichore, what about heroic, sacred, and choral song? This question, which he crosses out but next to which he puts a large check of approval, prompts Olson to cite two passages from *The Tempest*, citations which occasion another question "What kind of song is this verse"? The first passage consists of lines beginning with Prospero's injunction to Ferdinand "not [to] give dalliance / Too much rein." The second begins with the line that he fastened on in his 1949 letter to Frances Boldereff:

Of wheat, rye, barley, fetches, oats and peas;
thy turfy mountains, where live nobbling [*sic*] sheep,
and flat meads thatched with stover, them to keep;
thy banks with pioned and twilled brims

which spongey April at thy hest betrims
to make cold nymphs chaste crowns . . .

[cited as in Olson's Shakespeare manuscript]

Olson comes alive with exclamation marks. In response to "to make cold nymphs chaste crowns," we are dared to "[s]et that against all mellifluities! Against any of the *going on* of the verse of any of the two previous periods" (my emphasis). "That 'stopping' of song . . . !" "Of wheat, rye, barley, fetches, oats and peas" is consistent with the aspirations (the hopes and the breaths) of "Projective Verse" and of the "Objectist's Shakespeare" proposal: the commas confirm that "even the text punctuates with these percussives." This may be vernacular, but "it ain't Falstaff. And it isn't Richard either." "But what is it?"

In order to answer his questions, Olson both has to pull back a bit and to amplify his thesis. He also takes this opportunity once again to align form with content in unexpected ways. When he was a high school and college student, Olson was a champion debater; here, although this is but a first and often very rough draft, we still can see him marshaling evidence and arguing purposefully along several vectors. Starting with theme and character, Olson notes that "lust is most what they [Prospero, but also Leontes] have on their mind." This is their inheritance from Sonnet 129, from Troilus, Angelo and Hamlet, from Timon, Othello, and implicitly, from Lear. It is what "they'd most control in human affairs" and what "they most fear as taking out of life." Moreover, lust takes a toll not only on his characters, but on Shakespeare himself. After 1608, "it was lust which the Real had come to for him."

Now enters the formal vector, with Shakespeare composing a new verse which has the power to bank what Prospero calls the "fire in the blood." If lust threatens, virtue or innocence redeems. What lust takes out of life, virtue puts back in *by means of verse*, the choral and sacred song that Olson hears in the passages he cites. Olson is happy to concede that the late "plays & persons [are] artificial." Theirs is a "curious stiff romantic plotting." Dispensing with vernacular, with individualized speech and person, Shakespeare began to adopt "type creature[s]" and "type story, the 'romance.'" Indeed, with the exception of *The Tempest*, the late plays are not "important or successful as plays"; they are only "hugely important, as verse," as "sacred, heroic or choral verse!" Sacred—the last vector of the first chapter's proof—as opposed to secular. For starting in 1608, when lust had become the Real for Shakespeare, he also began to see "the secular's uselessness." "[J]ust when Puritanism & commerce & England had clearly come, when mercantilism was at her beginnings, he was through with" secularism. If secularism is the invigorating source of the real, the vernacular, and the unprecedented dramatic verse of the major tragedies, in the late plays, a "'prig' and an artificial story, an impossible, surely 'unrealistic' business" is made "vital" by sacred verse. Secular history underwrites *King Lear* and *Macbeth*, but *Pericles* is a romance "as old . . . as any material Shakespeare ever put his hand to," having arisen from "one of those springs of the muses."[20] And lust, which depth psychology had brought home to us by means of dramatic verse in the tragedies, now meets its match in the "flatness" of the choral "Third Verse" in Shakespeare's last plays.

For neither the first nor the last time, but in this instance precisely at the moment when he was working on his Shakespeare manuscript, Olson championed twentieth-century American poets'—Pound's, Crane's, Williams's and his own—"push to find out an alternative discourse to the inherited one."[21] With this same push he credits Shakespeare. The effort, early modern and postmodern, called for reinvention, with the understanding that invention consists less in making things new than anew. If First and Second Verse Shakespeares sponsor succeeding centuries of canonical English poetry, these Shakespeare chapters put Third Verse Shakespeare in the service of Olson's ambition to create the poetry of the mid-twentieth century. If he could explain, even redeem, the likes of *Pericles*, let alone of *The Two Noble Kinsmen*, if he could demonstrate their advances beyond *A Midsummer Night's Dream* and *King Lear*, then he would have a further, and bankable, warrant for his own poetics. The pleasure one takes as Olson goes about his business in the Shakespeare manuscript stems from the unflinching way he looks directly at the putative weaknesses and disappointments of late, late Shakespeare and, contrary to what was manifestly his experience with late Melville, finds so much poetic virtue. We can no more succeed in appraising *Henry 8* if we are captive to the poetics of, say, *King Lear*, than we can make sense of what Olson is up to in *The Maximus Poems* if we look at them through the lens of Wordsworthian mellifluousness. We can raise the stakes even further on Olson's behalf by conceiving of the new ways *King Lear* will appear to us from the vantage of both late Shakespeare and *The Maximus Poems*. For example, with Olson's help, we may be willing to acknowledge that innocent Cordelia, deprived of access to sacred or choral verse, is first silenced and then killed off by the dramatic verse she is required to speak, not just by Edmund's order. And if we listen, with Olson, not just for accent but for quantity in the late Shakespearean line; if we allow, with Olson, that Shakespeare, the poet of "the real and the natural," develops into a champion of the "artificial," even the "mechanical" ("QV," 272); we may yet hear or see what the great, Second Verse plays are deprived of. Olson's poetry asks us to listen to verse in ways that we perhaps have not listened before—in ways in which we may well prefer not to listen. Even if he fails to convince us that Third Verse Shakespeare is top dog, he certainly discloses more verses in the Shakespearean canon than are dreamed of in *King Lear*.

Olson's succeeding chapter drafts elaborate on the ways that the "motion" in the verse in the late plays compensates for their lack of "action," and on the ways Shakespeare's formal shifts "complement the content of his last plays because they aren't plots but motifs turning on the filial in order to forefend lust" ("THE NEW MORRIS"). In "THE SEDGED CROWN C̶R̶I̶S̶P̶ C̶H̶A̶N̶N̶E̶L̶S̶," we find that "youth, and its love for youth" comprise two of these motifs: "boy & boy" (Palamon and Arcite, or Guiderius and Arviragus), and "girl & girl" (Emilia and Flavina). A third is "the love of man & man" (Leontes and Polixenes), and a fourth is "parentness, and its care of youth," that is, "the love of father for daughter (Pericles and Marina, or Prospero and Miranda), and the "love of father for son" (Polixenes and Florizel). The nobleness of blood takes precedence over ardor; chastity and friendship trump Caliban ("the sort of monster all these plays have hidden in them"). There still is room for heterosexuality, but unlike its raging and volatile precursor in the major tragedies, now it is "idealized—or stiffened." (Speaking of stiffening, Olson enjoys reminding us that Hermione is "statuary almost through the play.") As a result, heterosexuality in the late plays "doesn't take to itself anything like the power of verse that" chaste, same-sex love gets; it merely resolves itself happily after having been "dependent on" the much "stronger motif" that is parent-child love. The "Shakespeare of 'friends'" has supplanted the "'dramatic' Shakespeare."

At the same time that Olson acknowledges the "diminishment of content" in the late plays, he tackles their "verse for itself." "The hardest thing of all is to say what it is." For one thing, the verse "behave[s] to a vertical which Shakespeare . . . added to blank verse." "The phrasings do not tend to finish themselves with the line, but to pass over into following lines and come to their ends rather at caesuras inside the line they end in rather than at the horizontal terminal a line of verse is, at least visually or by the law of rhyme." In the later "Quantity in Verse, and Shakespeare's Late Plays" essay, Olson will write, "[t]he late plays are motion, not action." They "move without internal combustion, or show any blades throwing the air. They come as quietly to a stop as they take off, vertically. They hover . . ." ("QV," 271).[22] This verticality pertains, as well, to what Olson makes out to be the interior rhyming typical of the late plays: "suddenly the language seems to be seeking rhymes inside the running of its thought up and down the distaff of any given speech." For another thing, Shakespeare now composes a "dry sweet music or a knotted crabbed music" that at once answers to the chastity theme and contrasts markedly with "fire in the blood" and with the "bluster" of *King Lear* ("THE HUMAN TITLE"). We can hear a "fierce going away from" the Second Verse and "the breaking off to celebrations of innocence & chastity and of youth as noble and beautiful only" in the "dried and flatted" Third Verse. Shakespeare's new metric consists of "stopped-down feet . . . joined to a humped syntax" which together produce "a difficult but most pleasurable song." It goes without saying that all of this is for the poetic good. The "modern psyche" and the dramatic verse that expresses it—Shakespeare being our best "evidence of the birth" of both—have "bedevilled" [*sic*] us for three hundred years and "only now [are they] going away." Bound cripplingly to the real, able only "to duplicate secular reality," to represent "outward things," the Second Verse is superseded by a verse in which "more nakedness shows through, more of the veins and the flowing of life in them is let through," even more than in *King Lear*.

Olson works hard "to make evident how an art of artifice can be at least as rewarding as the damned O." This "O" stands for "round" as opposed to flat, for action as opposed to motion, "event" as opposed to "pattern," "egotistical" as opposed to the "dual," and for the real and the dramatic as opposed to the artificial, the archaic, and the postmodern. Olson predictably and adamantly rejects arguments for post-1608 Shakespearean "prettification" and "decline" ("THE SO-CALLED MASQUE, AND W. SHAKESPEARE"). "This ["too damn easy"] graph of Shakespeare's life which has to go down" describes the current against which Olson swims. After all, he asks in a shrewd digression into what he calls the "literal," does not Shakespeare's company's acquisition of the Black-friars playhouse in 1608 signal an *expansion* of possibilities comparable to what the 1599 move to the Globe inspired? And does not the later move coincide with the evolution of the Third Verse, even as the earlier move coincided with the development of the Second Verse? Arguing in a somewhat less literal vein, Olson rejects the opinion that masquing in the late plays is proof of Shakespeare's decline into courtly "amusement." The masque, his research tells him, dates back to 1562, at which time it was a "form of amateur histrionic entertainment (note), originally consisting of dancing (note) and acting in dumb show (there, the real emphasis, dumb show), the performers being masked; afterwards including dialogue and song." Spectacle, song, dance (Olson compares the late-sixteenth-century "dance craze" in England with the American roaring twenties), pastoral, mask, entertainment, pageant, dumb show, jig, all of these were pervasive in England; and Shakespeare had his way with each of them, from Bottom to Sir Toby to Caliban. In a five-page set of notes entitled, "INTRO HE WAS A PLAYER"—probably intended as his introduction to the Shakespeare manuscript—Olson argues that Shakespeare was first a player, not a poet. Hence he was "adept at . . . leaping, tumbling, dancing," and music. In chapter 4, Olson wants us to imagine "the man who acted Hamlet coming out, afterwards, to do his stuff"—to dance a jig. Then, in an exhilarating burst of confidence, sounding I think a smidgen like Caliban but apparently celebrating on Shakespeare's behalf, Olson pencils in at the end of this chapter, "Hey! Hay foot, straw-foot, bring in, the girls!" ("THE SO-CALLED MASQUE, AND W. SHAKESPEARE").

Part and parcel of what Olson calls the "variety theater of England from 1562," Shakespeare's late plays call up from within the playwright a verse that "can be seen to hold in itself all the elements—dumb-show, or pantomimes, contrasti [disputations between allegorical figures], or talk, spectacles, dance, music, mythology & allegory, &, almost without exception, the central images & the central motif which mark the romance as it came from pageant and pastoral, & from masked comedy" ("THE BERGOMASK"). It is a "choric verse" characterized by "quantity more than accent" and by a "tenacity, almost an obduracy, of thought" unrestricted by "any dramatic exigency, either of a person or the situation in which the person finds himself" ("THE NEW MORRIS"). "The urgency of action is so reduced one can take time to let the verse work for itself." Amidst these claims, as if sensing that he still hasn't *shown* us Shakespeare's late verse working for itself, Olson pauses, rallies himself ("Let's get to work"), cites four and a half lines from *Henry 8* (1.1.141–45), and then parses them. These are the lines, as cited by Olson:

> We may outrun
> by violent swiftness that which we run at,
> and lose by overrunning. Know you not
> the fire that mounts the liquor till't run over
> in seeming to augment it wastes it?

His "analysis," as he terms it, runs to two-and-a-half typed manuscript pages (an excerpt reappears in "Quantity in Verse, and Shakespeare's Late Plays"). Its burden is that Shakespeare is "weaving accent, breath, [and] quantity." An example of the proof he offers looks like this:

As I hear it the accents are 'vi', 'swift', 'that', and 'run', in other words not the five feet blank verse goes by. And for good reason: that the quantity of syllables, how long it takes to say them, pull down the accent to a progress of the line along the length of itself, which progress—and which quantities—the thinking itself, the very idea of outrunning, demands. The quantity asserts itself immediately, with 'by' (long i) and 'violent' (not only long i too, but with two following syllables, which, though unaccented, are—the long o, and the heavy consonantal 'lent', 3 consonants to one vowel—slow to get through. So much so, in fact, that the first breath in the line has to be taken, even if it is a slight stop, before starting to say 'swiftness', the 't' on the end of 'lent' before the 's' of swiftness requiring the tongue to shift from upper teethridge (alveolar to you!) off it towards the combined lip and tongue position from which 'sw' may be said. To sum up, then: 'by violent', which is only one accent, and four syllables, already holds in itself that weaving of accent, breath, quantity which makes prosody, or the articulation of the sound of the words, the music it is. ("THE NEW MORRIS")

After laying in a good deal more of this, Olson concedes, "[A]ll right. I know this was thick. But it's done." What he has done is to reconfirm that Third Verse Shakespeare "does knot up his speech" and "'stops' his lines." Gone is the Second Verse "suave poet" of the "running-on" line. Third Verse Shakespeare subscribes to the principle that Olson compactly formulates in the opening lines of "Siena," a poem he wrote in 1948: "Awkwardness, the grace / the absence of the suave" (*CP*, 78). Third Verse Shakespeare's words "hold in themselves the flows *and the resistances* of life, feeling, thinking, acting" (my emphasis). Like Olson's own verse, late Shakespeare's lines "obey space-time" (see "time [and] . . . space-tensions" in "PV," 244 and "space-time" in the 1954 letter that Olson wrote to William Carlos Williams when he was "batting out" his Shakespeare manuscript [*Selected Letters*, 227–28]).

Here, as elsewhere, Olson emphasizes *poiesis* but refuses to confine himself to it. He argues that the Third Verse confirms that Shakespeare knew that he had reached a dead end: "lyric was as dead as the drama[tic]" ("THE INDIVIDABLE SCENE"). It took another year or so for Olson to articulate, in "Quantity in Verse, and Shakespeare's Late Plays," exactly what it was about the late plays that led not only to his observations about their verse but about the "matter of the[ir] thought" (271). As we have seen, early in that essay Olson argues that not just the verse of the late plays, but the plays themselves are "vertical" (271). Further along, he adds that they also are "flat" (279). Theirs is the flatness of "initiation . . . not drama" (279). Hence, while their "matter is innocence," it is not innocence like Cordelia's, with whom Shakespeare "let the world's real sit for portrait" (277) and through whom he "show[s] life as it is" ("THE NEW MORRIS"). Innocence in the late plays is not staged. Rather, it is a stage; it is one stage in one of the "*rites de passage*" (277) that each of these plays substitutes for drama. Not even lust, which opposes innocence in the late plays, introduces drama into them. As Olson remarks—succinctly and in response to widespread sentiments about the romances—lust in these plays "is not developmental, it drops, bang" (279). Again, we have to do with flatness (no development) and, like the "bang" in "Projective Verse" (244), with verticality (drops). When Shakespeare's "plays & persons" become "artificial," it remains for their verse to become "vital" ("THE DIFFERENCE OF MEN").

In both the manuscript and the subsequent essay, Olson turns to Dante's *De Vulgare Eloquentia* and *Epistola X* to elucidate the ways late Shakespeare "practice[s] the language" in order to make it vital. (Another sustained and important argument in both Olson's manuscript and his summarizing essay, one that I do not address, derives from Thomas Campion's 1602 attack on rhyme and his defense of quantity in *Observations in the Art of English Poesie*.) Taking his cue from both Dante and "Projective Verse," Olson listens to Shakespeare syllabically. But because the plays with which Olson is concerned represent Shakespeare's return to comedy after he had exhausted tragedy, Olson also zeroes in on Dante's belief that comedy "remove[s] those living in this life from the state of misery and lead[s] them to the state of felicity." Shakespeare's is, Olson acknowledges, a secular rendering of Dante's precept, a rendition of secular content in sacred form. It is also aesthetic. If felicity, or chastity or innocence, is an ethical matter that occupied Shakespeare from his earliest plays through the major tragedies, the means of expressing the *state* of felicity becomes an aesthetic problem that he struggles with at the end of his writing career. Olson believed that words "are more than handles by means of which we take hold of" ideas like innocence. "They are themselves 'holders' of our experience of those things, they are the transfer of force over from the things they stand for." "Language . . . is not a substitute for something else. It is the other thing of the thing" ("THE POEM UNLIMITED"). Innocence in the late plays, then, is a problem of *poiesis* after all. And from Olson's point of view, it is a problem that Shakespeare could not solve. "I don't think any Englishman . . . could have grappled successfully with the state of felicity—and thus comedy—until . . . this century" ("THE NEW

MORRIS"). Nonetheless, at the end of "Quantity in Verse, and Shakespeare's Late Plays" Olson still tries to fathom how the "form" innocence takes in these works is "powered" (281). He rules out the possibility that Shakespeare uses "any means or matter other than those that are local and implicit to" it (282). Moral argument and preconceptions ("outside power[s]," "weather from outside") dissipate the "intensity of the attention . . . equal to . . . innocence"; a "waste of energy, which is dispersal," they necessarily reduce "the intensity below the level of the implicit power of occasion or of thing" (281). When the right verse finally enables innocence to "yield what it is made of, . . . a thrust much more than sensuality ever gave" will emerge (281–82). Only then, in the verse at that moment, can innocence move "as one has known it does of its own nature" (282). Even though the essay concludes with a familiar Olsonian injunction, an uncommonly vatic note resonates: "Get that out with no exterior means or materials, no mechanics except those hidden in the thing itself, and we are in the hands of the mystery" (282).

About the mystery of "Mr. Big"'s post-1608 plays, Olson writes, "If they ain't drama, they at least are verse. We don't even know what they make" ("THE NEW MORRIS"). The assumption is that Shakespeare does not know either— because he did not live long enough, or did not keep at it long enough, to find out. One of the refrains of Olson's manuscript, the one that speaks loudest to its exigency ("how we practice verse now"), is that it has taken "the Americans 300 years to find out how to do it. So let's be easy on Grandfather [Shakespeare]. Let's look at him for what he did—to get us started, you might say!" That the verse of the late plays turns away from the verse of the previous periods proves that "the state ơf both the English language and verse were in <u>crise</u>." Suddenly, "blank-verse-drama was dethroned, the very *power* had become a bore" (my emphasis). Shakespeare's experiment with quantity ensued, but he "didn't [and couldn't] make the shift." Quantity is "what he was going to . . . even if he couldn't break out of the play-form, and thus did abide by blank verse" ("TO MAKE COLD NYMPHS CHASTE CROWNS"). Shakespeare is the "automobile I say hung, for 300 years, on the overhang." During those three centuries, "the language did freeze, did stabilize itself as a rational discourse system" at once "descriptive and logical." We have had to wait "until the modern was over" to discover that the postmodern (or the pre-postmodern) door is "open at this end for us." After three hundred years of lyric—"that small song of self expression" ("trick it out as best Keats could")—we arrive at Lawrence, Pound, Williams . . .

and Olson, that is, the first "essential 'invention' in the English-American possibility" since Shakespeare's late plays.

Olson's "<u>A Later Note on Letter # 15</u>," poem 2.79 in the epic-length epic
effort that is *The Maximus Poems*, presents us with one version of the story told
here. It begins with the state of English verse c. 1630:

> In English the poetics became meubles—furniture—
> thereafter (after 1630
>
> & Descartes was the value
>
> until Whitehead, who cleared out the gunk
> by getting the universe in (as against man alone

Eleven lines later, the end of the poem indicates that in 1962, poetry—and
Olson—were still finding their way:

> The poetics of such a situation
> are yet to be found out

V

JOHN BERRYMAN'S
SHAKESPEARE/SHAKESPEARE'S
JOHN BERRYMAN

In a *Paris Review* interview conducted in 1970 and published in 1972, Peter Stitt asked John Berryman, "How do your roles as teacher and scholar affect your role as poet?"[1] For Berryman, this was a "Very, very hard question." First, he identified A. E. Housman as one of his "heroes," a man whose "activities" as a "minor poet" and "great scholar" were "perfectly distinct." Then, apparently thinking out loud, Berryman reflected:

> In me they seem closer together, but I just don't know. Schwartz once asked me why it was that all my Shakespearean study had never showed up anywhere in my poetry, and I couldn't answer the question. It was a piercing question because his early poems are really very much influenced by Shakespeare's early plays. I seem to have been sort of untouched by Shakespeare, although I have had him in my mind since I was twenty years old.

Stitt demurred, and quoted lines from "Dream Song 147" that sound "very Shakespearean to me" ("Henry's mind grew blacker the more he thought. / He looked onto the world like the act of an aged whore.").[2] At first, Berryman graciously acquiesced ("I would call that Shakespearean"). But he did not quite back down. While Delmore Schwartz's early poems may be responsive to Shakespeare's plays, for Berryman to agree that one of his Dream Songs is "Shakespearean" is "Not to praise it, though, only in description. I was half-hysterical writing that song. It just burst onto the page. It took only as long to compose as it takes to write it down." To acknowledge influence would be immodest on two counts: it would smack of unwarranted self-praise, and it would falsify Berryman's method of composition—or the lack thereof. Of course, savvy readers of strong poets like Berryman inevitably will side with Stitt. Master of consistently dramatic, character-driven poetry that he was, Berryman could not possibly be "sort of untouched by Shakespeare." Long-time Berryman biographer and scholar John Haffenden is confident that "*Homage to Mistress Bradstreet* . . . took inspiration directly from *Lear*."[3] Kenneth Gross makes a strong case that "*The Dream Songs* . . . seems especially indebted to the striking range of mad-speech in *King Lear*."[4] Nevertheless, a close look at how Berryman read and then thought about, even dreamed about, Shakespeare indicates that it is not Shakespeare's writing, per se, so much as it is "all my Shakespearean study"—a devotion to the minutiae and the apparatus of Shakespeare scholarship—that insinuates itself into the work of Berryman the poet.[5]

That assiduous study commenced at Columbia College, under the tutelage of the poet and literary critic Mark Van Doren (whose *Shakespeare* appeared in 1939, three years after Berryman graduated). While Keats envied the "good Genius presiding over" his friend, the painter Benjamin Haydon, and dared to fancy that Shakespeare was his own "Presider," Berryman dubbed Van Doren "the presiding genius of all my work until . . . I fell under the influence of W. B. Yeats."[6] Near the end of his life, Berryman pronounced Van Doren "the hottest teacher of Shakespeare in the country . . . a critic of great & original power."[7] Berryman's filial regard for the professor who would later win the affection and respect of such Columbia undergraduate poets-in-the-making as Richard Howard, John Hollander, and Allen Ginsberg was deep and sustaining. Starting in 1933, when Berryman enrolled in Van Doren's writing class, and continuing long after his senior year at Columbia, when he took Van Doren's Shakespeare course, Berryman turned with trust and affection to "Mark / a personal friend."[8] "He is absolutely the justest person I have ever known . . . I absolutely reverence the man."[9]

Not to "let Mark down" ("Down & Back") was a perennial standard for Berryman, who by turns acknowledged and resisted his mentor's level-headed appraisals of him. Just two months before Berryman committed suicide by jumping off Minneapolis's Washington Avenue bridge, Van Doren wrote to tell him that he had supported Berryman's successful application for an NEH senior fellowship, but that he was convinced that Berryman would "never finish the Sh book" for which it had been awarded. For decades, Shakespeare had been a signal medium through which the two men confided in one another. Now, in equally admiring and admonitory lines, Van Doren summarized his outlook on their life-long conversation, beginning with an allusion to *Hamlet*:

There will always be metal more attractive: poems, novels, a memoir, a collection of pensées—God knows what else. You have this illusion that you are a scholar, but you know damn well you are nothing of the sort, any more than I am. Scholarship is for those with shovels, whereas you're a man of the pen, the wind, the flying horse, the shining angel, the glittering fiend—anything but the manure where scholars have buried the masterpieces of the world. You're for the masterpieces, and you know that nothing else matters one tiny little bit, one pitiful little jot, one tit, one tittle. (*Life*, 402)

When Berryman wrote back, he conceded that he had never "finished anything important except the Sonnets, the Crane, the Bradstreet poem, and The Dream Songs" (no mean accomplishment, as both he and Van Doren well knew). As for what he had failed to complete, it was due to the "DOLDRUMS, proto-despair" and to "the opposite, fantastic hysterical labour, accumulation, proliferation" ("labour": Berryman's spelling and his accent changed irrevocably in England). Amid plea and boast, a third reason followed:

I have seldom known you wrong about anything but you couldn't be more wrong about me as a scholar. Mark, I am it, Dr Dryasdust in person. The man I identify with is Housman, pedantic & remorseless . . . and I mean to deal with him some time. . . . Third is over-ambitiousness. Part of this is temperamental grandiosity . . . but more of it . . . is legitimate self-demand on the largest conceivable scale. Presenting myself with any topic whatever, I require to present, or to explain, as the case may be, *everything*. This sometimes holds matters up for years—always to advantage (provided they ever get done). (*Life*, 402–3)[10]

Twenty-five years prior to this, in March 1946, a laboring, accumulating, possibly hysterical or manic Berryman wrote to Van Doren that he had just "collated 24 copies of the First Folio [*King Lear*] in Washington . . . and am only just able to see my hand in front of my face, ha ha" (*BS*, 242). Given that no Berryman edition of *King Lear* and no Berryman life of Shakespeare ever came to fruition, his scrupulous if comically parenthetical "provided they ever get done" can only have been tendered as half-grudging grist for Van Doren's mill.[11] And yet, Berryman's lifelong commitment to manure and to dust, to "*everything*," was more consequential than even Van Doren could see.

Thanks to Van Doren's last-minute rescue effort, Berryman was able to move from Columbia College to Cambridge University as the Kellett Fellow for 1936–38. His English tutor, George ("Dadie") Rylands, was an accomplished actor, a director (who inspired Peter Hall, John Barton, and Trevor Nunn), and Virginia Woolf's host at the King's College luncheon described in *A Room of One's Own*. Berryman would not have been alone in judging him "one of the 3 or 4 most acute critics of the 1930s of Shakespeare's *poetry* & style" (*BS*, *xii*).[12] "He was kind to me stranded," writes Berryman in "Transit"; "even to an evening party / he invited me, where Keynes & Auden / sat on the floor in the hubbub trading stories" (*CP*, 197). Although in 1937 he protested that "It's awfully silly . . . ever to do anything but read Shakespeare—particularly when we've only one lifetime" (*Life*, 85), Berryman read very widely while abroad (from Chaucer to Yeats, from Ronsard to Rimbaud). He was nearly always composing poems, and occasionally publishing them (Robert Penn Warren took five for *The Southern Review*; Eliot rejected what he sent to him at *The Criterion*). He drank with Dylan Thomas and he sipped tea with Yeats. He took in plays (including Olivier's "unbelievably bad" Hamlet and his "damn bad" Macbeth) and then tried his hand at writing them. Working on his one-act *Cleopatra: A Meditation*, Berryman let on as how "Shakespeare was magnificent (and wrong), I hope to be interesting as well as right" (*Life*, 92). It was while he was at Cambridge that Berryman first announced that he was "very anxious to edit *Lear* . . . no edition worth drains exists."[13]

His Shakespearean through-line would extend to the Harness Essay Prize, which he did not win but for which he wrote more than seventy pages on "The Character and Role of the Heroine in Shakespearian Comedy," and to the prestigious and remunerative Charles Oldham Shakespeare Prize, which he won in 1937. In the course of preparing for his prize essays, he worked his way through Folio facsimiles and "such Quartos as I have, the Cambridge 1863–6, some Furness volumes, some Arden, the erratic New Sh as far as it goes, . . . Johnson, Richardson, Hazlitt (hell take him), Coleridge, Bradley, Greg."[14] And so it went. From 1944 to 1946, Berryman was awarded Rockefeller Fellowships for his projected critical edition of *King Lear*. Several years of immersion in the play's vexed textual history led him to believe that its cruxes were "susceptible of permanent solution," that "the establishment of a text at every point responsible and highly probable is a matter now merely of labour and insight."[15] Prodigious study and note-taking, detailed correspondence with the aforementioned W. W. Greg— the *éminence grise* of the New Bibliography—and "temperamental grandiosity" led Berryman to believe that his edition would be "closer to Shakespeare's intentions than any other in existence." Even in 1952, when he was willing to admit that he had been "insane in thinking at the outset that I could do the three- or four-year job in two years," he remained convinced that he had almost pulled it off: "Still, by not sleeping the second year I came near the end."

In the 1950s, once again engaged in extensive Shakespeare research, Berryman began to write substantial chunks of a biography. Guggenheim Foundation support for this project followed in 1952. When he applied for fellowship renewal in 1953, he reported that "my critical biography of Shakespeare . . . has moved forward . . . and nine chapters of it are now drafted."[16] According to Berryman's "Plan of Work," he would be writing for "the general cultivated public." For such an audience, it would be necessary to pursue

> many broad enquiries: documentary, historical, paleographical, bibliographical, editorial, theatrical, linguistic, genetic (sources), critical (including questions of value, comparison, style, form, substance, versification, image-study, etc.), psychiatric and psychoanalytic, ritual, symbolic. . . . The biographer must be capable of a book . . . neither unduly confident nor perpetually reserved, presenting an image unified and acceptable to a reader sick of quarter-Shakespeares. . . . [This will require "many years" of work] because nothing less than passionate absorption will enable the student to persevere through everything irrelevant and lunatic to a mature working acquaintance with any of these fields of enquiry, and the process will have to be repeated again and again.[17]

Five years later, in July 1958, Berryman began a "Preface" (in this instance, for a *Shakespeare Handbook*) in which he acidly dismisses those who fail to see that "Shakespeare was a human being and wrote out of his heart and his own brain."[18] "This book" will stand four square against the C. J. Sisson "Mythical Sorrows of Shakespeare" school according to which the playwright was "a man who felt nothing." Instead, as he had been arguing in a series of Shakespeare lectures (the 1951 Hodder Lectures at Princeton, the 1952 Elliston Lectures at the University of Cincinnati, and summer-school lectures at Harvard in 1954), Berryman would unabashedly align biography with art. About Marlowe, Jonson, and Shakespeare, he had written that the "connexions, now illuminating, now mysterious, between the artist's life and his work . . . [are] denied only by very young persons or writers whose work perhaps really does bear no relation to their lives, *tant pis pour eux*."[19] For his part, Berryman would continue to read Shakespeare's plays and sonnets with full regard for the "man whose son died, who was publicly ridiculed and insulted, who followed a degrading occupation, whose mistress got off with his beloved friend, whose patron was condemned to death and imprisoned for years, whose father died" (*BS, lviii*).

In 1971, on the heels of teaching a University of Minnesota seminar on *Hamlet*, Berryman was again fully invested in his Shakespeare project—now *Shakespeare's Reality*. In his five-page, single-spaced, 10-point type "Description of proposed study" for the NEH fellowship that he was indeed awarded, Berryman rehearses every imaginable reason why he is the right man for the job. He charts a route leading from his student days under Van Doren and Rylands ("poor Dadie, used to adoring chumship from his tutees which I didn't vouchsafe him at all"), to the Oldham prize, to his correspondence with Greg ("it only took me one year instead of 3–5 to make myself a first-rate textual critic"), his Rockefeller fellowship, his invited lectures, his volumes of award-winning poetry, classes he taught on Shakespeare ("Harvard's big graduate Shakespeare . . . dealt with 22 plays in 34 lectures—idiotic, but that was what I did") and the New Testament and "classical medieval Renaissance literature & art & thought (from psychology to folklore to polit. Science to cosmology)," to his familiarity with "Post-Freudian developments," with the "art-science of Biography" from Plutarch to Erikson on Gandhi, and with Shakespeare films ("Oh I have seen Hamlets"). Even as he pitches the biography, Berryman off-handedly allows as how "[s]ome time, after the eight books I have now in hand to finish next, I'll go back to *Lear*, revising the 120-page Introduction and completing the commentary. No hurry"![20]

But in fact, Berryman's *Lear* had lapsed for good, and so did *Shakespeare: A Critical Biography* and all of its successive or projected avatars and companions: *A Shakespeare Handbook*; *Shakespeare's Friend*; *Shakespeare: An Attempt at Critical Biography*; *Shakespeare's Identity*; *Shakespeare's Reality*; *Shakespeare: A Study of Imagination*; *Shakespeare's Reading*. A multi-volume "fine printed edition of" *The Dramatic Works of William Shakespeare* was broached. *Shakespeare's Murderer*, *The Utopian Theme in Shakespeare*, and *Shakespeare's Dream World* may have been intended book-length projects. Contracts and advances were forthcoming from Farrar, Straus and Giroux, from Viking, and from Thomas Y. Crowell. If everywhere there are signs of Berryman's grandiosity, the three hundred and fifty pages of prose collected in John Haffenden's *Berryman's Shakespeare* confirm that none of this was idle. Not to be forgotten, besides all of the poetry for which he is best known, is that Berryman could and did complete a biography (*Stephen Crane*, 1950). His essays and occasional pieces, collected in *The Freedom of the Poet*, encompass Marlowe and Nashe, James and Babel, Yeats and Pound, Dreiser and Fitzgerald, and a good deal besides. And yet, tellingly, with the exception of "Shakespeare at Thirty," an essay published in *The Hudson Review* in 1953, none of Berryman's work on Shakespeare was printed during his lifetime.

Had John Berryman not committed suicide in 1972, it is possible that Robert Giroux, the friend and then publisher who sat with him in Van Doren's Shakespeare class, would have nursed or cajoled a finished manuscript from him. Despite the line in his NEH application about going back to *Lear*, and despite the fact that he had in his files an introduction that ran to well over one hundred pages plus a mostly completed text with apparatus and partial commentary, it is highly doubtful that Berryman would have picked up where he left off work in the 1940s. The appearance of George Ian Duthie's edition of *King Lear*, about which Berryman had numerous and valid reservations, pretty well took the wind out of his editorial sails. The often-mentioned critical biography is another matter. Even as late as May 1971, in a letter to Giroux, Berryman's list of ongoing projects included "*Shakespeare's Reality*—'74?" (*FP, viii*). Still, what may be his last words on the subject, written in his journal when his "Tho'ts [were] constantly of death" (Mariani, 498), are anything but optimistic: "I thought *new* disappointments impossible but last night (Thurs.) suddenly doubted if I really *have* a book 'Shakespeare's Reality' at all, despite all these years" (*Life*, 418).

The criticism on offer in *Berryman's Shakespeare* gives us a fair idea of what parts of such a book would have looked like. Berryman tasked himself to read everything he imagined that Shakespeare himself had read, as well as every English play known to have been written between 1570 and 1614, not to mention swaths of theater history, English history, and volume after volume of twentieth-century scholarship. All of this learning informs his essays. So, too, does an Edward Dowden–inspired developmental understanding of the always intertwined life and works, based on a more or less conventional account passing from one period to the next ("early," "second," "middle," "tragic," "the crisis," "the end"). A variety of themes—"the *Utopian* theme" (51), "sexual loathing" (101), "the Displacement of the King" (120)—are explored, sometimes with an eye to Shakespeare's two "nervous crises" (100), sometimes taking into account the playwright's "ferocious or even a desperate frame of mind" (102). *Hamlet*'s "common theme," the "death of fathers," is not just Claudius's, but it is Shakespeare's (110–11). Having spent a fair portion of his waking and dream life trying to make sense of his own father's apparent suicide in 1926, it was Berryman's common theme, too. Less conventionally academic, and more telling, is Berryman's willingness to stand in judgment or comment against the grain.

"Richard [III] is only first-class journeyman work, a performance we admire rather than feel with" (16); "during the six years of his [Shakespeare's] supreme *normal* achievement, from 1594 to 1600, his literary practice *was* conventional, and perhaps his life was" (66). Of Henry's speech at the start of *1 Henry 4*, Berryman quips, "Shakespeare writes thus when he is bored" (72). "The incapacity to organize experience [in *Antony and Cleopatra*] (comparatively, that is) combined with the grandiosity and the rapid alteration of subject suggests to me in the poet not only degrees of fatigue and evasiveness but a remnant of hysteria" (138). There is much that is moving about the inescapable autobiographical force of this last observation, from "alteration of subject" and "fatigue" right down to "grandiosity" and "hysteria." But there also is much to admire about Berryman's Eliot-like refusal to turn everything that he found flawed in Shakespeare into evidence for the Bard's uncanny or redeeming method. What Haffenden calls Berryman's Shakespeare lectures and essays (regarding the latter, Berryman more modestly calls his piece on *Macbeth* a "sketch" [319]) are almost always interesting, but they require our patience in the face of their unceasing biographical (and autobiographical) claims. Paradoxically, Berryman can be most convincing when he is least plausible, when his immoderate devotion to "the life" effectively cancels itself out. The second state of the Droeshout Shakespeare portrait, writes Berryman, "achieved at last that hard, foxy, *false* appearance which has gravelled us all and sent so many weak-minded persons scurrying about in search of the 'real' (the titled) author" (40). Then, too, Berryman's recourse to no-longer fashionable theme criticism can sound flat-footed, at best serviceable in the student-filled lecture halls for which it was originally intended. More rewarding are passages like the two pages Berryman devotes to *Macbeth*'s "By the pricking of my thumbs, / Something wicked this way comes" (319–20, including a fine gloss on "By"), or his recognition that as early as *2* and *3 Henry 6*, "a bewildering, unprecedented variety of human experience is deployed *without confusion*: intrigue, ambition, pride, penance, a raving death, wrangling, the supernatural, the amusing inconsequence and brutality of the common people, hawking, murder, domestic life, treachery, nobility, resignation, the businesslike (curt, natural, manly), the ominous, the contemptuous, the exalted" (10; my emphasis).

It is safe to say that every reader will walk away from *Berryman's Shakespeare* with his or her own handful of durable insights. I have mine, but I will confine myself to just one set of remarks, exemplary for their shrewdness and their unsentimentality. Initially, the subject is Falstaff, but then Berryman unexpectedly widens his lens. In "Shakespeare's Poor Relation: *2 Henry IV*," he writes that Falstaff has run away from armed combat. He has gloriously lied about it. He seeks credit (at Shrewsbury) for what he has not done in the way of battle. He is prepared to steal horses in order to get to his friend's coronation. He looks on companions as prey: of Shallow he says: "If the yong Dace be a baite for the old Pike, I see no reason in the law of nature but I may snap at him." The very sharp word "snap" defeats any Huckleberry Finn view of Falstaff. And yet does all this misdoing amount to much?" (337)

Berryman then notices the "coldness" in the young king's "I know thee not, old man" speech, and he homes in on Henry's "Make lesse thy body (hence) and more thy grace." By turns bemused, scrupulously historical, and uncompromising, Berryman concludes:

> From a partaker [Henry] in these riots, this [Henry's newfound abstemiousness] is *good*, or seems so to me; I doubt that an Elizabethan playgoer would feel any sanctimoniousness here, being committed to monarchism (and nervous already about the succession to Elizabeth's throne). *One might argue, even, that this word "grace" is too often at Shakespeare's disposal for this kind of situation—Caliban you remember promises to be wiser thereafter and "seek for grace."* (338; my emphasis)

The exacting judgment that Shakespeare might be facile, that he might cut corners in passages that are in plain sight, at even the most familiar moments, is breathtaking. It is one thing to argue that Shakespeare could fudge motivation (witness Macbeth's "black and deep desires"; Iago's "What you know, you know"). It is another to suggest that he was prone to moral finesse. Haffenden dates the unfinished essay from which I have quoted to 1969–70, but in one of his last footnotes to his introduction, he quotes from a letter that Berryman wrote to Giroux back in 1955. Even then, Berryman was advising his friend that "[a] number of passages in my book go into this strange & unattractive moral smoothness of Shakespeare's" (367, n. 123). Of this, one would have been happy to hear a good deal more.

When "that multiform & encyclopedic bastard" Shakespeare was on Berryman's mind (*BS, xxxiv*), he felt exhilarated and devoted—or besieged and resentful. With his undergraduate pal E. M. ("Milt") Halliday, he "systematically stud[ied]" the Sonnets "at a rate of one per day."[21] In a letter to his mother from

Cambridge, he quips, "Jeez, he could write, dat guy!!" (June 25, 1936).[22] Like Keats, "haunted . . . intensely" by a passage from *King Lear*, Berryman writes that Hermione's words "have haunted me for days" (*Letters*, 100; April 18, 1937). From Princeton, on October 3, 1944, he writes to tell her that Shakespeare must be "merry with wicked joy peeping over Olympus at sorrowful scholars" (*Letters*, 211). And late in his life, in a Step One declaration that he presented to his AA group, Berryman writes, "Replacements for drinking: work on my Shakespeare biography mornings & afternoons—I drink v. little when doing scholarly work or writing prose: 2 or 3 drinks a day" (*Life*, 375). Hours spent studying Shakespeare could feel ruinous to Berryman, but they also made for a salutary discipline (recall Virginia Woolf: "Shall I read King Lear? Do I want such strain on the emotions? I think I do."), and when there was communion back and forth across the page, there were moments of pleasure, too.[23] He was susceptible to Shakespeare's "active continual joy" in language.[24] In a 1958 letter to Russell Cooper, probably unsent, Berryman wrote, "I am working on Shakespeare from ten to fifteen hours a day and am very happy" (*BS, lviii*). In 1965, he told an interviewer that Shakespeare taught him "How to be, or try to be, gorgeous" (*RB*, 97).

The archive at the University of Minnesota gives us a good idea of what Berryman was actually doing, day in day out, when he read Shakespeare. It is voluminous. Berryman kept thousands and thousands of pages of his notes, seemingly every piece of paper he ever jotted, wrote, or typed on. He also marked up page after page in volume after volume of his books—there is Berryman commentary in a goodly percentage of the approximately one hundred and fifty Shakespeare volumes that he owned. Sometimes, Berryman avails himself of margins and inside covers to take notes or make lists. He responds to words, phrases, and to characters more often than to actions. He engages in hundreds of spirited, one-sided conversations with editors. Occasionally their work meets with his approval but more often than not, he is (gorgeously) impatient and in disagreement. No matter what, there is always room for one or both of his two recurring marginal responses: his skeptical, argumentative "eh?" and his hesitant "HM" (hmm). Frank Kermode's 1954 edition of *The Tempest* provides a fair sampling of Berryman reading with pen in hand but, in this instance, mostly willing to ignore the emendations and variants on which he was prone to dwell. When in his introduction Kermode writes that "Prospero, like Adam, fell from his kingdom by an inordinate thirst for knowledge" but that learning also helps him to repair his ruin, Berryman responds with "no! no sense of sin in Prosp." This kind of acute micro-analysis crops up only now and then in these volumes. There is another one beside Prospero's "To cry to th' sea that roar'd to us; to sigh . . ." where Berryman writes, "a new style!" Pointed but less memorable are his one-word notations: "jerks" appears in the margin beside a comment from Kermode about the way Guarini and Fletcher "trifled" with pastoral tragicomedy; "marvellous" is his response to Miranda first lamenting the "foul play" she and Prospero endured then wondering if "blessed was't we did?" "Cf. Lowell's style" next to lines spoken by Ceres reveals Berryman's friend and rival on the horizon when he was reading no less than when he was writing.

It was much more common for one passage in the plays to recall another for Berryman. Rosalind's "'Tis not your inkie browes" calls to mind Hamlet's "'Tis not alone my inky suit." Oliver's "being the thing I am" reminds him of Parolles's "simply the thing I am / Shall make me live." Berryman admires the way Shakespeare gives Orlando a half line ("But heavenly Rosalind") at the very end of 1.2: "what an instinct!—to keep Orl. speechless (he has <u>done</u>) and give him this moving exit, wherein he finally <u>speaks after the couplet</u>." In notes on the inside back cover of an Arden edition of *Antony and Cleopatra*, which Berryman appears to have marked up when he was in England, he judges it "a simple story, consisting chiefly of <u>betrayals</u>." It is "A disillusioned work, & for all its beauty rather disheartening." On a slip of note paper inserted in his facsimile edition of the *Troilus and Cressida* first quarto, Berryman writes that it is "like <u>Meas.</u>, marvellous here & there profound, but gritty." His reactions to Shakespeare's sonnets were more idiosyncratic. Berryman, whose 117 "Sonnets to Chris" were eventually published as *Berryman's Sonnets*, was underwhelmed by Shakespeare's sequence. While "three or four challenge perfection . . . most of them are very moderately good or bad, and I think their mediocrity has been insufficiently appreciated" (*BS*, 43). Berryman's marginalia in his copy of Ingram and Redpath's *Shakespeare's Sonnets* were terse and often disengaged. There are a host of "poors" and "mediocres" and "trivials," a series of more particular reactions, such as "bitter," "spiritless," "tense," and "defiant," and an occasional "superb" or "grave and fine." Perhaps Berryman was saying to Stitt that he approached Shakespeare the poet-playwright as a scholar-critic because it left him the breathing space he needed as a poet. Eileen Simpson, Berryman's first wife, remembers him asking, "Will *Lear* crowd verse out of my brain? Will *Lear* devour my writing time?"[25]

The gap between what Berryman called his study and his poetry never closed entirely, but it tended to narrow when he was reading the plays, running up red flags that only a scholar-poet could or would raise. As Dr. Dryasdust, Berryman wrote to the Rockefeller Foundation in 1949 that "The truth is I suffer from a respect for textual technicians which is excessive." He always thought of himself as what he called a "textual critic," better still, a "critical editor."[26] Convinced that editing was "a job for literary critics" (*BS, xxxiii*), he was often far more caustic with generations of editors than Keats was with Dr. Johnson. Where a note in the *New Variorum of Shakespeare's Henry the Fourth Part 1* suggests that several readings in the second Folio edition of the play may have been heard by a reviser from the mouths of actors, Berryman writes "or they <u>may</u> have been dictated by Sh's ghost; but they <u>prob. weren't</u>." Where John Dover Wilson writes in his edition of *Love's Labor's Lost* that he does not "hesitate to avow" that the Quarto was printed from Shakespeare's autograph manuscript, Berryman snaps, "Do you ever hesitate?" The eighteenth-century editor William Warburton suggested that Cleopatra speaks of never having to palate more the "dug," as opposed to "dung." Berryman plasters his response across the top of the page: "'dug' is unforgivable because it does <u>not make sense</u>: neither the beggar nor Caesar any more tastes, grown, any dug! Nor ever will!" The 1880 New Variorum *Lear* has Sir Joshua Reynolds saying that "The words, 'No, no, no life,'" are spoken "not tenderly, but with passion." Berryman underlines this and writes in the margin, "no: with despair; = '<u>no life</u> in her!'" When W. J. Craig writes in his introduction to the Arden *Lear* that "I have very seldom ventured to introduce new readings," Berryman, probably thinking of his own aspirations, asks, "Why did you 'edit' the play then?" More clipped and typically tart marginal reactions range from "Yes!" and "very good" and "Hurrah hurrah" to "quite sufficient" and "not impossible" to "you fool" and "Idiotic & bad" or "ungrammatical, besides unwarrantable," "another armchair note," or "fantastic ignoring of desperate crux." The Berryman who felt compelled to "explain . . . *everything*" had no tolerance for ignoring. While the evidence from his *Lear* work is predictably legion, an example from *Antony and Cleopatra* confirms his vigilance. Caesar says of Antony's death that "The breaking of so great a thing should make / A greater crack. The round world / Should have shook lions into civil streets" (5.1.14–16). Unhappy with an Arden note that justifies the short line, Berryman wonders whether or not "round" should be "ravind," which he associates with *Macbeth*'s "ravined [ravenous] salt-sea shark." In any case, there is more work to be done since "'round' is <u>inadequate</u>" to the occasion.

Berryman the Shakespeare professor was as conscientious about "everything" as was Berryman the Shakespeare editor, biographer, and critic. In a set of notes in which he drafts a proposal for a University of Minnesota course on "The Age of *Hamlet*," he foresees an "Emphasis on the year 1600, when the play took its final form." The idea is to "bring everything feasible to bear on *Hamlet*, and then to use the play, thus enriched, as a text for the study of Shakespeare's mind and the late-Renaissance view of Man."[27] A separate folder devoted to this course provides an idea of what is meant by "everything feasible." On three sheets of five-by-eight-inch note paper, Berryman inks a chronology in which 1600–1601 is divided into months, each month subdivided into as many as a dozen days. 21 March: "Essex kept tight at home"; 30 April: "Fr. King trouble w. mistress." We can also get a sense of what transpired in the *Hamlet* classroom. At the top of one page, Berryman reminds himself to "Apologize for my harshness over Pol." He then lists four topics he plans to cover, including "self-representation in Pr. Hamlet?"; "a) facts of 1601: Essex executed . . . fa[ther] died—Fa-son relation in Ham. The closest he ever represented b) late Eliz'n disenchantment." Berryman's much earlier "My Harvard Sh" notes dwell on plays and characters in familiar, less historically-minded ways. Falstaff is "a dialectical character . . . (next to Hamlet) the most complicated and least readily formulated. 1) Does he mislead Hal, or Hal him? 2) Even his age? old or 'young'? (essentially) 3) a liar etc. or more honest w. himself than Hotspur?" "No other play is so persistently reflective" as *Troilus and Cressida*, Berryman writes, "but the reflection does not go anywhere either." Its "style is forced, ultra-Latinate, almost undifferentiated as to character, and capable not only of freq. self-parody but positive silliness." *Antony and Cleopatra* is without "dram. pressure, comparatively; to speak truth, a want of passion." Needless to say, none of these notes tells us what Berryman sounded like when he read Shakespeare. Philip Levine has written of Professor Berryman's "haunting and unique cadences" (*RB*, 40), but this probably does not pertain to Shakespeare. Neither may William Meredith's recollection that "[w]hen John read aloud, the etymology of the word *aloud* was brought forcibly home."[28] Only Robert Lowell gets us a very little bit closer: "John could quote with vibrance to all lengths, even prose, even late Shakespeare, to show me what could be done with disrupted and mended syntax."[29]

Better than anyone else, Berryman knew that in the battle between "everything" and "everything feasible," his "fantastic hysterical labour, accumulation, proliferation" tended to prevail. According to Simpson, shortly after Berryman received his first Rockefeller Foundation check in support of his edition of *King Lear*, he fretted, "Can I control my bloody obsessiveness?"[30] Whether or not he spoke precisely these words, they probably are not far off the mark. Stamina bordering on mania is what comes through in Berryman's letters. In October 1944, he wrote to Van Doren that "*Lear*'s renovation is going on rapidly & ruins me altogether for anything else. I am willing, however, to be destroyed in this cause: I hope to have some permanent effect." In April 1945 he was spending

"15 hours a day" on *Lear* and in August he wrote to his contacts at the Rocke-feller Foundation that "I have been on the Cape at Truro for two weeks with my wife for a nominal vacation, but n [*sic*] fact I worked five or six hours a day at variant-analysis" (*BS*, 226–27). In a letter to his mother from May 1946, not much has changed: "I posted fifty pages of tough close argument to Greg the other day and am now rushing through the text proper, this week so far I've written twelve of text, five of apparatus, eighteen of commentary, and I mean to be done in a month of 15-hour days unless I break up" (*Letters*, 222). "Henry's" acknowledgment that "There's always the cruelty of scholarship" (Dream Song 119) speaks feelingly not just to what Shakespeare has done to Berryman but to what Berryman would like to do to Shakespeare. The *Lear* work entailed many "Ah ha!" moments, but just as often, it felt punitive. Probably riffing on Cassio ("there be souls must be saved, and there be souls must not be saved," *Othello*, 2.3.96–98), Berryman wrote to Van Doren that "[a]ll scholars who are not to be saved should be set in Hell to edit 'King Lear,' the First Quarto" (*Mariani*, 163). From Princeton, Berryman wrote to his mother that his chances of making pro-gress on the edition improved once he was given an office: "far from ideal, but a table, book-space and privacy" (*Letters*, 209). Simpson makes it sound more proximate to Hell: "a closet of a room, the Ball Room (named for Professor Ball, not a joke about its size), in the basement under Chancellor Green [Princeton's pre-Firestone library], and reachable by way of a long, dark tunnel through which ran asbestos-covered hot-water pipes."[31]

According to an unusually laconic account of Berryman's own, his "Rocke-feller project" entailed preparing "a new full-dress edition of *King Lear*, a play of which the text in all existing editions is shamefully unsatisfactory: the establish-ment of text and commentary on it are the main labours" (*Letters*, 209). Since, more than sixty years later, editors are still at odds with one another, sorting out claims about the *Lear* 1608 and 1619 Quartos and the 1623 Folio, it comes as no surprise that Berryman was overreaching. In his introduction to *Berry-man's Shakespeare*, John Haffenden does a superb job of describing the morass of textual scholarship, as it stood in 1944, into which Berryman threw him-self (*BS*, xv–xxxiv). Haffenden also gives us Berryman's "Textual Introduction" in its 1946 state and technical correspondence between Berryman and Greg (whose *The Editorial Problem in Shakespeare* Berryman reviewed for *The Nation* in 1943). The letters reveal Berryman's considerable emotional investment in the minutiae of editing as well as the very high level of imaginative analysis that he could bring to bear (see my introduction, as well). There is, for example an exchange between Berryman and Greg regarding the "slayer begin threats /

state begins thereat" crux at Q *Lear* 4.2.57. Berryman thinks that "'state' must be right (the compositor probably thought he saw 'slare' and interpreted it); but 'thereat' has every appearance of correct syntax, and 'threats' is a plausible misprint for it" (241). As for "begin[s]": when Berryman proposes "begird," Greg comes back with a conjecture of his own ("bestirs") (241–42). Berryman is won over immediately and responds with a rousing "Hurrah! I feel sure that with *bestirs* you have reached Shakespeare." And yet, he cannot help but wonder whether "the amazing copy simply had *besir*." This transatlantic give and take could conceivably go on, but for now, Berryman graciously concedes: "Poor 'begirds' I whistle off, though I'm happy my analysis helped to the true one" (242). While Haffenden's delightful selection gives us a good deal more of this, it simply cannot convey the daunting intensity—the staggering particularity—of what Berryman, in his *Paris Review* interview, called "my Shakespearean study."

No written description can do justice to the notes Berryman generated across all of those fifteen-hour days. He certainly could generalize about *Lear* (about its textual provenance, at least; there are only four pages in all of *Berryman's Shakespeare* that count as conventional literary criticism of the play); but day-in and day-out, he concentrated on individual words. One after another after another. Even though Berryman believed that it is unfair and inaccurate to distinguish work on cruxes and emendations from literary criticism, hence interpretation, he himself was of the opinion that neither Q nor F underwent anything "that should be called literary revision" (*BS*, 179). So when he was reasoning his way through "upward of 1,200 serious variations" (*BS*, 179), he was examining in their minute particulars not just the likes of begin/begird/bestir, but "vntender" vs. "untented," "peruse" vs. "pierce," "alapt" vs. "attaskt" vs. "at task," even "ye" vs. "you" and "Ha" vs. "yea." If pointing and line division—mispunctuation and mislineation—are part of this picture, they pale in comparison with the attention given over to word-level variants, "sophistications," and "equivalents." Berryman even schooled himself on typesetting—to the point that he could hold his own with skilled analytical bibliographers (witness: "The argument [from Q2 & F] to show that the so-called 'invariant' sheets of Q—B, I, L— also existed in corrected & uncorrected states is very difficult.")—and for some time, he had a pony in the race between the memorial and the stenographic reconstruction of Q *Lear*. Still, the "fantastic labour" that "attaskt" his eyes, his ears, and his imagination was word work. Close optic and phonic variants were all-consuming. Even when Berryman aggregates, as he does in the margins and end-papers of his editions of *Lear*, and still more exhaustively on note page inserts, willy nilly, his basic unit remains the word.

Like a language poet, he files and stacks the words of *King Lear* into columnar poems. The six-by-nine-inch sheet atop the recto and verso of which Berryman wrote "<u>Sh</u>. only in <u>Lear</u>" is, first and foremost, evidence of sheer work (fig. 5.1). How many hours did just this sheet consume? Are the many, many comparable pages of seemingly relentless, painstaking research stashed among the Berryman papers signs of inspiration or plodding? Reading Donne's line, "Hither with christall vyals lovers come," Berryman wrote that he wanted "to get down and bite a large piece from the poker when I see that" (*Life*, 77). The *Lear* project gave rise to a different kind of transport, something closer to trance but far from the shock that kept Samuel Johnson from returning to the play until *he* began to revise it as an editor. Berryman's lists and charts and textual notes answer to the deep identification that compels one to rewrite the master's words, or they are evidence of the identification that derives from doing so. Taken together, the *Lear* sheets reveal Berryman reconfiguring and (in a way that Pierre Menard would have appreciated) rewriting Q and F. They constitute what I would call Berryman's Shakespeare.

With its expanded range of reference, another sheet—"<u>once only</u> in Sh."— makes for an even more impressive, hectic word-hoard (fig. 5.2). It is more all-over canvas and more painterly than "<u>Sh</u>. only in <u>Lear</u>." It is the work of a hypomanic editor, obsessed but not out of control. In notes that he drafted for a letter to his friend Sally Appleton, Berryman wrote that "Perh. the essential thing abt. poetry is that it is both rebellious (malice, fury, contempt, ungoverned grief & pain, ruleless desire, arrogance, *un*successfully forbidden knowledge) and the servant of order" (*Life*, 254). Scholarly frenzy and rule compete on pages like this one. Words fall into place even as they come unmoored from their sponsoring texts. It is easy to lose sight of the extent to which characters and plot have simply vanished.[32] Underlined play titles and occasional exclamation marks constitute the only evidence of drama (at age twenty-two, Berryman had already determined that "the Elizabethan aim was not character"). On another sheet, at the top of which Berryman wrote, "<u>Shakespeare</u>: a study of imagination," he proposes an introduction in which he will answer the question, "<u>How</u> to study Sh?" The first task is "To <u>assemble</u> & <u>use</u> the superb equipment worked up by generations of critics." Precisely toward the word "equipment" Berryman directs an arrow, descending from a corner of the page where he has written, "NED [*New English Dictionary*], for ex.—not only as scholarship but <u>criticism</u>!"

The prose in Haffenden's *Berryman's Shakespeare* is unarguably one sort of (familiar) Shakespeare criticism. It is acute and learned and sometimes memorable, but it is not consanguineal with Berryman's verse. Untouched by the

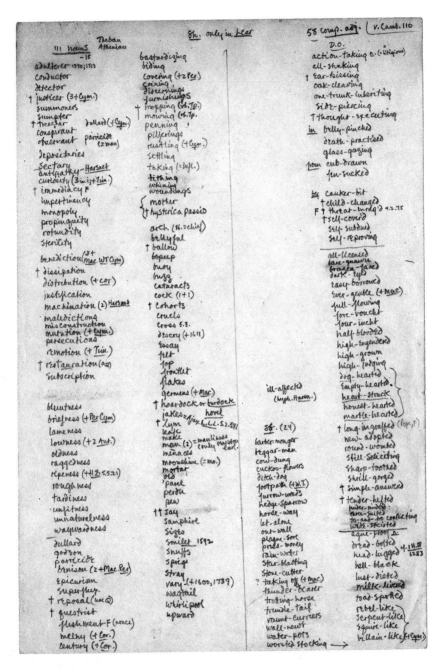

Figure 5.1: John Berryman's "<u>Sh.</u> only in <u>Lear</u>." John Berryman Papers (MSS 43). Courtesy of the Literary Manuscripts Collection, University of Minnesota Libraries, Minneapolis, Minnesota. © Kate Donahue.

Figure 5.2: John Berryman's "<u>once only</u> in Sh." John Berryman Papers (MSS 43).
Courtesy of the Literary Manuscripts Collection, University of Minnesota Libraries,
Minneapolis, Minnesota. © Kate Donahue.

poems, it mirrors Berryman's contention that his poems were "untouched by Shakespeare." The "criticism" on the two sheets of *King Lear* notes, however, is patently related to the semantic disruptions and jaggedness as well as to the structural equipoise of Berryman's verse. The poet-editor met the poet-playwright via intense work on variants and emendations conducted on note pages brimful with Shakespeare's rearranged words. While Edgar and Gloucester may prefigure Henry in Dream Song 120 ("I totter to the lip of the cliff"), it is Shakespeare's "enormous sounds"—which "downward & up bring real" stuff like "Loss, deaths, terror"—which Berryman amplifies in the mixtape that is the complete *Dream Songs*. Not Berryman the Shakespeare critic, but Berryman the Shakespeare editor, the relentless curator of Shakespeare's quarto and folio variants, outfitted Berryman the dream song poet.

Berryman did not follow Keats's example of inserting a poem of his own in one of his Shakespeare editions; instead, he got himself onto the pages of *King Lear* by cataloging its cruxes and emendations. The broad and inviting margins in his 1927 edition of *The Tragedie of King Lear* are replete with page after page of his conjectures and his punctilious transcriptions of entire Quarto passages. At times, these notes are so meticulous that they call to mind the apparatus familiar to any reader of a variorum edition of the play. But when we quit the pages of the editions that Berryman unfailingly marked up and return to his notebooks, or to separate sheets of his *Lear* notes, handsomely laid out leaves of deracinated language poems once again emerge into view. The page headed "outer Forme of 'I'" is one of the loose sheets inserted into Berryman's 1885 facsimile edition of Q *Lear* (fig. 5.3). While a student trained in analytical bibliography could straightaway construe a page of this sort, what most readers will find noteworthy is the exquisite composure of this page. That this is the *poet* John Berryman's handiwork is but one reason to apply an exercise described by Stanley Fish, whereby a list of words with a seemingly unpoetic provenance is conjured into verse. If Berryman often sounds like an American Hamlet, anguished, self-lacerating, violent, defiant, despairing, arrogant, childish, self-absorbed, suicidal, brilliant, witty, fierce, sulking, generous, charming, ambitious, courtly, morbid, and wretched, the reconfigured *Lear* that appears on "outer Forme of 'I'" bespeaks Berryman's modesty, clarity, and serenity. The handwriting is delicate; the lineation is accommodating. It is an elegant bento box of variant readings. On the very next sheet in this series, where four irregular columns are devoted to typographical errors, to sophistications, and to "right" and "wrong" conjectural emendations, Berryman drew an artless, awkward-looking, 5/8-inch question mark. For its part, "outer Forme of 'I'" is

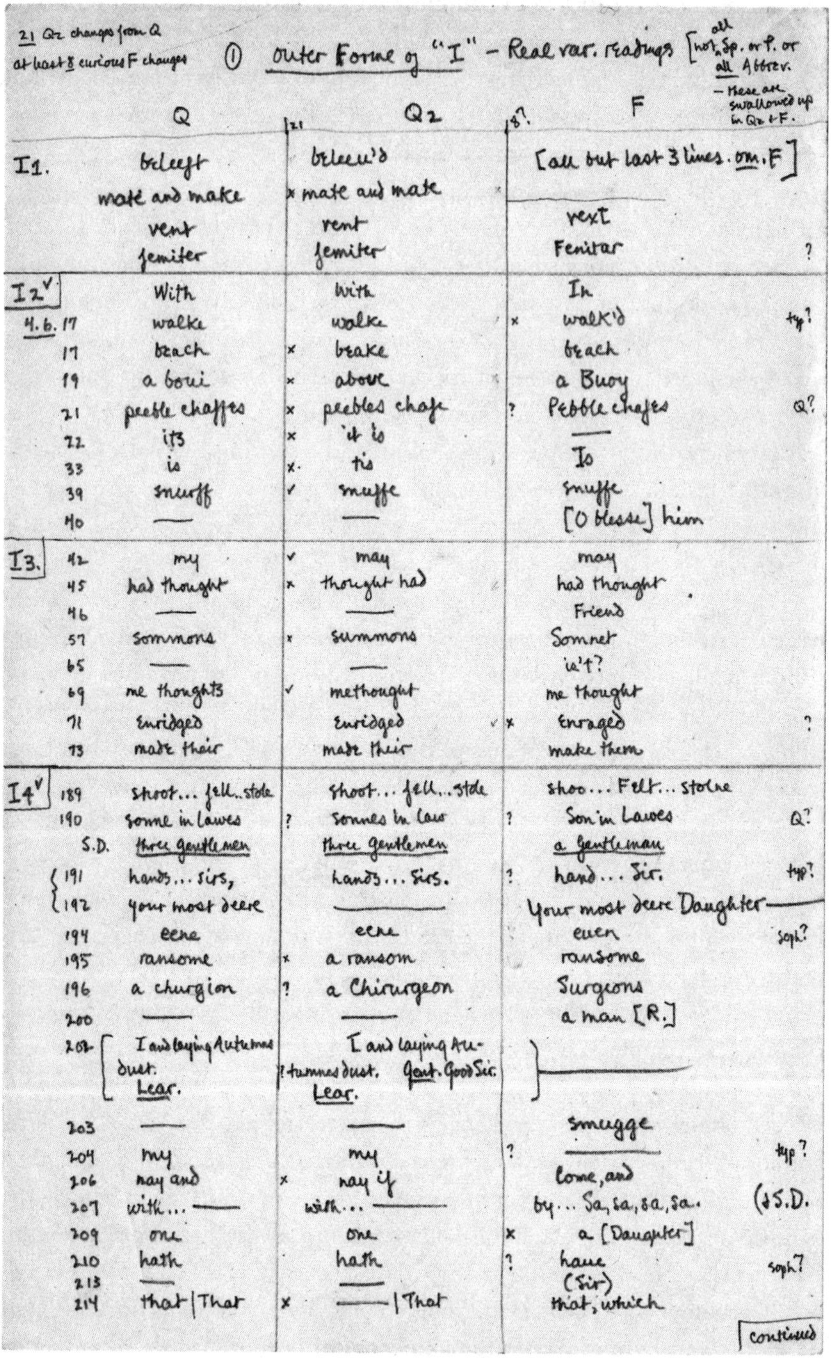

① outer Forme of "I" — Real var. readings [all not in Sp. or P. or all Abbrev.

— these are swallowed up in Q2 & F.

		Q		21	Q2	8⁷.	F	
I1.		beleeft		beleeu'd			[all but last 3 lines om. F]	
		mate and make	x	mate and mate				
		vent		rent			rext	
		Jemiter		Jemiter			Fenitar	?
I2ᵛ		With		with			In	
4.6.	17	walke	x	walke			walk'd	typ?
	17	beach		beake			beach	
	19	a boui	x	above			a Buoy	
	21	peeble chaffes	x	peebles chafe	?		Pebble chafes	Q?
	22	it's	x	it is				
	33	is	x.	'tis			Io	
	39	snueff	✓	snuffe			snuffe	
	40	———					[O blesse] him	
I3.	42	my	✓	may			may	
	45	had thought	x	thought had			had thought	.
	46						Friend	
	57	Sommons	x	summons			Somnet	
	65	———					is't?	
	69	me thoughts	✓	methought			me thought	
	71	Enridged		Enridged		✓x	Enraged	?
	73	made their		made their			make them	
I4ᵛ	189	shoot... fell.. stole		shoot.. fell.. stole			shoo... Felt... stolne	
	190	Sonne in Lawes	?	Sonnes in Law	?		Son in Lawes	Q?
	S.D.	three gentlemen		three gentlemen			a gentleman	
{	191	hands... sirs,		hands... sirs.	?		hand... Sir.	typ?
{	192	your most deere					Your most deere Daughter —	
	194	eene		eene			euen	soph?
	195	ransome	x	a ransom			ransome	
	196	a churgion	?	a Chirurgeon			Surgeons	
	200	———					a man [R.]	
	202	[I and laying Autumns dust. Lear.		I and laying Au-turnes dust. Gent. Good Sir. Lear.	?		]	
	203	———				?	smugge	
	204	my		my			come, and	typ?
	206	nay and	x	nay if			by... Sa, sa, sa, sa.	(JS.D.
	207	with... ———		with... ———				
	209	one		one		x	a [Daughter]	
	210	hath		hath		?	haue	soph?
	213						(Sir)	
	214	that	That	x	———	That		that, which	

[continued]

Figure 5.3: John Berryman's "outer Forme of 'I.'" John Berryman Papers (MSS 43).
Courtesy of the Literary Manuscripts Collection, University of Minnesota Libraries,
Minneapolis, Minnesota. © Kate Donahue.

free of any such ungainliness. Its question marks are manicured. Even the polite "continued" in the lower right corner has a room of its own. Taken as a whole, the sheet achieves its structural integrity by means of its alignment of large and small variants.

When Peter Stitt asked about the structure of *The Dream Songs*, Berryman responded that it consists of "a personality" and "a metrical plan." He had already told *Harvard Advocate* interviewers that the plot is "the personality of henry as he moves on in the world."[33] While it is not difficult to identify thematic preoccupations and clusters within the sequence, one would be hard-pressed to specify an overarching narrative. Consequently, it has been suggested that the poems' interrelationships are arbitrary or improvisational, or perhaps cumulative. Berryman's "Shakespearian study" points in another direction: each of *The Dream Songs'* variously rhymed six-line stanzas (typically, but by no means always, two five-beat lines followed by a three-beat line, then two more at five and another at three) is a *variant* on those with which it shares the page, and each poem is itself a *variant* on the original 77 and the eventual 385. Line by line and stanza by stanza, Dream Song 190 works then reworks "young . . . old" and "old . . . young" poets, Keats and Yeats and Yeats and Keats. "It is hard & hard to get these matters straight," says Henry. As a structural element, a variant is less linear than a narrative but more technically satisfying than a theme (think of Bach's variations). If Dream Song 190 takes up the survival of the poet and the "stoppage of a voice," not just its own stanzas but Dream Songs 67, 77, 78–91, 133, 145, 191, 201, 259, and 278 vary, emend, and gloss it. They are what Berryman the Shakespeare editor called new readings, sophistications, inversions, equivalents, additions, strange variants, corrections, and corruptions.

Eileen Simpson writes that Berryman first tried his hand at "dream songs" in 1943, when he wrote a short series of "Nervous Songs."[34] This would put the *Lear* work in tandem with their gestation and so point to the moment when Berryman's study passed into his poetry. In his interview with Peter Stitt, Berryman says that he "invented the [*Dream Songs*] stanza in '48 and wrote the first stanza and the first three lines of the second stanza, and then I stuck." He "finally got going" again in 1955. The "new sort of poem," writes Paul Mariani, was "in large part the result of the 650 pages of dream analyses he'd compiled over the past nine months" (298). If this is so, then Shakespeare enters the picture from yet another direction. In September 1955, Berryman wrote to his mother that he was "keeping on with the dream-work, . . . I have done a great part of more than

150 dreams . . . and I am stale and wish to come up. . . . Also last night I began Shakespeare again" (*Letters*, 292; this refers to the critical biography project). But Berryman's papers make it clear that Shakespeare was already both latent and manifest in what he was calling his "self-analysis." That Shakespeare wrote 154 sonnets and that what Berryman would call his "St Pancras' braser" project numbered 154 dreams is no coincidence.

"'St Pancras' braser'" is a phrase that Berryman recalled from the third dream he wrote up. Each time the dream appears in his typewritten notes, it begins

'St Pancras' braser' (or brazer, cf. brazier)
is all I can now remember, in a long speech
<u>seen</u> rather than heard . . .

For reasons that Berryman himself was never able to work out, these were the seminal words (over time, he associated braser not just with brazier but with brazen [bull], razor, blazer, bras[sière], St John's brazier, St Martin's brazier, St Peter's brazier, and Robert Glenn Shaver, his maternal great grandfather!). Nor is it clear why he never acknowledges as *fons et origo* the first line of the inaugural dream of the entire series, a line featuring Shakespeare, specifically, "Herschel Baker lecturing on Sh." The page atop which Berryman writes "<u>Initial</u> fragments" gives a reader a fair idea of Berryman's method (fig. 5.4). He typed each of his dreams in what appears to be verse form, the poet-editor in him occasionally relineating a dream when he recopied it. Then he would extensively free-associate with each and every word, sometimes for pages on end.

As for what Berryman intended to do with the completed analyses, he himself evidently never made up his mind. On the first of a series of four, 5.5 × 8.25 inch note pages, under the title "St Pancras' Braser," he writes, "I don't know for whom I am writing this exactly. It can't be published during my mother's lifetime in any case. I may show the ms. to certain friends as I go on—if I go on—and ask their advice. . . . But it is likely to be too personal & painful in the recounting for the game to be worth the candle just as entertainment."[35] In one set of notes, he tells himself that he has the makings of a book, not an essay "as I've always thought." In other notes, he cautions himself: "NOT intellectual interp.: emotional"; "Quote some amusing dr[eams].'s, & some nightmares, <u>without</u> analyzing." Elsewhere, still trying to imagine a dream book but perhaps having moved a step closer to *The Dream Songs*, Berryman enjoins himself to give up "Structure," to adopt "Stories," "Scenes," and "Panoramas (<u>not</u> reaching to sc. or story—both of wh. are comprehensive)." One more note page,

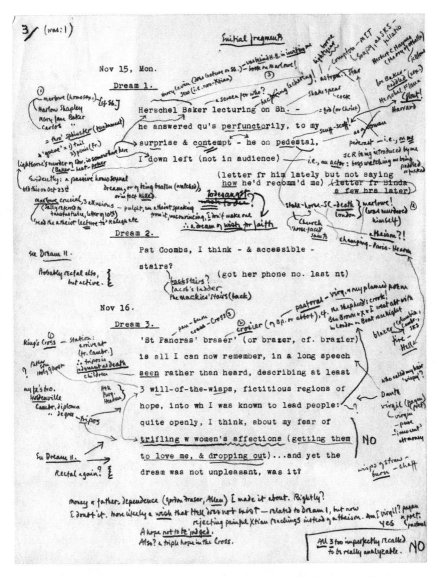

Figure 5.4: John Berryman's "'St Pancras' braser.'" John Berryman Papers (MSS 43). Courtesy of the Literary Manuscripts Collection, University of Minnesota Libraries, Minneapolis, Minnesota. © Kate Donahue.

unaccompanied by any dream, has Berryman again thinking in terms of verse, and of venues—*Partisan Review* or *Mademoiselle*, no less:

> Publish this dream & its interp? (wd only have to expurg. it slightly, & say so) as my 'poem' for my 40th birthday

> Yes—it wd fascinate—PR esp. or even Mlle or New Yorker? Write it well, v. well—easy & amusing. [Apparently] not as autobiog. or Science: just a poem. Yes, absol—excellent idea!—& money, & composition. The first open result (exc. negative ones—not drinking, not panic, not loving, not despair) of my analysis of myself.

Just as Berryman was loathe to abandon his Shakespeare projects, he kept toying with the St Pancras' book. Writing apparently in the mid-1960s, he forecast an "only partly censored account of a self-analysis . . . intended as a contribution to the meagre scientific literature of the subject." He remembers that he was "between jobs, in a strange city, with some money and the fully free time and resolution that dream-interpretation demands." Then, in words that sound just like a description of Berryman at work on *King Lear*, he continues: "For several months I gave my dreams eighteen hours a days [*sic*], sometimes in exultation, sometimes in tears. . . . I have never returned to the task . . ." This comports perfectly with an earlier calculation, on a page dated Nov 15–Dec 22, 1954, where Berryman sounds the familiar Shakespeare-study notes of "proto-despair" and "grandiosity": "38 [dreams] in two months; wd be 228 a year! intolerable."[36]

Berryman's dream analysis looks back with resentment and pity toward his father's (John Allyn Smith's) alleged suicide by gunshot when Berryman was twelve years old, with hostility toward his stepfather, "Uncle Jack" Berryman (Berryman's mother married John Angus Berryman three months after her first husband's death), and with confusion toward his mother. In August 1955 he wrote to her that he had been "dealing solely with dreams, of which I have now alas 120 since November." "I am unblocking slowly," he added (*Letters*, 291). Consisting of highly mediated autobiography in the form of dream poems, the analyses look forward to *The Dream Songs*. Amid all of the static and clutter, Shakespeare is conspicuous. As manifest content, he is limited to an appearance in Dream 1. But as latent content, as a link in one or another of the hundreds of associative chains forged over hours of self-analysis, Shakespeare and his plays figure recurrently. And this—Shakespeare's latency, his usefulness as textual gloss—has a curious structural aspect. In the 1940s, Berryman spent his days poring over editions in which Shakespeare's text filled the upper part of each page while Berryman's (and his predecessors') commentary crowded at the bottom. Now, in the self-analyses of the 1950s, Berryman's own dream verse, not infrequently with "Shakespearean" line numbers running down the left or right margin, gets top billing while Shakespeare participates in the glossing down under. The dream analysis, which may have unblocked Berryman and enabled *The Dream Songs*, is the locus of Shakespeare's Berryman. Here, Shakespeare provides his would-be editor with substantive annotations to this edition (also unfinished and unpublished) of Berryman's life and (dream)work.

The page headed "half-dream" looks just like an Arden Shakespeare page (fig. 5.5). Berryman has relineated what appears to be a prior record of this "half-dream," a sheet which he marked up by hand much as he marked up the "'St Pancras' braser'" sheet. On the earlier sheet, Shakespeare plays a marginal part. "[D]o" in line 8 is associated with *Macbeth*'s Third Witch's "I'll do, I'll do, and I'll do." In the upper right corner, Berryman writes, "'do' = threat to sailor (weird sisters) 'I'll drain him dry.'" This in turns leads Berryman to couple the "cere" in his "insincerely" with Macbeth's famous "sere." From "bore" in line 9 he arrives at boar, which leads him not to Shakespeare's *Venus and Adonis*, but to "dull" and so to "Anthony Dull, a constable *LLL* takes Costard into custody." Meanwhile, something—the bed, the cottage, the witches, or "bit" (in the margin: "?bite")—triggers what Berryman calls "torture-themes": "Procrustes' bed," "Iron Maiden," and its "prongs." "[[V]ag. dent.," "my penis" and "breaking me betw. their (lips, thighs[)]" follow down the left margin. As so often, the entire dreamscape pertains, somehow, to the "fa[ther] dead" in the left margin. Because Jimmy Worden's father died "normally," Jimmy is "friendly & guiltless." Because *his* father did not, Berryman in his marginalia is "friendless & guilty." In "half-dream," Berryman takes a second crack at Dream 11. Dutifully, *pace* Dr. Freud, he detects homosexuality (on the previous sheet, "rectal interc." and "anusing" appear in the margins); but more intriguing is editor Berryman's conjecture for the word missing in line 10. What keeps getting interrupted is not so much "E's letter" as it is Berryman's own boring writing. Even the ever-so-Shakespearean textual lacuna where "write" ought to appear is an interruption. Fittingly, Shakespeare is available to fill the gap, to provide an "interesting . . . story," the "sad story of my father's death" lifted from *Richard 3*. While it would be far-fetched to say that Berryman has brought the meaning of his father's death into clearer focus, he has found in Shakespeare a host of roles into which he can project his father and himself (parenthetically, his mother—"Mo."—too). Berryman is *1 Henry 4*'s Douglas, the would-be regicide (he poignantly recollects that

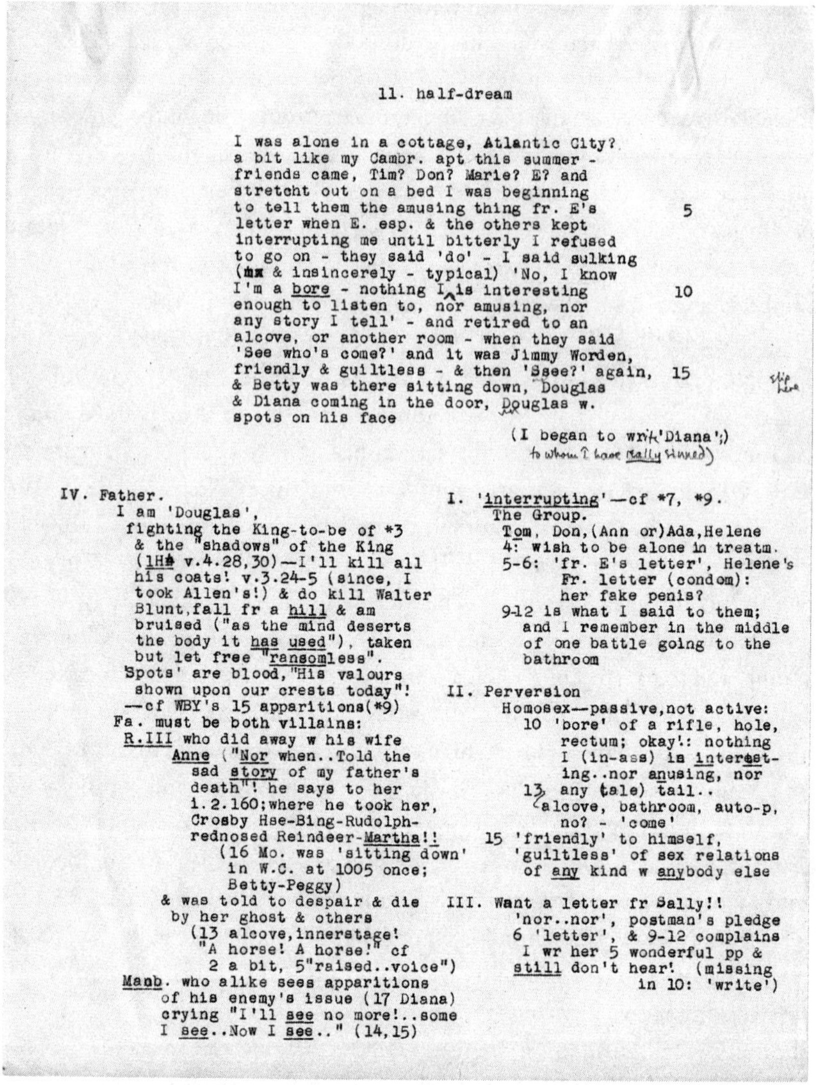

11. half-dream

          I was alone in a cottage, Atlantic City?
          a bit like my Cambr. apt this summer -
          friends came, Tim? Don? Marie? E? and
          stretcht out on a bed I was beginning
          to tell them the amusing thing fr. E's   5
          letter when E. esp. & the others kept
          interrupting me until bitterly I refused
          to go on - they said 'do' - I said sulking
          (mx & insincerely - typical) 'No, I know
          I'm a <u>bore</u> - nothing I is interesting   10
          enough to listen to, nor amusing, nor
          any story I tell' - and retired to an
          alcove, or another room - when they said
          'See who's come?' and it was Jimmy Worden,
          friendly & guiltless - & then 'Ssee?' again,   15
          & Betty was there sitting down, Douglas
          & Diana coming in the door, Douglas w.
          spots on his face

                              (I began to wrk'Diana';)
                              to whom I have really sinned)

IV. Father.
    I am 'Douglas',
    fighting the King-to-be of *3
    & the "shadows" of the King
    (1H♯ v.4.28,30)—I'll kill all
    his coats! v.3.24-5 (since, I
    took Allen's!) & do kill Walter
    Blunt.fall fr a <u>hill</u> & am
    bruised ("as the mind deserts
    the body it <u>has</u> <u>used</u>"), taken
    but let free "<u>ransomless</u>".
    Spots' are blood,"His valours
    shown upon our crests today"!
    —cf WBY's 15 apparitions(*9)
    Fs. must be both villains:
    R.III who did away w his wife
    Anne ("<u>Nor</u> when..Told the
        sad <u>story</u> of my father's
        death"! he says to her
        1.2.160;where he took her,
        Crosby Hse-Bing-Rudolph-
        rednosed Reindeer-<u>Martha</u>!!
        (16 Mo. was 'sitting down'
        in W.C. at 1005 once;
        Betty-Peggy)
    & was told to despair & die
      by her ghost & others
      (13 alcove,innerstage!
      "A horse! A horse!" cf
      2 a bit, 5"raised..voice")
    Manb. who alike sees apparitions
      of his enemy's issue (17 Diana)
      crying "I'll <u>see</u> no more!..some
      I <u>see</u>..Now I <u>see</u>.." (14,15)

I. '<u>interrupting</u>'—of *7, *9.
   The Group.
   Tom, Don,(Ann or)Ada,Helene
   4: wish to be alone in treatm.
   5-6: 'fr. E's letter', Helene's
   Fr. letter (condom):
        her fake penis?
   9-12 is what I said to them;
     and I remember in the middle
     of one battle going to the
     bathroom

II. Perversion
    Homosex—passive,not active:
    10 'bore' of a rifle, hole,
       rectum; okay!: nothing
       I (in-ass) is <u>interest</u>-
       ing..nor <u>amusing</u>, nor
    1½ any (tale) tail..
       alcove, bathroom, auto-p,
       no? - 'come'
    15 'friendly' to himself,
       'guiltless' of sex relations
       of <u>any</u> kind w <u>anybody</u> else

III. Want a letter fr Sally!!
     'nor..nor', postman's pledge
     6 'letter', & 9-12 complains
     I wr her 5 wonderful pp &
     <u>still</u> don't hear! (missing
        in 10: 'write')

Figure 5.5: John Berryman's "half-dream." John Berryman Papers (MSS 43).
Courtesy of the Literary Manuscripts Collection, University of Minnesota Libraries,
Minneapolis, Minnesota. © Kate Donahue.

Douglas is "taken but let free 'ransomless'"); he is Sir Walter Blunt, "marching in his [father's] coats" (5.3.25); he is Hal, his father's resentful defender; he is the despairing villain, Richard III; and he is the grieving Anne. For his part, Berryman's father "must be both villains": the apparition-seeing Richard and Macbeth. Hence, to Shakespeare's Berryman may be added Shakespeare's John Smith. Beneath the guilty surviving son's name (Berryman) lurks the repudiated father's name (Smith—Berryman well knew that he ought to have been a John Smith), itself now underwritten by the name William Shakespeare.

It is to be expected that penises and vaginas, patricidal and matricidal imaginings, and masochism and sadism would pepper Berryman's self-analysis of his dreams (a one-line dream from August 14, 1955, covers many bases: "I smasht Father's genitals w stone"). For seven years, he had been a patient of Dr. James Shea, a Park Avenue psychiatrist. Much later, in his NEH statement, he trumpeted his familiarity not just with psychoanalysis but with its "Post-Freudian . . . socialization." Given his literary critical practice, it also makes sense that he would be looking for themes, "self-pity & fear of punishment" or "exile" in Dream 3, "Death naturally! you fool!!" in the case of Dream 8. Berryman even worked up a coding system which allowed him to sprinkle his margins with "s-p" (self-pity), "Sch" (Schadenfreude), "s-d" (self-defense), "O" (Oedipal), "p" (paranoia), and "h" ("homosex"), and the like. Years of reading Shakespeare contribute a series of resonant characters and scenarios: Antony ("I am Antony too—I lead astray") contending with the flaming shirt of Nessus and Antony deserted by Hercules (emblems of rage and unfaithfulness); Brutus (who "killed Fa. Caesar"); the Henries (Hal the father-defending Prince; Henry VI the "weak son"; Dream 1 prompts Berryman to quote Hal/Henry's "not today, O Lord, / O, not today, think not upon the fault / My father made . . ."); Lear ("wicked da. [Da = daughter] arraigned by injured king"); Macbeth ("fa.-murder by me: Banq. by mo: [Dunc.] both Daddy"; "Lady Macb. i.e., she killed my father?—as I once suspected, & accused her"); The Tempest's Ferdinand ("thought his father dead"); Love's Labor's Lost's Berowne ("bear own [baby]"); Hamlet ("enticing Phantom—he beckons me to go now [as the Ghost did to Hamlet—also killed by my Uncle, uncle Jack]"); Richard III "who did away w his wife"; etc. But it is, finally, Berryman's own Shakespeare-style editorial work on his dream texts that takes up the largest part of "'St Pancras' braser.'" Arden edition–like pages give way to Variorum edition–like pages on which, beneath two or three lines of copy text, dozens of notes climb right up the page (fig. 5.6). At one point, glossing Dream 19 ("It seems to me this is the best job I've been able to do on any dream so far"), Berryman quotes Macbeth asking

it seems I remember as a
fragment of a dream (lately,
but when I don't know)

Ann w. glasses falling off her nose

Figure 5.6: John Berryman's "it seems I remember as a." John Berryman Papers (MSS 43). Courtesy of the Literary Manuscripts Collection, University of Minnesota Libraries, Minneapolis, Minnesota. © Kate Donahue.

the Doctor, "Canst thou not minister to a mind diseased?" Then, thinking of the lines "Therein the patient / Must minister to himself," Berryman responds, "Well, I say, I can—& am—& praise myself for it." Having applauded himself, he proceeds to accept praise from Shakespeare. Identifying himself with King James, he writes: "me—K. Jas(!) touching for K's evil, healing, & v. highly praised [by Sh] for it." Again, Shakespeare's Berryman.

When he extruded himself into Henry in all of his *Dream Songs* iterations, Berryman's "Shakespearean study" touched his method, whether or not it touched his matter. Both his *Lear* work and the Shakespearean contributions to his dream work share numerous glossarial hallmarks: variants, equivalents, cruxes, conjectures, and emendations. If Shakespeare failed to provide Berryman (or Delmore Schwartz, for that matter) with long-lasting equipment for living, his work on Shakespeare's writing did give Berryman much more than a penchant for dramatic impersonation.

What gall had he in him, so to begin Book VII
or to design, out of its hotspur materials,
its ultimate structure
whereon will critics browse at large, at Heaven Eleven
finding it was not cliffhangers or old serials
but according to his nature

This, the first stanza of Dream Song 293, confirms that *The Dream Songs'* browsable "hotspur materials" are "ultimate[ly] structur[al]," not substantive. What "gall" there is in Berryman's 385 dramatic poems has little to do with their trading on Shakespearean matter, or "materials." If he did not stop rewriting Shakespeare words when he gave up his edition of *Lear,* he certainly did when he abandoned his "Self-Analysis." As for succeeding years given over to research on the critical biography of Shakespeare—years that overlapped with the composition of *The Dream Songs*—nothing to do with this effort would have constituted influence. No, the "gall" has to do with adopting and then adapting a method of "design," an architecture of response to Shakespearean variants that, "according to his nature," Berryman found so compelling.[37] Although Berryman himself never made the connection, "'The Care & Feeding of Long Poems'" (Dream Song 354) drew heavily on habits of textual scholarship rooted in his "Shakespearean study."

VI

ALLEN GINSBERG ON
SHAKESPEARE'S FUNNY
MOUTHINGS

That English-speaking poets might reckon with Shakespeare's verse when they write their own is unsurprising. But this hardly accounts for all of the time they spend with the Bard in mind. We have seen that Samuel Taylor Coleridge carried on a conversation with Shakespeare in copious notebook entries and extensive marginalia in four editions of the plays. He also gave his most notable series of lectures on Shakespeare at the London Philosophical Society in Crane Court in 1811–12.[1] T. S. Eliot's writing on Shakespeare is often cited, but it is rarely noted that one of his two most famous essays—"Shakespeare and the Stoicism of Seneca"—was first given as a lecture. Eliot wrote to G. B. Harrison that when the text was printed, he hoped that Harrison "would put in somewhere, I don't care where, a statement that this was an address read before the Shakespeare Association—otherwise it seems to me much too pretentious; and the fact that it was a paper read aloud may incline readers to pardon certain faults of form and style."[2] At the invitation of John Dover Wilson, Eliot went on to deliver two lectures devoted to Shakespeare at Edinburgh University in 1937.[3] These talks were devoted to *Pericles* and *Coriolanus*. Eliot's poems "Marina" and "Coriolan" are readily available, but his lectures remain unpublished. More than five hundred people regularly attended W. H. Auden's Shakespeare lectures at the New School for Social Research in 1946–47. Auden even held discussion classes each Saturday for students who were taking his class for credit.[4] In 1949, he led a seminar on the Sonnets at Swarthmore. And as Neil Corcoran notes, "[T]he Shakespeare essays in *The Dyer's Hand* derive from Auden's lectures as Oxford Professor of Poetry from 1956 to 1961."[5] Of course, other poets have taught Shakespeare—I have glanced at John Berryman's notes for his 1970 *Hamlet* class at the University of Minnesota, along with Berryman's immodest plans to use the "text for the study of Shakespeare's mind and the late-Renaissance view of

Man." So many hours spent preparing and delivering Shakespeare lectures cannot help but have deepened these poets' long-standing and avid reading of the plays and poems. It is a truism among teachers that they often do not "know" their subject until they teach it. At the very least, a poet who lectures about Shakespeare knows the works differently from a poet who does not.

What version of these elusive transactions can we detect in Allen Ginsberg's classroom commentary on Shakespeare? In the mid-1940s, Ginsberg studied at Columbia University with Mark Van Doren, the poet and critic who stood by Berryman. He wrote in his journal that he "wormed through some of Shakespeare" in 1948.[6] In 1949, he read *Macbeth* and commented in a letter to Jack Kerouac on the "irony of neglected and forgotten misunderstandings and complacencies returning like ghosts to wreak vengeance."[7] Since Ginsberg was facing imprisonment because he had allowed Herbert Huncke and his friends to store stolen goods in his apartment, the "misunderstandings and complacencies" may have been Ginsberg's as much as Macbeth's. While yeoman storekeeper on a Military Sea Transportation Ship resupplying the Distant Early Warning line in the Bering Straits, Ginsberg wrote a letter to Gary Snyder in June 1956, in which he mentions his mother's death, wonders whether he will "see God in the white floes and brilliant black light," and reports that he has been "reading thru Shakespeare on board, beginning to end chronologically."[8] From Paris a year and a half later, he wrote to his father that he was reading *Timon of Athens, Coriolanus*, and *Pericles*, "trying to finish all the obscure plays I'd neglected."[9] And yet, even though in 1966 he wrote that Shakespeare was a "primary source" for him, Shakespeare does not figure largely in either his voluminous letters or his notebooks (surely nowhere nearly as large as, say, William Blake, Jack Kerouac, and William Burroughs).[10]

Ginsberg liked to tell the story about a Christmas night in 1944 in Greenwich Village, when his friend Lucien Carr, "a degenerate fellow student whom I was in love with," regaled Burroughs with his version of a "totally alcoholic fight" during which Carr bit off "some bull dyke's earlobe." Burroughs responded by quoting from *Troilus and Cressida*, "'Tis too starved a subject for my sword." Ginsberg made this out to be his *ad fontes* Shakespearean moment: "I got my Shakespeare originally from Burroughs. The first Shakespeare I ever understood was out of Burroughs' mouth."[11] Burroughs domesticated Shakespeare's language for Ginsberg. Suddenly, it was both approachable and serviceable. Perhaps this explains why from then on, there seems never to have been a moment when Ginsberg betrayed even a modicum of anxiety in relation to Shakespeare.

Instead, reading Shakespeare gave him pleasure, and opportunities to confirm his own hunches, eventually convictions, about prosody.

Thirty-one years later, in a Naropa classroom, there remained a mimetic aspect to Ginsberg's appreciation of Shakespeare. He told his students that Sonnet 97 "was Kerouac's favorite sonnet and among the most celebrated of all the Shakespeare sonnets."[12] In 1980, he told them that *Love's Labor's Lost*'s "And birds sit brooding in the snow" was "Kerouac's favorite line in Shakespeare."[13] Ginsberg triangulated even Lionel Trilling—his dearest and most loyal Columbia professor—with the works of William Shakespeare. In a fleeting *mise-en-scène* that Ginsberg recorded in one of his notebooks, he recalls a dream from which he awoke on January 13, 1976:

> I was in Trilling's bed, I borrowed it for a nap, sort of presumptuous, I realized once I got into it, because it was made up of many layers of covers and many layers of books and newspapers—at the foot two large volumes of Shakespere [*sic*], Freud under one of the thin pillows [Trilling first published "Freud and Literature" in 1940], another layer of pillow & 2 Vols of Collected Keats Letters [Trilling's selection of Keats's letters came out in 1950], I couldn't keep track, since once I got in bed I lifted blankets & rearranged them to cover me disturbing the order of the bed-library. When I tried to put it all back in order I realized I couldn't remember how it was all packed in from the first—Then Trilling came in looking vigorous & youthful 50's [Trilling had died just two months earlier, at the age of 70]—He didn't seem to mind as much as I thought, the disturbance of his couch—and his end tables & bookshelves nearby.[14]

The "sort of presumptuous" Ginsberg, who in a 1980 class on the Sonnets compared his own love life to Shakespeare's, now beds down with the Bard; but his presumption has less to do with his intimacy with Shakespeare than with his interloping in Trilling's "bed-library." Freud is on hand, and the "bed" becomes a "couch," so perhaps Ginsberg is concerned that he has recruited Trilling as a pander/Pandarus.[15] That the word *order* appears twice here, as does some form of *disturb*, suggests that a genealogical claim is at once being struck and resisted. Shakespeare plays a foundational ("at the foot" of the bed) role but he is not under the pillows. Equally passive-aggressive is the relationship between the fatigued but disruptive Ginsberg (he needs a nap) and the surprisingly vigorous but recently deceased Trilling. The revered professor who was never given to coddling Ginsberg has been displaced from his own bed. However, because Trilling's former student's bedmates ratify Trilling's own cannon, he remains mostly unperturbed: Ginsberg has not disturbed the essential order of things after all. Was it oneiric tact, a desire to placate, or a desire to fit in that kept Ginsberg's unconscious from introducing the likes of Rimbaud into Trilling's bed? So to augment the "company of immortals" (see below) might have made for a less forgiving Trilling.[16]

A year and a half after his Burroughs-Shakespeare minor epiphany and while he was still studying at Columbia, Ginsberg ventriloquized his aspirations in his journal. "Waiting in mess hall for the morning" on July 22, 1946, he wrote out a long, psychomachic conversation between his "Muses" and his "Conscience." With everything from authenticity and spirituality to aesthetics and social action tumbling onto these unaffected pages, "Muses" finally attempt to console Allen by telling him that he and they "perhaps . . . shall join the company of the immortals." These include Homer, Plato, and Shakespeare, each of whom knew that "poetry can be an harmonious and active life."[17] A similar conviction, again expressed in relation to Shakespeare, surfaces when Ginsberg writes about an "attained unity of being which insures knowledge and pleasure in the world." This unity was "the common genius of Homer, of Shakespeare, of Mozart. There is a word for it which nobody really understands, and it is objectivity."[18] On the one hand, this sounds quite a bit like the Coleridge who lamented his own "almost daily throwing off . . . desultory fragments"—his "Over-activity of Thought"—but who found that in Shakespeare, the "[h]eterogeneous united as in Nature."[19] It was Shakespeare's great virtue that he could resolve "many circumstances by into one moment of thought to produce . . . Unity."[20] Ginsberg, whose own notebooks are replete with self-castigation for spreading himself too thin, would spend many years trying to find "unity" through Buddhist meditation. Like Coleridge, he caught glimpses of this achievement in Shakespeare's plays. On the other hand, the unity about which Ginsberg writes entails a more experienced than theorized "active life" and "pleasure in the world." An enviable generosity toward others and heartfelt political engagement were the hallmarks of Ginsberg's way of being in the world. That one word for this might be "objectivity" suggests that Ginsberg's affiliations were as much Modernist (Pound) and Eastern as they were Romantic (Blake). Among his prosodic touchstones were the sorts of objectivity that he discovered in haiku and in Shakespeare's verse.

In April 1947, Shakespeare pops up on one of Ginsberg's many reading lists ("Sonnets, *Romeo*, *Richard II*, and *Midsummer Nights' [sic] Dream*"). A month later, next to "*Tempest*" he wrote, "Read and reread for a week—Shakespeare."

Then, in July, while visiting Neal Cassady in Denver, Ginsberg wrote in his journal a handful of lines shadowed by Shakespeare's Sonnets as well as the sexual and artistic doubts and ambitions of a twenty-one year old:

> N.Y. Scraps / And my mind *presides* / on what my will prophecies.
> Loneliness: Liveliness is a weary promise, / My pleasures as all
>   melancholy.
> Whoever comes, henceforth, for me / I will in fear and anger flee.
> So in this 21ˢᵗ year I praise creation.
> Someday finish the great sonnet: / Lord, forgive my passions, they
>   are old / and restive as the years that I have known.[21]

In May of the next year he wrote to Jack Kerouac, "I think I am going to write a sonnet sequence. I want to read Petrarch and Shakespeare, Spencer [*sic*] and Sidney . . . and write a series on love, perfectly, newly conceived." At a time in his life when he was asking for forgiveness for his "restive passions" and wanting to "celebrate my 'lovers' in all various manners, intellectually, wittily, passionately, raptly, nostalgically, pensively, beautifully, realistically, 'soberly,' enthusiastically, etc." (a series that nicely forecasts Ginsberg's classroom commentary on Shakespeare's Sonnets more than thirty years later), it makes sense that Ginsberg found a warrant for those precise desires and for his verse in Shakespeare.[22] It is also no surprise that, a decade later, Ginsberg took his place in a long line of melancholy lovers who let Shakespeare plead on their behalf. Feeling blue in Peter Orlovsky's absence, he wrote, "But if the while I think on thee, dear friend, / All losses are restored, and sorrows end."[23]

Even when taken together, these disparate gleanings, while they speak to Ginsberg's on-again, off-again dialogue with Shakespeare's verse, lack the quality of sustained attention. For this, we must turn to the classes that he taught at the Jack Kerouac School of Disembodied Poetics at Naropa (now home to the Allen Ginsberg Library and an Allen Ginsberg Graduate Fellowship). The classroom recordings are replete with Ginsberg's unrehearsed, colloquial comments (his students' questions and comments are sadly uninspired). Always winsome and often wise, he is unembarrassedly unencumbered by critical history or fashion. Neither is there any sign of a Coleridge, an Eliot, or Auden opining on Shakespeare. We hear nothing that one would call magisterial. Even Ginsberg's way of reading Shakespeare out loud lacks polish; but so, apparently, did Coleridge's, and slowly, one comes to the conclusion that Ginsberg's articulation was every bit as motivated as was the way he recited his own poems. As for the pedagogical setting, throughout his life, Ginsberg teetered back and forth, thinking one moment that he was a poet-prophet, thinking the next that he was, as Kerouac put it, "a hairy loss." When it came to teaching, he also had doubts: "Teaching: I am not a scholar and feel as if I'm filling up time with unworthy students . . . with merely repetitive general recollection of ideas I once had thought."[24]

But this is unduly harsh. In Ginsberg's Shakespeare classes there is an abundance of intelligence and pleasure, also plenty of method in his clowning. It is, for instance, under the aegis of William Carlos Williams's "no ideas but in things" that Ginsberg analyzes the Shakespearean passages to which he calls his students' attention. The point is to get them to notice what, adapting Henry James, he calls "the solidity of specificity" in Shakespeare's verse. Having discovered what Cézanne called his "*petites sensations*," Ginsberg found in Shakespeare's poetry what he tried to capture in his own: an apperception of eternal truths (for Cézanne, the sensation of *Pater Omnipotens Aeterna Deus*) derived from close, in Ginsberg's case, trance-like observation of the quotidian.[25] The Sonnets he admires for their logopoeia, Ezra Pound's word for "the dance of intellect among words." In *The Tempest*, he hears the sounds of Shakespeare's beguilingly artful but seemingly unself-conscious "easy genius." When it came to Shakespeare's poetry, then, not Auden's "verbal contraption" but Pound's linguistic dance proved most congenial to Ginsberg. If Charles Olson found a warrant for his poetics in Shakespeare's late plays, Ginsberg found confirmation for his own praxis wherever he heard or felt something that he called "funny" in Shakespeare's lyrics. The Shakespearean verse that he pauses to consider has the mouth feel of song and the physical presence of dance.

The delight that Ginsberg takes in the "shrewd intelligence" of Shakespeare's Sonnets, their "slyness" and "sharpness," is palpable throughout his March 6, 1980, Naropa Basic Poetics class.[26] Each of these words speaks to Ginsberg's admiration for the carefully calibrated simultaneity of artifice and self-exposure in the Sonnets. One moment he is in the thick of a class devoted to "basic poetics," but the next, he identifies Sonnet 20 ("A woman's face, with nature's own hand painted") as "somewhat of a key to Shakespeare's series" of "somewhat gay sonnets." Reading out loud, he lifts his voice each time he approaches the feminine endings of successive lines. His line-by-line paraphrase gets a laugh when he explains that "An eye more bright than theirs, less false in rolling" means that "his boyfriend [who] rolls his eyes while he's coming while he's being blown is less false . . . than some girl that fakes orgasm." This sort of casual, familiarizing take on the poem, at the same time that it intentionally rags the poem's high-brow provenance, obscures just how closely Ginsberg is paying attention. For instance, he points out that "more" and "less" mitigate the apparent opposition between men and women (as does the poem's prosthetic and fungible prick—"one thing [added] to my purpose nothing"). Moreover, even if it is a "male chauvinist poem," the young man's credibility is hardly unimpeachable. Sonnet 20 may have been Ginsberg's starting point because the story it tells, its myth of origins, cues the subsequent poems as an account of "a cycle of the heart." And this licenses Ginsberg to approach the series as a "love story," a "novel" or "drama" fully comparable to an affair Ginsberg himself had with "a kid" he was "hung up on." (Eve Sedgwick, who writes that Shakespeare's Sonnets "have been a kind of floating decimal in male homosexual discourse," reminds us that most readers have interpreted the sequence as a "relatively continuous erotic narrative" and that "since the nineteenth century it has been easiest to read the Sonnets as a novel.")[27] A "faggot poem," which Ginsberg savors and with which he can identify, Sonnet 20 appeals to him because it is "courteous and charming." I think that this surprising characterization stems from what Ginsberg takes to be the speaker's (for Ginsberg, Shakespeare's) proximity and distance from the young man—and Ginsberg's, too (his closeness and distance from both the kid he once was "hung up on" and the young man of the Sonnets). "Courteous and charming" correlate with the Sonnets' particular kind of "knowingness" but also, as Ginsberg says, with their "sweet[ness]." The artfulness and openness, or honesty, with which Shakespeare's sequence manages both knowledge and affect constitute what Ginsberg recognizes as their "wit," their "funny intelligence." And "funny," which comes up again and again in Ginsberg's Shakespeare classes, speaks to their consummate poetic achievement: the Sonnets' formal pleasures are pitched perfectly to their humane content.[28]

From Sonnet 20, Ginsberg jumps to Sonnet 29 ("When, in disgrace with fortune and men's eyes"). Once again, he reads out loud, pausing to comment and playing for his student-audience both the ever-so-slightly erudite commentator and the self-deprecating comic. Thus he says that line 7 ("Desiring this man's art, and that man's scope") probably pertains to Ben Jonson and Francis Bacon. To Allen Ginsberg, too: "I wish I had Creeley's intelligence or I wish I had Kerouac's art or I wish I had Harpo Marx's friends." The sweetness of Shakespeare's sonnets is also present in Sonnet 29, which Ginsberg points out proceeds from "myself almost despising" to "happiness" and a redeeming "sweet love." Shakespeare has "found someone who really answers the call of his heart . . . somebody that really turns him on . . . went to bed with him . . . a young kid, apparently." However, there is a strong autobiographical countercurrent of "loneliness" and "self-despair," of "dust and ashes." Ginsberg reflects that we (Shakespeare included) spend much of our lives lonely, envious, feeling inadequate and insecure; "that's exactly how everybody feels about themselves." It is how Ginsberg himself feels "more than half of the time." So it is unsurprising that for him, the triumphant "lark at break of day" is a consoling, vaguely Wordsworthian poet of what he calls "the dawn of eternal recollection." The tonal complexity of Ginsberg's best poems carries over into his brief comments on Sonnet 29. Although quickly discussed in an unintimidating and apparently unpremeditated way, it turns out to be a poem about what Ginsberg chooses not to call, in present company, *agape, acedia,* and *poiesis.* In short order, he executes a slightly goofy pedagogical *tour de force,* appearing to trifle with the poem even as he homes in on what led him to single it out in the first place—its vulnerability, bitterness, and hope.

Skipping to Sonnet 33, Ginsberg recaps the entire sonnet sequence's "little love story novel." It begins with "some kind of roundabout sex proposition" that the "boyfriend" should procreate; it moves on to a promise to immortalize him; and then it evinces signs that he has been warmly responsive to Shakespeare. "However," and Ginsberg draws out this word, "there have been some slights": "His boyfriend has gone out with somebody else, or didn't come on time one night, or missed a date, or didn't come or didn't make him come." Or it goes like this: "Maybe he [Shakespeare] only made it with him once for an hour ["he was but one hour mine"—33.11] . . . but he was just so totally delighted that he wrote these great sonnets . . . but then the next day, you know, he didn't answer the telephone." Or this: it begins "with a glimpse, falling in love, big crush, making out, total delight, a little problem, forgiveness, getting together again." Or, finally, this: "He's going through the wracks and torments of everybody's ordinary, deep, early love affair." "I was in a situation like this, really hung up on some kid, in 1975, going through big torments . . . from total love to disappointment and then renewal and then more hope." Without saying why, Ginsberg turns from renewal and hope to the "ominous" and "sado-masochistic relation" in Sonnets 57 ("Being your slave, what should I do but tend") and 58 ("That god forbid that made me first your slave"). This pair of "naked, completely open" poems of "abasement" Ginsberg again, openly, connects with his own history ("has anybody ever been in this relationship? . . . "I have").[29] But Ginsberg is thinking about his own history as a poet as well as a lover. Having read both poems aloud, often not quite suppressing amusement at what he has just called "kinky," he remarks that although Shakespeare is "totally abased," it is "amazing that anybody could write so clearly" about erotic abjection. Like the so-called plain style, clarity requires considerable art. To write as "totally truthfully" as Shakespeare did required him "to have hit it directly." His was the artist's perennial problem of finding forms sufficient to the truth.

With the clock ticking, Ginsberg picks up the pace, turning the pages of the sonnet-novel more rapidly, reading and paraphrasing Sonnets 64, 73, and 94 as installments in a relationship that has begun to sour, that requires desperate persuasion and suffers the corrosive effects of time and mortality. Perhaps because his students are flagging, Ginsberg sketches out the lineaments of a story of jealousy and disappointment populated by a rival poet, a dark lady, and the "base infection" (94.11)—the syphilis—that she gives Shakespeare and the young man ("my love is as a fever"—147.1). Shakespeare becomes "a little bitter," then "totally embittered." "Things have gone badly." Himself now tiring, Ginsberg asks out loud, "What time do we have?" and then skips ahead to Sonnet 116, which bobs up as his lifeline because it contains the "most perfect examples [of] logopoeia." Reading it out loud, Ginsberg is suddenly revved up and emphatic. He pauses only long enough enthusiastically to comment that now we can "get to the heart of the logopoeia."

Having recited the poem, Ginsberg explains that what captures his fancy is its "pure language play": first, the "switches" he hears in "alters when it alteration finds" (116.3), then "remover to remove" (116.4); but most of all, "bending sickle's compass come" (116.10). "That's really pretty," he coos; it's "good witty language." None of Ginsberg's recitation in class up to this moment prepares us for the way he compresses and accelerates the phrase "bending sickle's compass come" each and every one of the many times he repeats it. The successive "ik kuh kuh," the *s*'s at the start and finish of "sickle's" which resume in the double *s* in "compass," the "come" after "*com*pass"—these quicken the fatiguing Ginsberg at just under an hour and ten minutes into his class. When he truncates the word "come," it is as if he were saying "yum." All of a sudden he sounds—really sounds—happy, tickled. He digresses for a minute to talk about Father Time's sickle, even adverting to illustrations of a scythe-wielding skeleton crowned with roses in *The Rubáiyát of Omar Khayyám*, but his paraphrase of consecutive words from "rosy" to "come" (116.9–10) has less to do with explaining them than with revealing their tangy orality. "Compass"/"encompass"/"*rondure*"/"time compass"/"space compass"/"physical compass"/"compassionate compass." Rather than paraphrase as he so often does, this time Ginsberg simply riffs. He keeps repeating the talismanic phrase, telling the class to "dig how we get this *funny* syncopation" (my emphasis) as a result of its "total vernacularity." Six months after this class, in a letter to Gary Snyder, Ginsberg was praising his friend, the rancher-poet Drummond Hadley's "long melodious vernacular lines," so when he spoke of Sonnet 116's "vernacularity," Ginsberg was probably thinking about rhythm and sound as much as diction.[30] In the Naropa class, he is still teaching, but he also is relishing sheer sonic effect, to the point that seemingly out of nowhere, he counterpoints the slightly amended phrase (which now has become "[Time's] bending sickle's compass come") with "Tom Hayden's helicopter's wheel"! From basic poetics we have moved on to Ginsbergian poetics: for a few minutes, the "little love story novel" of the Sonnets turns decidedly surreal. Or "aurreal," since it is not so much an image (the compass of a sickle, the wheel [?] of a helicopter) as that which sounds "trippingly on the tongue" that Ginsberg has leveled at.

In the fifteen minutes of class time that remain, he adds Sonnets 129, 144, and 152 into the mix. Characterizing 129 as a "rant," he seems to be thinking about pitch at least as much as affect, and certainly more than content. Reading the first line and a half, his voice rises in volume until he shouts the phrase "lust in action." The sonnet's famous series ("perjured, murd'rous, bloody," etc.) gives Ginsberg more chances to rant. "Full of blame" matches his violent vocalization of "lust in action." With iambs scarce on the ground, Ginsberg is free to introduce his own "funny syncopation," attacking "extreme" then "proved" then "joy," "dream," and "well know." He accelerates through what he takes to be the sonnet's crucial line—"On purpose laid to make the taker mad" (129.8)—as if the velocity he felt in "bending sickle's compass come" were still resonating in his ears (indeed, in a 1976 Naropa History of Poetry class, Ginsberg explicitly compared the speed of the two lines).[31] He again asks the students to "dig the sound," the "fantastic melopoeia" of line eight. And then he repeats it, for its "fantastic witty language," at once "simple" and "funny," like a "weird slogan that goes in one ear and out the other." In the earlier class, he demonstrated "the funny kind of assonance in 'ur,' 'ayd,' 'ake,' 'ake,' 'ad.'" The line is "like a tongue-twister, except such a funny mind Shakespeare had, a funny ear, a funny mind, funny tongue."

The comic Ginsberg who grounded the vatic Ginsberg continually responded to what he found funny about Shakespeare's verse. Here and elsewhere, "funny" connotes curious or idiosyncratic, or simply worthy of attention; but Shakespeare's wit—his art—does also amuse Ginsberg, so "funny" is apt. Poetic "genius is funny," he quotes Kerouac as having said. Reciting first "On purpose laid to make the taker mad," then Horatio's "in the dead vast [Q1; in Q2 and F, "wast"] and middle of the night," Ginsberg comments that there is "a strange humor about the juxtapositions of the words that is like amusing funniness, considering the suchness [or "thusness"—*Tathata* (Sanskrit) plays a prominent role in Ginsberg's Buddhist thinking] of the language, or what the words feel like and how you put them together in a weird way that enters the brain for like the first time . . . so you get a funny vocal tone and voweled breath."[32] From hendiadys ("vast and middle"), where a conjunction dilates a "weird" Shakespearean juxtaposition, Ginsberg associates his way aurally to "Tom Hayden's helicopter's wheel." He often called attention to his own compressed and clashing phrase, "hydrogen jukebox" ("Howl"); in 1966, he told his *Paris Review* interviewer that such juxtaposition enabled him to "reach the different parts of the mind that are existing simultaneously." So "funny," Ginsberg's on-the-spot response to the Sonnets, is both vague and it is analytical. He explores the "funny mind [of] Shakespeare" by sorting out the ways the Sonnets crossed the sonic (what Shakespeare and Ginsberg hear) with the erotic (what Shakespeare felt). "Funny" also pairs subjective with objective; it gets at the ways the Sonnets are at once naked and sly. It is predictable that, given the choice between Pound's "Only emotion endures" and Louis Zukofsky's "Only emotion objectified endures," Ginsberg chose the latter (in his words, "Only objectified emotion endures"). This was to acknowledge the Sonnets' autobiographical *art*. Hence, when Ginsberg told his students to find "a form for your emotion outside your own body," he was not telling them to discount their experience but to give it an objective shape that alone could eclipse solipsism. This is what he had in mind in 1950, when he told William Carlos Williams that he aimed for "a renewal of human objectivity," a goal he hoped to achieve though formal, particularly sonic, means.[33] "Ode to the West Wind," he reminded his class, is a "big block of sound that makes you feel emotional."

"[V]oweled breath" and "block of sound" speak to Ginsberg's lifelong interest in prosody, to what in "Howl" he called the "vibrating plane." Describing his "breathing" in that poem's Moloch section and in parts of "Kaddish," he explained that the "rhythmic . . . units . . . that I'd written down . . . were basically . . . breathing exercise forms . . . which if anybody else repeated . . . would catalyze in them the same . . . *affects* or emotions."[34] In "Notes Written on Finally Recording 'Howl,'" Ginsberg wrote that "[i]deally each line of "Howl" is a single breath unit. . . . My breath is long—that's the Measure, one physical-mental inspiration of thought contained in the elastic of a breath."[35] The credible etymology of "sonnet" that Ginsberg gave his students—"a little ringing," "a song of some kind"—confirms that he was hearing and sounding out Shakespeare's poems. Starting in the 1960s, Ginsberg often accompanied himself on a hand-pumped harmonium; at Naropa, he would sing the songs he was explicating. In several of his Shakespeare classes, he brought up the two limpid, pitch perfect songs that conclude *Love's Labor's Lost*; but surprisingly, he tended to ignore their acoustical elements. What was funny about Shakespeare's songs was their "specificity, particularity, tangibility, corporeality, actuality."[36] If these songs "have a funny kind of literality," it is because of "crazy Shakespeare, or funny Shakespeare['s] . . . historically accurate observation." "Winter" in particular is memorable for its "almost William Carlos Williams-like kitchen sink mindfulness."[37]

> *Winter*. When icicles hang by the wall,
> And Dick the shepherd blows his nail,
> And Tom bears logs into the hall,
> And milk comes frozen home in pail,
> When blood is nipped and ways be foul,
> Then nightly sings the staring owl,
> Tu-whit, tu-who—a merry note,
> While greasy Joan doth keel the pot.
>
> When all aloud the wind doth blow,
> And coughing drowns the parson's saw,
> And birds sit brooding in the snow,
> And Marian's nose looks red and raw,
> When roasted crabs hiss in the bowl,
> Then nightly sings the staring owl,
> Tu-whit, tu-who—a merry note,
> While greasy Joan doth keel the pot.
>
> (*Love's Labor's Lost*, 5.2.895–912)

Having read (not sung) the song out loud, Ginsberg comments that "without having said it, we've got the generalization Winter." The entire season is incarnated in a "series of tangible, corporeal, sensory, tactile, sensible, actual, directly treated visual fact minute particulars, [a] phalanx of particulars, specificities, facts. Close to the nose. Close to the nose. Absolutely close to the nose." "Close to the nose," Ginsberg's reformulation of Williams's "no ideas but in things," is his acknowledgment of "those *things which lie under the direct scrutiny of the senses*."[38] "[P]halanx of particulars"—the antidote to "lack of specificity" or "mediocrity"—is Ezra Pound's Aristotelian phrase ("generalities cannot be born from a sufficient phalanx / of particulars" [Canto 74]).[39] Those among Ginsberg's airy students who have not noticed how his own poetry works, Ginsberg admonishes to "stick with reality if you want to write unreal poetry." The poet must make a "presentation of situation in fact." "Let's begin somewhere real," Ginsberg says, "instead of somewhere up in the air where we can't begin at all. . . . If there's no place with feet and a floor and carpets and senses, then it's hardly possible to talk."

Ginsberg's students had before them only the selections in their *Norton Anthology of Poetry*, and not many of them would have known *Love's Labor's Lost*. Latter-day auditors of the Naropa tapes who do know the play will recognize that Ginsberg's stipulation about "feet and a floor" speaks to the fatuousness of the play's Ferdinand, Berowne, Dumaine, and Longaville, not to mention Don Armado. Hence Ginsberg's recognition that the two songs at the end of the play articulate Shakespeare's oblique but unmistakable criticism of his courtiers as well as the princess and her ladies. For Ginsberg as for Shakespeare, logopoeia could lean toward "honest kersey noes" (*Love's Labor's Lost*, 5.2.414) and "honest plain words" (5.2.743) or toward "maggot ostentation" (5.2.410) and "sharp wit" (5.2.399). When he reads the Sonnets, Ginsberg understands this distinction in terms of sweetness and wit (and so follows in the footsteps of Francis Meres, who in 1598 wrote of Shakespeare's "sugred sonnets" and of the "sweete and wittie soul" of Ovid that "liues in mellifluous & hony-tongued" Shakespeare").[40] Having read "Winter," Ginsberg asks his students to notice both its "absolutely solid" diction and its (destabilizing) puns. What Ginsberg now calls "the method of writing poetry by Shakespeare" consists of a proportionality between authenticity and artifice.

In the 1975 History of Poetry class, Ginsberg has something of a hard time backing up his argument, not because of his students but because Gregory Corso was in attendance. Playing the imp to the hilt, Corso keeps interrupting Ginsberg, sounding ever so much like George and Nell, the obstreperous, meddling characters/actors planted in the audience in Francis Beaumont's 1607 *The Knight of the Burning Pestle*. Ginsberg explains that when the "staring owl" in "Winter" "nightly sings . . . 'Tu-whit, tu-who,'" it "is obviously a pun, like nothing to do but make love in the middle of the night." Twenty-five years later, at the start of his introduction to the Penguin edition of the play, Peter Holland writes that this owl "may be calling 'to it,'" encouraging sex; may be making a statement about the play so far: there has been *too* much *wit*, *too* much *woo*ing; and may itself be a pun, since "owl" was pronounced "'ole,' thereby punning on 'hole'" and so making another of the play's sexual jokes (Ginsberg himself connects the owl with a phallic awl).[41] When Corso shouts out that it is just an owl, Ginsberg responds, "Yes, of course, but what is the owl saying?—"Make love"—"Tu-whit, to-w[o]o." Without missing a beat, Corso shrewdly cites Coleridge's asexual owl's "Tu whit! Tu-who!" at the start of "Christabel." A slightly exasperated but still accommodating Ginsberg says that Coleridge was imitating Shakespeare and then tries to move on. But like a burr, Corso once again dismisses the pun, insisting that "Tu-whit, tu-who" is mere onomatopoeia. Only now does a touch of condescension creep into Ginsberg's voice when, in a last ditch effort to champion Shakespeare's wit, he first concedes that "Of course it's onomatopoeic," then calls it "funny little pun-sense." Ginsberg improvises a bit of spur-of-the-moment wordplay in the spirit and defense of Shakespeare's.

The campaign on behalf of the song's wit temporarily having been concluded, Ginsberg begins to bore in on its poetics, exemplary because the song is a tissue of "accurate observation." The keynote of its "William Carlos Williams-like kitchen sink mindfulness"—its "imagism"—is "Shakespeare's own kitchen wench: 'greasy Joan [who] doth keel the pot.'" Here is Ginsberg: "Kerouac kept asking 'Who's "greasy Joan'? I wanna meet 'greasy Joan.' I wanna fuck greasy Joan.' It's just those two words conjured up this person. In two words, a complete structure in the air with her job, kneeling at the pot, greasy. No wonder greasy, because she's got to clean out the pots, so she's got all this grease up to her elbow." And now, Ginsberg takes in the song's entire "phalanx of particulars":

> "greasie Joan" working there, wind blowing, coughing, while the Parson's saying, "Well, everything's alright, folks. Keep it low." Birds sitting "brooding" in the snow, Marian's nose red and raw, crabs hiss in the bowl, "tu-whit to who," the owl again, Joan back there still at the pot. What's so great about that is the accuracy, the focus, the concentration of attention, like a Zen *haiku*—every line worthy of *haiku*, every line a fact, every line a sensory detail.

Ginsberg's Shakespeare warrants Williams's "no ideas but in things" because Shakespeare uses "things"—"present[s] more fact"—to get at even the "unconscious function" of "Tu-whit, tu-who." It is the facticity of "And birds sit brooding in the snow," Ginsberg says, that explains its "tragic" effect. Indeed, that effect utterly depends on accuracy and detail ("Let's begin somewhere real"). Is it because "greasy Joan['s]" brief but graphic cameo gives us a glimpse of life downstairs in *Love's Labor's Lost* that Ginsberg and Kerouac fall for her? In the end, Ginsberg argues, both comedy and tragedy (itself another "abstract generalization"), as well as the riposte of community homespun to courtly artifice, can only emerge from a poetry of "situation and fact." Greasy Joan "keel[s] the pot" and, for just a moment, Ginsberg pauses to make sure that his students know what it means to keel.

Ginsberg had a good bit more Naropa class time in which to discuss Shakespeare on August 18 and 20, 1980. With his paperback copy of *The Tempest* in hand, he taught two classes in four sessions for which we have about five recorded hours.[42] That summer, Naropa offered a "Rotating Shakespeare" class. Ginsberg finished out the course, having been preceded by Alice Notley on *Twelfth Night*, Anne Waldman on *Troilus and Cressida*, Clark Coolidge on *Titus Andronicus*, Diane di Prima on *A Midsummer Night's Dream*, Larry Fagin on *Measure for Measure*, Dick Gallop on *Richard 2*, Philip Whalen on *Pericles*, and Reed Bye on *Hamlet*. Prior to his own first class meeting, Ginsberg began to mark up his edition of the play; on the inside cover, he wrote, "For Teaching Naropa Summer 1980." At some point, underneath "THE TEMPEST" on the first page of play text, he wrote the word "Envy," an uncommon keyword for a play that has been discussed in terms of everything from revenge and forgiveness to, more recently, colonialism and otherness. Ginsberg may have suspected as much, since toward the start of his first session on the play, he seems slightly hesitant. He says that envy is the "origin of the play" and its "psychological motif," but he wonders out loud whether his interpretation comports with "tradition[al]" readings of the play. So he ticks off some evidence: Sebastian and Antonio are incontrovertibly envious of their brothers. Gonzalo's "commonwealth" (at the bottom of the page in his Penguin edition, Ginsberg calls it "Shakespeare's Utopia") is designed to put paid to envy. Envy is the "psychological trap that Prospero was trapped by when his brother usurped his throne" (later in the day, Ginsberg will say that Prospero's envy for "spiritual accomplishment" led him to neglect worldly business; when he renounces magic, he renounces "envy of magical power"). "With Caliban ["pure envy"] there's the continual theme of envy and jealousy and contention for superiority and inferiority." "The corruption of Sycorax also was envy." A "primordial earth mother," she was plagued by the "envy of beauty or envy of lightness or envy of humanity." This reading goes some way toward explaining an otherwise cryptic marginal comment that Ginsberg made in his copy when he came upon the only appearance of the word *envy* in the entire play. He drew a box around the word and then, starting from the line in which

Prospero asks Ariel, "Hast thou forgot / The foul witch Sycorax, who with age and envy / Was grown into a hoop?" (1.2.257–59), he drew an arrow and wrote, "This Play." At the bottom of the page he added, "ariel [*sic*] the servant of envy!" In the second classroom session on the play, Ginsberg explains that because Ariel is the servant of envy, and because Ariel stands for the imagination, the imagination itself "was originally born as the servant of envy." It follows that at some point, envious "magical imagination" has to be "dismissed"—as Prospero dismisses Ariel—so that the "direct perception" ("the flat fact description") that prevails in "Winter" can do its work.

When Ginsberg indentures the imagination to envy, he apparently has in mind his own development as a poet as well as his more mature reservations about the poetic imagination ("the universe is already sufficiently imaginative"). "I developed my poetic imagination out of envy of people around me that I thought were really smart and I tried to imitate and wanted to get their powers. And so I began observing how they did it." "They" were Burroughs, Kerouac, and Cassady, and although they were "ignorant of theory," they did have "direct perception of things that were right in front of their noses, close to the nose." They had the "granny wit" on display in "Winter." And for this, "the extra-magical power" of imagination is unnecessary. If "the mind is already back to its own base, there is no need of imagination." Of course, even though Ginsberg does not say so, Caliban is even more closely related to Sycorax than Ariel is. And it is Caliban's language that comes closest in *The Tempest* to what Ginsberg prized in "Winter" ("let me bring thee where crabs grow . . ." [2.2.164ff.]). So "pure envy" though he may be, Caliban is endowed by Shakespeare with verse that is close to the nose. Caliban, too, confirms that the royal road to *poiesis* runs through observation, not the imagination.

Ginsberg comes at envy from another angle when he puzzles out Miranda's response when Prospero tells her that she is "ignorant of what thou art": "More to know," she protests, "[d]id never meddle with my thoughts" (1.2.21–22). Prepping the play for class, Ginsberg had penciled a rectangular box around "meddle with my thoughts." In front of his students, he comes up with a curiously finicky paraphrase ("[T]he thought of more to know did never meddle with my other thoughts"), then comments, "[I]t's a funny thing, meddling with thoughts." Again, "funny." After a long pause during which you can almost hear Ginsberg thinking, he tries once more, this time recurring to envy: "[A] thought envious of more information, uh, would be considered meddling." And one last time, more obscurely now: "[S]he may have meant moral, 'to whom moral speech did never meddle with my thought.'" Ginsberg is working his way to what he now calls the play's "basic theme": "the nature of thought forms and consciousness." To explain this even less "traditional" interpretation of *The Tempest*, it helps to know that for Ginsberg, the "craft or art [of *poiesis*] is being shrewd at flashlighting mental activity. . . . The subject matter is the action of my mind."[43] Miranda's line has also led Ginsberg to think about the practice of meditation, that is, about the *form* of thinking. For the meditator, he observes, there is "a funny piece of physiological noticing of the process of thinking": thought is intervallic. To illustrate this, Ginsberg jumps to the speech at the end of the play in which Prospero tells us that "every third thought shall be my grave" (5.1.312). Prospero's "third thought" chimes for Ginsberg with Miranda's "meddle . . . thought." Father and daughter are accidental phenomenologists; "both have the same quality of perception" about the "nature of consciousness itself." Thoughts meddle, or they come in thirds. From meditation, Ginsberg had learned that "thought forms are discontinuous." They arise, "flower," "dissolve" and then a "gap" opens up. "Then another thought rises and dissolves." Thoughts "flicker." As Prospero puts it, "[a]ll which [we] inherit shall dissolve" (4.1.154).

Lest he has begun to sound too abstract, a deadpan Ginsberg moves "close[r] to the nose" to illustrate thoughts in thirds: "One thought will be a salami sandwich, another thought will be what time is it, and the other thought is, 'Ah, this human body is temporary and this body will be a corpse.'" For the meditator, every third thought is a "gap." For Prospero, the third thought is what Ginsberg calls his "empty moment"—his yet untenanted grave. But that grave has been present from the start of the play when, with the ship going down and the mariners crying, "All lost," the Boatswain responds, "What, must our mouths be cold?" (1.1.52). Commenting on the same line that Keats underscored in his Whittingham edition of *The Tempest*, Ginsberg applauds Shakespeare for composing with things as opposed to ideas. Reciting again from "Winter," he explains that Shakespeare consistently opted for the concrete "exemplification of an abstraction." His is "a process of simplification rather than complication." His poetics are premised on "primary arithmetic," not "higher mathematics." He relies on pattern-forming "details of cause and effect" which give rise to generalizations. In sum, his "easy genius" derives from his "unobstructed sight" and from his "unobstructed mind" ("the mind . . . back to its own base").

The generalizations ("the psychological philosophy") to which *The Tempest*'s details give rise are "heart's sorrow" and "clear life" (3.3.81–82), two "emotional . . . [or] awareness antidote[s]" to the "wraths" caused by "envious action." But, as with the Sonnets, what really jazzes the poet Ginsberg is less the play's lesson about life than the ways Shakespeare's "little philosophies of life *are built into the syntax*" (my emphasis). The poet's ear is attuned to quirky, "funny" bits of language in the play, what Ginsberg calls its "little elegancies" and "little delicacies." In the aggregate, then, his four sessions on *The Tempest* are an intentionally "spotty" (his word) tour of the play's local felicities. Ariel's readiness to "ride / On the curled clouds" (1.2.191–92) conjures clouds in Tibetan paintings for Ginsberg; it is so "accurate . . . so simple, like sewing or something." He classifies it among Shakespeare's manifold "arrangements and combinations," noting that "imagist poets have been working for eighty years trying to describe a cloud." Prospero's "the minute bids thee ope thine ear" (1.2.37) gets three or four minutes of Ginsberg's attention. Lacking a "logical connection," it is a "surrealist image." What with the peculiarity (the "mixed metaphor") of a minute bidding—let alone bidding an ear to open—it has a "very funny pictorial quality." How "sweet" to have a minute *bid* thee do anything. As with "bending sickle's compass come," which he worked and reworked five months earlier, Ginsberg keeps repeating and repeating "ope thine ear," three "Creeleyesque" stressed monosyllables that "aren't too staccato." You get this a lot in Shakespeare, he says, and it is "a good sound to absorb." More to himself than to the class, Ginsberg rhymes (remember "Tom Hayden's helicopter's wheel") "bids thee ope thine ear" with "show thy foot to air," then "put thy hair in here." He is laughing out loud now, perhaps at his own illogic, which answers more to what he hears than to what he understands in Shakespeare.

"The dark backward and abysm of time" (1.2.50) is another phrase that pulls him up short. A "funny rhetorical trick," this famous hendiadys is for Ginsberg part of Shakespeare's surrealist enterprise. But such poetics are not quite arbitrary. By collating "vast" and "middle" with "backward" and "abysm," Ginsberg can demonstrate that in both cases, Shakespeare gives us spatial coordinates. Twice, he "breaks your brain open." Of course, this was the ambition of "hydrogen jukebox," which he now explains derived from Shakespeare via Yeats's "murderous innocence" ("A Prayer for My Daughter") along with "some intervention of surrealist thinking." The hendiadyan "and" is a placeholder for the "mind-blowing" thought that Ginsberg says necessarily results from the even "swifter conjunction" that is "hydrogen jukebox." Form and content thus yoked "short-circuit the brain . . . to make you think fresh." This is the lesson to be drawn from Cézanne's juxtapositions of colors and it is the "trick" of Burroughs's cut-ups. It is the way of "all great metaphor," too. Burroughs comes to mind, as Kerouac often does, because both writers taught Ginsberg to listen to the Shakespearean demotic, and to what he says Kerouac called the "uncanny" in Shakespeare's language. This was also true of Corso, with whose long poem "Clown" Ginsberg begins his second session on *The Tempest*. In Corso's verse, he hears the same "crispness" that he hears in Shakespeare's. Corso's "Tang-a-lang boom! Fife feef! Toot!" (Ginsberg calls this the reduction of an entire toy circus clown band into one line of verse) he compares with Shakespeare's "tu-whit, tu-who." Corso's "cadence" and "condensation" (his wit) also compare well with Shakespeare's, although Corso does not have "the burden of having to fill out the blank verse line." If once again Ginsberg fixes his attention on versification, it is because he wants what his students hear to condition what they think.

Ariel's "full fathom five" is grist for the same mill. The spirit's song may be Shakespeare at what Ginsberg calls his most "mysterious," "poetical," "exquisite," "magical," and "philosophical"; it may be where Shakespeare gives us an "inkling" of "the whole universe of change"; but for all that, Ginsberg responds most wholeheartedly to its "chiming" and to its "nursery-rhymish form." Having summarized commentary on Shakespeare's politics (his "disgustingly antidemocratic view . . . but then he's also done the same thing to the aristocracy"), he gives an exuberant recitation of Caliban's "triumphant revolutionary song" ("No more dams I'll make for fish"—2.2.176). Yet Ginsberg's plaintive response—this is "really sad"—addresses Shakespeare's political allegiances only obliquely. What he instead keeps calling to his students' attention are the play's easily overlooked lines—their "pretties" most of all. He reads out loud Alonso's "pretty funny" "You cram these words into mine ears against / The stomach of my sense" (2.1.106–07). Beside these lines in his copy of the play, Ginsberg wrote, "Curious phrase." Alonso's "I myself could make / A chough of as deep chat" (2.1.264–65) he calls "a funny piece of mouthing that Shakespeare presents for an actor" and then repeats or runs variations on it no fewer than eleven times. "Mouthing" is apposite because Alonso is talking about Gonzalo's prating, also because Ginsberg has such a good time sounding out the phrase from "chough" to "chat," from *ch* to *ch* and from *ff* to *at*. Turning to another line that caught Keats's attention, Antonio's "They'll take suggestion as a cat laps milk" (2.1.287 [they will fall right into line]), Ginsberg comments, "That's a funny, fast, exact movie." Again and again repeating "a cat laps milk" ("it's good sound . . . for an actor it must be great"), he says that "you could mouth it with any suggestion of contempt . . . or humor." To single out passages about "chough," "chat," and "lap[ping]," to dwell on their mouth feel, is to lodge content not so much in form as sound. Rather than explain, Ginsberg vocalizes his point that Shakespearean prosody can be a real mouthful. This is the Ginsberg for whom it was a "revelation" to listen again and again to a tape of Pound reading Canto 45.

He would count the lengths of vowels and notice their "musical possibilities," straining to hear the ways that Pound "vocalizes . . . the tone leading of vowels" (melopoeia). In short, he was "simply paying attention to what's being said by mouth."[44]

It was the catalogue of Shakespearean "elegancies" that the best among the Naropa students would have realized that they could find only in a class taught by Allen Ginsberg. But he must have known that it was otherwise for the majority of his students and tailored his classes to them. In the fourth and final session on *The Tempest*, Ginsberg devotes a lot of time to the wedding masque that Prospero produces to celebrate the nuptials of Ferdinand and Miranda. He walks his students through an almost line-by-line paraphrase of the masque and then Prospero's "Our revels now have ended" speech. He talks about the message from "Great Nature," about Prospero's "visionary seizure" and his "vision of transitoriness and the ultimate void and emptiness of existence." And yet Ginsberg's interest in Shakespearean prosody seems to have gone deeper than his interest in Shakespeare's vision, also deeper than he let on to his Shakespeare students. About eight months after the *Tempest* classes, he heavily marked up and underlined in black and red ink Iris's speech at the beginning of the masque (4.1.60ff.). At the bottom of the page, he wrote "Note Quantity." Either in April 1981 or back in August, when he was re-reading the play for his Naropa classes, he annotated phrases like "thatched with stover" and "pioned and twilled brims." His scansion notation blankets the lines when Juno and Ceres sing. "You sunburned sicklemen, of August weary" is underlined. Perhaps Ginsberg was remembering Olson's "Quantity in Verse, and Shakespeare's Late Plays" (written in 1956; first published in 1966), in which Olson singles out "Thy banks with pioned and twilled brims," noting the "consonants forced to the vertical." In language strikingly consistent with Ginsberg's, Olson extolls Shakespeare's "monosyllables at their quietest and sweetest" in Iris's "Of wheat, rye, barley, fetches, oats, and pease." In his unpublished Shakespeare manuscript, Olson describes these syllables as "percussives"; in the published essay, he wrote that the "thinking and weighing in of the quantity stop twist and intensify the speech, thus increasing the instancy."[45] At Naropa, Ginsberg spoke often of Shakespeare's "direct" and "grounded" verse (William Carlos Williams, too, was "grounded").[46] When he reads Shakespeare out loud in class, his pitch rises and falls unpredictably from the start of a line to its end; his enunciation of vowels and syllables is always marked, as if he were grafting quantity onto stress and accent. Students may have wondered what he was up to when, five or ten times in a row, each time with a different inflection, he repeated a line, varying its rhythm and meter, and the lengths of individual syllables, even substituting words for those that Shakespeare wrote. He was recruiting Shakespeare for the prosodic "community effort" that extended all the way from the "seed syllables" of Sanskrit ("their deployment, physiologically in the body during their pronouncing, is crucial") to Olson ("the line itself is connected with the breath in that the whole body's intention is mobilized") and to Pound (whose "rhythmic change" occasions a "a change in body apprehension").[47] Ginsberg was reading Shakespeare by feel, by ear, and by mouth.

I mentioned at the outset that in 1966 (seven years after he completed "Kaddish"), Ginsberg wrote that Shakespeare was for him a "primary source." At first blush, there does not seem to be much evidence for this in his letters, notebooks, or poems. However, if we attune ourselves to rhythm and mouth feel, if we take our cue from the way Ginsberg "rhymed" "[Time's] bending sickle's compass come" with "Tom Hayden's helicopter's wheel," it is possible to find the way back from "Kaddish" to Shakespeare. Helen Vendler unsurprisingly finds "the rhythm of the Hebrew Kaddish . . . at the end of the first part of the poem."[48] But Ginsberg was not a practicing Jew—he had to ask his father to get him a copy of "The Mourner's Kaddish." He had, however, been reading Shakespeare for more than ten years when he sat down to write his own "Kaddish," so it is reasonable to assume that Shakespeare's verse was also in his ears. Instructed by Ginsberg's Naropa pedagogy, in which idiosyncratic ("funny") rhythmic and sonic calls invite commensurate responses, I juxtapose "Kaddish" with *King Lear* not because the play is demonstrably a source for, or influences, the poem but because as an analogous examination of human frailty and mortality in which voicing counts dearly, it deepens our understanding of Ginsberg's poetics.

It will help to start with one of Ginsberg's characteristic metrical "rhymes." Shortly before the passage to which Vendler refers, Ginsberg imagines his mother Naomi's lobotomist with "an idiot Snowman's icy . . . Sharp icicle in his hand." Then he particularizes this "strange ghost . . . Death": "a dog for his eyes—cock of a sweatshop—heart of electric irons."[49] The three prepositions in this blazon are at variance with the compression—the stark juxtapositioning—that is one hallmark of Ginsberg's prosody at the level of the phrase. More typical is a series like this one, also from "Kaddish," in which once again Ginsberg describes his lobotomized mother: "the roar of bonepain, skull bare, break rib, rot-skin, braintricked Implacability" (9). Yes, there is a preposition here, too, but the subsequent contractions best represent Ginsberg's *modus operandus* (elsewhere:

"marred of heart, mind behind, married dreamed, mortal changed" [11]). For sonic as well as substantive reasons, it is instructive to compare the way Ginsberg "rhymes" his dog-cock-heart sequence with Edgar's "False of heart, light of ear, bloody of hand, hog in sloth, fox in stealth, wolf in greediness, dog in madness" (*King Lear*, 3.4.93–94). Several hundred years after the fact, an Olson or a Ginsberg comes along and jettisons Shakespeare's prepositions. Ginsberg takes an inventory like Edgar's and experimentally condenses it to light ear, hog sloth, fox stealth, and so on. Here, in the poet's mind and ear, was the laboratory in which modernism wrought changes on Shakespeare. Velocity and compression create disturbances in the iambic field.

In the classroom, Ginsberg grabs hold of a word or phrase of Shakespeare's and tampers with its sound and rhythm, sometimes plays fast and loose with its meaning. The word "Nothing" ricochets through *King Lear*, starting with Lear's obtuse "Nothing will come of nothing" in response to Cordelia's two "nothing[s]" (1.1.87–90). Responding to "Naughtless" Naomi (10), hoping to "cut through" (11) the closed circuit of her nothingness, Ginsberg asks Jehovah, the "only One blessed in Nothingness" to "Take this, this Psalm, from me . . . now given to Nothing" (11–12). Naomi is pursued by Hitler and Mussolini. Poor Tom is pursued by "[t]he foul Flibbertigibbet. He [that] begins at curfew, and walks till the first cock . . . gives the web and the pin, squints the eyes, and makes the harelip, mildews the white wheat, and hurts the poor creature of earth" (3.4.114–18). Naomi is tormented by "Trotsky mixing *rat bacteria* in the back of the store" (18; my emphasis) and by "'Old Grandma . . . dressed in pants like an old man . . . On the fire escape, with poison germs" (14). "The foul fiend hath . . . laid knives under [poor Tom's] pillow and halters in his pew, set *ratsbane* by his porridge" (3.4.53–56; my emphasis).

Not just Naomi's "skull bare," but her eyes and her mouth have a Shakespearean cast. The first strophe of "Kaddish" begins, "Strange to think of you, gone without corsets & eyes" (7). At some point, Ginsberg memorized Ariel's song, so the "sea change . . . rich and strange" (1.2.401–02) that Ariel describes—"Those are pearls that were his [Alonso's] eyes" (*The Tempest*, 1.2.399)—might have been in his ears. Perhaps there is a faint recollection of Lear's "If thou wilt weep my fortunes, take my eyes" (4.6.176). Naomi's "hideous gape of bad mouth" (10) recalls both "My Lady Worm's, chopless [jawless]" (*Hamlet*, 5.1.83–84) and Yorick, now "abhorred" in Hamlet's "imagination": "Here hung those lips that I have kissed I know not how oft. . . . Quite chopfallen?" (5.1.177–82). Ginsberg writes that he "gaspt" when he saw Naomi, post-stroke and post-lobotomy, her "One hand stiff," that same "hand dipping downwards to death"

(29). Lear himself tells his weeping daughter, "I will not swear these are my hands" (4.7.56)—as if he, too, has suffered a stroke. In one of the most excruciating lines in the play, he tells Gloucester that his hand "smells of mortality" (4.6.133). The *odor mortis* that permeates Shakespeare's play has blown into Ginsberg's poem.

As *odor di femmina*. If Naomi's bonepain pales in comparison with the notoriety of her "long black beard around the vagina" (34; also her "big slash of hair" and her "ragged long lips between her legs"—24), what can we say about "Her smells" (24)? "What, even, smell of asshole?" (24). "Now wear your nakedness forever" (30), Ginsberg in full Blakean, prophetic voice, tells his mother. But he already has admitted that when she was "oft naked in the room," he would "stare ahead, or turn a book ignoring her" (24). The smells themselves of Ginsberg's strophes are infused with the odor of their anguished and ruthless *locus classicus* in *King Lear*:

> Down from the waist they are centaurs
> Though women all above.
> But to the girdle do the gods inherit
> Beneath is all the fiends.
> There's hell, there's darkness, there is the sulphurous pit; burning,
> scalding, stench, consumption. Fie, fie, fie! pah, pah! Give me an ounce
> of civet; good apothecary, sweeten my imagination!
>
> (4.6.124–31)

Absent most of Lear's rage, Ginsberg takes his gagging misogyny down several notches, but not so far down that he refuses to stage moments of indecorum at "varicosed, nude, fat" (22) Naomi's expense. Smell, often said to be our oldest sense, helps both poets reach toward something taboo, hence unspeakable (and female?), that conjoins *eros* and *thanatos*.[50] That ineffableness, already present in the sound of Lear's "fies" and "pahs," recurs in his howls (howls that endowed Ginsberg with "Howl"), in the sound of Ginsberg's pleonastic caws and Lords at the end of "Kaddish," and in his stupefied response to Naomi, "as if she were dead through funeral rot": "'The Horror' . . . to see her again—'The Horror' . . . 'The Horror!'" (30). Not just the sound that we attribute in English to crows but both the epizeuxis and the phonic resources on display in *King Lear* vouch for Ginsberg's "caw caw" and his "caw caw caw" (36). At the limits of language, an insistent, inhuman vocalization that Ginsberg has heard in Shakespeare takes over. It is what he heard in Lear's "howl, howl, howl, howl" (four times in

Quarto, three in Folio), his "kill, kill, kill, kill, kill, kill!" (Q and F), in Folio Lear's "never, never, never, never, never" and in Quarto Lear's "O, O, O, O!" Five lines from the end of "Kaddish," Ginsberg confronts the same agonizing, eloquent inarticulateness that we respond to at the end of *King Lear*: "Lord Lord O Grinder of giant Beyonds my voice in a boundless field in Sheol" (36). If there is a smell to mortality in these two verse dramas, it also has a sound, by turns discordant (howling and grinding) and haunting (a voice in Sheol, the chthonic dwelling place of the dead).

The roster of Shakespearean shards in "Kaddish" also includes figurations of the end of time, "Time rent out of foot and wing an instant in the universe" (36). The poem begins with Ginsberg "Dreaming back thru life . . . accelerating toward Apocalypse, / the final moment" (7). *King Lear* ends when Kent asks, "Is this the promised end?" and Edgar completes the query, "Or image of that horror?" (5.3.269–70). For Ginsberg as for Shakespeare, the end of a life and the end of time both do and do not coincide. Ginsberg imagines himself "as old as the universe—I guess that dies with us—enough to cancel all that comes—What came is gone forever every time" (8–9). When Edgar says that Lear "is gone indeed," Kent says that he "but usurped his life" (5.3.321–23). If in "Kaddish," "Death . . . is the end, the redemption from Wilderness" (12), is it she who dies (Naomi) or he who survives (Ginsberg) who is redeemed? It is said that Cordelia "redeems nature from the general curse" (4.6.205), and Lear believes that Cordelia's survival would "redeem all sorrows" (5.3.273). But he also says that Cordelia will "come no more" (5.3.314). One thing that we know survives Naomi is what she writes in her last letter: "The key is in the sunlight at the window in the bars the key is in the sunlight" (33). Here is how Ginsberg inflates this: "But that the key should be left behind—at the window—the key in the sunlight—to the living—that can take / that slice of light in hand—and turn the door—and look back see / Creation glistening backwards to the same grave, size of universe" (33).

More in keeping with the sound and equipoise of Naomi's unassuming prose is the conclusion of *King Lear*, with its own self-effacing look backward and forward:

> The weight of this sad time we must obey,
> Speak what we feel, not what we ought to say.
> The oldest hath borne most; we that are young
> Shall never see so much, nor live so long.

>   (5.3.530–33)

Naomi's letter, like the words "to the living" (33) that Edgar speaks here at the end of Folio *King Lear*, vouchsafes only a quiet, subdued response to suffering and death. Just as her simplicity cautions against those moments in "Kaddish" when Ginsberg gravitates toward "Visions of the Lord" (36), with an uppercase *V* and an uppercase *L*, so Edgar's couplets lower the volume of Lear's "Blow, winds, and crack your cheeks! Rage, blow!" (3.2.1) and modestly qualify his own bout with despair ("The worst is not / So long as we can say 'This is the worst'"—4.1.27–28). The key in the sunlight is as guileless as Lear's fantasy that he and Cordelia will sing "like birds i' th' cage" (5.3.9); in other words, what Ginsberg learned by listening to what Shakespeare wrote was not just how to ratchet things up but how to tone them down. Short on consolation, the poem and the play make do, bearing witness to those who have "borne most" in sometimes broken, sometimes heartbreakingly unaffected verses. Naomi "on the grass," her "long black hair . . . crowned with flowers" (29), converges with the "phalanx of particulars" that is Lear,

> Crowned with rank fumiter and furrow weeds.
> With hardocks, hemlock, nettles, cuckooflowers,
> Darnel, and all the idle weeds that grow
> In our sustaining corn.
>
> (4.3.3–6)

as Ginsberg joins Shakespeare, "seek[ing]" both "Peace for Thee"—for those "Tortured and beaten in the skull"—and "Peace for Thee, O Poetry" (29).

VII

TED HUGHES READS THE
COMPLETE SHAKESPEARE

Time and again when reading from the *Complete Works* of Shakespeare, we notice something particular or recurrent: thematic motifs, wordplay, rhyming couplets, disguises, soliloquies, beleaguered masculinity, meta-theatricality. The possibilities are legion. Different flames kindle for each of us. We understand what we have noticed in terms of literary conventions, habits of mind, or what we think of as typically Shakespearean. Perceived dramaturgical patterns or philosophical inclinations operating "below the level of 'plot' and 'character'" help us to correlate the succeeding lines of a speech or a scene, of an entire play or a narrative poem.[1] They constellate seemingly unrelated moments from a variety of plays. Their persistence encourages us to suspect that they gesture beyond themselves to deeper matters that their individual appearances adumbrate only imperfectly or incompletely. Like figures in a carpet, they enable us to organize our perceptions even as they prompt us to be on the lookout for more of the same. Like lenses, they filter our perceptions, intensifying parts of the spectrum. Repeated elements orient us when we feel as though we have lost the thematic trail. They reassure us that we are, after all, onto something noteworthy. Taken together, they can feel like a cluster of favors or insights granted to those of us sufficiently alert to have descried them. But this is to suppose a benefactor, and if not explicitly, then tacitly, to decide that the designs and themes that capture our attention are evidence not just of matters of consequence but of a presiding genius for whom they also are consequential. Must they not index Shakespeare's own abiding concerns, his hobbyhorses, even? Can they not tell us something about the man himself: his beliefs, his allegiances, his philosophy? Or do they just tease us, as when W. H. Auden's Caliban (in *The Sea and the Mirror*) steps out onto the stage to taunt us at the precise moment when it was Shakespeare whom we were expecting: "you instinctively *do* ask for our so good, so great, so dead author to stand before the finally lowered curtain and take his shyly responsible bow for this, his latest ripest production, [but] it is I . . . who will always loom thus wretchedly into your confused picture."[2] Although we tell ourselves that we should know better, we hanker for a glimpse of, maybe even limited access to, the Bard and to what he was thinking.

What happens, then, when we are provided with evidence not for a Shakespearean theme (for example, what G. Wilson Knight calls the "hate-theme"), nor for a developmental account of Shakespeare (for example, what Knight calls "the Shakespeare Progress"), but for *the* Shakespeare theme, the one that reveals *the* master plot that transcends what Knight called the "visionary unit" that is each play?[3] How do we respond when an intelligent, indeed a commanding, poet tells us that he has found the way to Shakespeare whole, that for well-nigh all of Shakespeare's major works he has detected the "equation" or "tragic equation" (*passim*), the "basic flexible formula" (1), the "perfect archetypal plot" (2), the "skeleton key" (2), the "mechanism" (3), the "patterned field of force" (3), the "mythic power circuit" (13), the "nervous system" (21), the "sacred symbolic language" (57), the "elemental law" (127), "algebraic method" (197), the "kit" itself (213)? These are but a dozen samples from the first half of *Shakespeare and the Goddess of Complete Being*, the poet Ted Hughes's massive and meticulous examination of Shakespeare's "DNA" (175).[4] Has Hughes given rein to his own hobbyhorse? Should poets (say, Charles Olson or Allen Ginsberg) be given special license to read Shakespeare idiosyncratically? Set beside Louis Zukofsky's *Bottom: On Shakespeare*—a *sui generis* compendium that argues that all "of Shakespeare's writing embodies a definition . . . of love as the tragic hero"—Hughes's volume is an epitome of accessible discursive reasoning.[5]

Some of us read Shakespeare searching for the Bard genome. This Shakespeare is susceptible to deciphering and decoding. For others, Shakespeare's writing is immune to precisely these procedures. Keats commends Shakespeare's negative capability, both his high comfort level when it comes to uncertainty and his refusal to reach after methods or formulas. This is also Keats's implicit advice to us as to how we ought to read Shakespeare. The nineteenth-century poet tacitly excuses our more or less inchoate and unformulated, our ad hoc, approaches to the *Complete Works*. By comparison, Ted Hughes sets out to expose our failure of nerve and vision. To his friend Lucas Myers, Hughes complained that most poetry lacks "wholeness—men make their whole style out of one filament of the thick rope of human nature. You get the rope solid in Proverbs, ballads, songs, Shakespeare."[6] More than thirty years later, Hughes was still thinking about wholeness. Drafting a "BLURB FOR SHAKESPEARE AND THE GODDESS OF COMPLETE BEING," he calls attention to the "many patterns in Shakespeare's carpet. This is an attempt to see the Complete Works . . . as a single, tightly-integrated, evolving organism."[7] If anything, this blurb is an understatement. Reading with astounding urgency and brio, Hughes produced a comprehensive version of the *Complete Works* that transmutes it into a capacious, sweeping drama set on a "mythic plane" (*SGCB*, 85), populated by avatars of Venus, Adonis, Tarquin and Lucrece. Riveted to one another, a Catholic source myth edited for Puritan consumption (*Venus and Adonis*) and a Puritan source myth as interpreted by Catholics (*The Rape of Lucrece*) combine to generate a cross-corpus tragic equation that represents "a fundamental polarity of human existence" (*SGCB*, 18). The simultaneously prophetic and shamanic Bard judges and sets out to heal Protestant England following its attack on Catholicism (the Goddess); because this attack cost England its soul, Shakespeare was compelled to keep replaying it from *All's Well that Ends Well* to *The Tempest*.

No wonder the poet-critic who wrote *SGCB* knew that he was going to be looked at askance—worse still, dismissed. Between April 23 (by no means co-incidentally Shakespeare's birthday) and June 14, 1990, Hughes wrote more than fifty very long letters to Donya Feuer (then a director and choreographer at the Royal Dramatic Theatre in Stockholm and a frequent collaborator with Ingmar Bergman) in which he essentially wrote *SGCB*. In his letter dated May 31, 1990, Hughes writes, "I hope I don't seem to be arguing that the living complex of these plays is nothing but the allegorical staging of the private theology of an eccentric, syncretic Occult Neoplatonist." This refers to Shakespeare, but Hughes speaks unmistakably about himself as well. A few lines further on, he admits that "anybody can find anything in Shakespeare's plays. Most especially they find themselves." Almost exactly a year later, in a May 27, 1991, letter to Christopher Reid, his editor at Faber, Hughes writes that over the many years that he has been nursing his thesis, he has felt as though he were making his "appeal" from the "dungeons," and that when he has floated it, it has met with "twenty years of blank stares." Hence, "it could be . . . that I've overdone it." On June 21, 1991, Hughes acknowledges to Gillian Bate, his copy editor, how very close to his argument he has become: "My eyesight has been in a way refashioned, writing this book—I'm now totally adapted to this peculiar world, like one of those shrimps living in the sulphur and fantastic temperatures of deep-sea volcanoes, and I no longer feel to have any confident idea of just how the final thing will appear in the old world where I used to live." Again he speaks as if he had emerged "to write my book like somebody after twenty years in jail making an appeal. . . . So I can't really get rid of a certain lingering expectation that my every sentence will meet only a pitying gaze and the same old deaf ears."[8]

None of this is to say that Hughes was having serious doubts about his argument, or that he was intimidated by the responses from academics that he already had gotten or that he well knew were forthcoming. To Peter Redgrove, he boasted that "[n]ot one scholar in a hundred knows Shakespeare well enough to guess whether I have something or haven't" (*Letters*, 321; October 27, 1971). "What my book has revealed to me among scholars," Hughes wrote to A. L. Rowse, "is their galactic ignorance of anything outside their specialised corner in their University library. And their incapacity of seeing any problem unless they already know the answer" (*Letters*, 609; April 15, 1992). "Academics," Hughes wrote to Reid on November 14, 1991, "with their nostalgia for woodwork hobbies and being a dab hand at fixing a car, always assume that they alone take the practicalities of the stage into account and really know what they are, or were. So I feel I shall be exposing my argument to that bit more arrogant idiocy if I don't pull a bit of rank, just a hint."[9] Pulling rank in this case would have had nothing to do with Hughes's clout as a well-known poet and everything to do with Hughes's theater experience, his having worked with Peter Brook as "an ideas man, providing germs of plots and suggestive dramatic situations which the actors then explored. . . . Some days we got through five or six of my 'plots.' From my notes, it seems that I produced hundreds" (*SGCB*, *xi*). Hughes imagined that his frenetic production schedule might have approximated Shakespeare's best practices. Did not Shakespeare use a "prototype plot consciously"? Certainly, Hughes goes on to write in his inaugural, April 23, 1990, letter to Feuer, the "Greek Tragedians constructed their plots according to definite well-proven patterns." Noh dramatists, modern TV writers, even "modern pulp fiction writers often construct their works according to a standard template that guarantees a high charge of effective dramatic energy." Surely this is the habit of any writer "contracted to a heavy production line of dramatic story-lines (as Shakespeare was)," one who "automatically invents, sooner or later, a basic successful formula of constants and variables."[10]

Nor should we think that Hughes was oblivious to the cries of foul that he expected from those who are committed to reading each of Shakespeare's plays as a separate entity, or from those who place a high premium on Shakespeare the realist. On the former count, Hughes simply asks Feuer to "[f]orgive this violation of the separateness of each play, and for any effect of claustrophobia that my argument may induce. I yield to nobody in my delight in the uniqueness and unique spacious complexity of the world of each of the plays."[11] On the latter—and given where Hughes was heading, the more important—count, Hughes was pretty much unrepentant. In this same letter, he made it clear to Feuer that he knew from the start that he was going to be "rather dogged on the narrow trail" and that he was apt to "try your patience by excluding consideration of everything in the plays except the role of the equation." In order for him to work effectively with his template, he had to ignore the "realist" for the "mythic" Shakespeare (*SGCB*, 35). "Accordingly, I propose to . . . separate the two Shakespeares. That is to say I am temporarily lifting away everything that might have been written by a kind of Dickens, everything that Tolstoy might have approved." Moreover, "[i]f the reader insists that the realist in Shakespeare cannot be separated in this way—in imagination, playfully—then my book must remain closed. This act of separating the two Shakespeares is, as it were, the first rule of the game that I am inviting the reader to play" (*SGCB*, 38). "Those who keep my rules in mind . . . will understand that I am simply exploring something else altogether, in an attempt to open up the [mythic] crypts and catacombs that have been—in our cultural enthusiasm for the upper architectural marvels of the realistic Shakespeare—somewhat ignored and neglected" (*SGCB*, 39). As it turns out, Hughes's enterprise is hardly playful, and his exploration is anything but simple. He may ask us to believe that what he is about to map out "can be found fairly readily" or "observed by anybody who will play the game" (*SGCB*, 39); but he is honest enough to advertise (in his characteristic idiom) the "tangle of my route, for which I am making my own crude map. . . . I rely on hand-torch and divining rod through the tunnels of the wild pig" (*SGCB*, 34).

If I were to estimate a ratio of bravado and conviction to defensiveness and diffidence in Hughes's reading of Shakespeare, I would plump for something like four to one; when he has gotten up a really full head of steam, say three hundred pages into the more than five hundred that make up *SGCB*, the ratio doubles. After all, Hughes was steeped in myth. Certainly, it underwrote much of his own poetry; it also affected the way he read poetry. In the response he drafted to John Carey's damning review of *SGCB*, he insisted that myth is "body and soul for Eliot, Yeats, Keats, Coleridge, Blake, Milton, . . . as for Shakespeare. But Carey stares at it like a Hans Caspar blinking at a box of alphabet letters, or like a bouncy, pink-necked young subaltern of the Raj squinting at a Hindu Temple" (Carey's review appeared in the *Sunday Times* on April 5, 1992; Hughes's rejoinder, on April 19). Myths organized Hughes's account not just of culture but of human history itself. No surprise, then, that he would write to a skeptical academic like Richard Proudfoot that "I always set Shakespeare within a mythic background—countersunk it—like a water skeeter on the river of myth. I also understood myth to be the language of the deeper life."[12] And no surprise that the rhizomes of myth should infiltrate the tunnel vision of *SGCB*. According to Hughes, myth dominates plot in Shakespeare, and it explains "the helplessness of the characters' humanity, under the compulsion of his or her [*sic*] mythic destiny" (*SGCB*, 211). If we have failed to see this, it is because we are the realist offspring of Dickens and Balzac. And if we suspect that Hughes has simply strapped his huge mythic apparatus onto the *Complete Works*, we do well to acknowledge that is was not quite his starting point. He did not ram Shakespeare, lock, stock, and barrel, into a fully formed "tragic equation." No doubt Robert Graves's *The White Goddess: A Historical Grammar of Poetic Myth* (1948) was as ever-present to Hughes the reader of Shakespeare, as was Hughes's homemade version of what would come to be known as sociobiology. Still, it was something more local, something he noticed very much within one play after another, which called out to him for an explanation. This pattern caught his attention a full twenty years before he published *SGCB*, at an earlier moment when he was intentionally running roughshod over the unity of individual plays.

In 1971, Hughes published *A Choice of Shakespeare's Verse* (Faber and Faber) in England; in the United States, this compilation was entitled, *With Fairest Flower While Summer Lasts: Poems from Shakespeare* (Doubleday). Both editions were reissued, with a revised introduction, in 1991 (with the same title from Faber; in the States, as *The Essential Shakespeare*, from Ecco Press). The 1971 version of the introduction, entitled "The Great Theme: Notes on Shakespeare," was also reprinted in 1995 in *Winter Pollen: Occasional Prose*, to which I will refer.[13] One might expect that the burden of Hughes's introduction would be a defense of extracting and collecting passages from the plays, but on this matter, Hughes expends relatively little energy. Given the scope and ambition of *SGCB*, it is somewhat ironic that in 1969, when he first pitched his idea for a Shakespeare anthology to his editor at Faber and Faber, Hughes protested that he did not think that "extracting 'beauties from the plays' is so reprehensible, except to the fanatics who read their complete Shakespeare steadily and constantly" (*Letters*, 288; February 19, 1969). "Out of context," Hughes writes, "we have to admit, they are different words. Fallen from the visionary world of the play, they have to make their meaning out of the rubbish-heap and more or less chaotic half-digested turnover of experience, the flux of half-memories and broken glimpses, in their reader at the moment of reading. And suddenly we notice what densely peculiar verbal poetry they are" (*WP*, 103). We may rest assured that "the higher poet" of the plays is "unimpaired," that the "Complete Works are still intact"; but the latter-day poet's anthology of Shakespeare fragments can give us "a whole poet where before we had only one of his hands" (*WP*, 104).

Hughes wants credit for liberating "a new teeming of possibilities" from Shakespeare's verse and for presenting "some of the best of it straight" (*WP*, 104–5). To frame his poetry in this way is to reveal that Shakespeare's language has

> the air of being invented in a state of crisis, for a terribly urgent job, a homely spur-of-the-moment improvisation out of whatever verbal scrap happens to be lying around, which is exactly what real speech is. The meaning is not so much narrowly delineated as overwhelmingly suggested, by an inspired signalling and hinting of verbal heads and tails both above and below precision, and by this weirdly expressive underswell of a musical neargibberish, like a jostling of spirits. The idea is conveyed, but we also receive a musical and imaginative shock, and the satisfaction of that is unfathomable. (*WP*, 105)

In the heavily revised 1991 introduction to the Ecco Press edition, Hughes writes that

> [t]he effect is always to . . . suspend the rather massively molded finality of each line's verbal physique over a gulf of inner apprehension and nervous self-awareness—more revelatory of emergency in the body's chemistry, more tightly and squarely responsive to the immediate occasion, more purely the timbre and tremor of the electrocardiograph made audible than can easily be found elsewhere.[14]

This jibes with Virginia Woolf's intuition that "Shakespeare is writing, it seems, not with the whole of his mind mobilized and under control but with feelers left flying that sport and play with words so that the trail of a chance word is caught and followed recklessly. From the echo of one word is born another word."[15] It also tallies with my own sense that Shakespeare was nothing so much as a huge mobile ear, complete with tiny legs and arms, perambulating through the streets of London, aggressively vacuuming up words by the hundreds. But if what Hughes writes in these passages are fine samples of his own spirited, hectic prose, the sort of prose that we appreciate from the *poet* Ted Hughes, his remarks tell us little about the *mythographer* Ted Hughes's subject.

That subject, it turns out, is what in hindsight Hughes recognized as the germ of *SGCB*. What happened when he pulled together his selection of Shakespeare's "top pressure poetry" (*WP*, 104) was that Hughes was struck by a "single fundamental idea," a "symbolic fable . . . which each of his plays in some form or other tells over again." "Plucking out" fragments of Shakespeare's verse judged for their "poetic intensity," Hughes happened upon Shakespeare's "great recurrent dream" (*WP*, 106; to Richard Proudfoot, Hughes wrote that he "deal[s] with the plays as if they were Shakespeare's own great dreams"; to Donya Feuer, that he wanted "to make a portrait of what a psychiatrist might call Shakespeare's Eros").[16] This defining idea, this fable which emerges into view for Hughes before he even starts to chart Shakespeare's mythic dimension, is initially "a particular knot of obsessions" (*WP*, 106). All of the busyness of the poetry enmeshed in the plays obscures what only a selection of the verse can make "nakedly plain"—and now Hughes shows his hand—"that the poetry has its taproot in a sexual dilemma of a peculiarly black and ugly sort" (*WP*, 106). This is the "cruel riddle" that neither Shakespeare nor Hughes can "rest from trying to solve. Dramatists in those days were prolific, but it was evidently something more than commissions that roused him to mount thirty-eight or more such tremendous and tormented campaigns" (*WP*, 107). And—it must be said—something more that roused the poet Ted Hughes to write hundreds of pages of prose that he suspected cost him his health—in a letter to Marina Warner, Hughes wonders whether "writing critical prose actually damages my immune system"; rather than having "refashioned" his eyesight, he found himself "in bed blind in my right eye when I was writing the chapters about the Eye in King Lear" (*Letters*, 729; August 19, 1998). Carol Hughes (Hughes's widow) confirms that "Ted poured his life blood into the work [*SGCB*]—and paid a heavy price, shingles on his scalp and into his eye . . . the aftermath bothered him on & off for the remainder of his life."[17]

What Hughes sketches out at considerable length in the rest of his introduction, and what he methodically probes in *SGCB*, is the "dark matter" (*WP*, 106) of which the great symbolic fable consists. In brief, that "knot" is the "sexual disgust" (*SGCB*, 121) that sickens Shakespeare's male protagonists (almost contemporaneously, in notes dating from 1970, John Berryman wrote of the "terrible sex nausea" first evident in *Hamlet* and surviving through *Lear* and *Timon*).[18] And the "fable" is the mythic scenario within which that nausea first worsens, then subsides. Hughes was convinced that every great plot and character in Shakespeare's writing originated in *Venus and Adonis* and *The Rape of Lucrece*. For Hughes, Shakespeare's own life (his biography), Shakespeare's times (the English Reformation), and Shakespeare's works, *all* of them, explicitly follow a rigorous trajectory enacted by the goddess of complete being in the two narrative poems (in her incarnations as mother, sacred bride, and queen of hell), in conjunction with a puritan moralist, a violent boar that metamorphoses into a murderous rapist, and a transcendental flower.

Sacred bride, boar, flower: surely this must raise literate readers' antennae. Pursuing Hughes reading Shakespeare is a demanding but salutary test of one's willingness to grant him his donnée. We are asked to follow someone who passionately fleshes out a thesis that we may find by turns unconvincing and uncongenial. But in recompense, we get to know a Hughes who is anything but naive, who deserves great credit for his willed un-suspiciousness. Hughes's generosity leads him to read Shakespeare without even the faintest whiff of skepticism, even as he conjures a Shakespeare who himself has been inoculated against doubt. Neither Hughes the reader/mythographer nor his Shakespeare is ever an ironist; neither is ever responsible for anything whatsoever that smacks of cynicism. Like the Serbian poet Vasko Popa, whom Hughes was championing in the 1960s, Shakespeare (and perhaps by implication, Hughes himself) is one among those few who "have managed to grow up to a view of the unaccommodated universe, but it has not made them cynical, they still like it and keep all their sympathies intact." Such writers manage to "precipitate out of a world of malicious negatives a happy positive" (*WP*, 222–23). There is most certainly a hell to be confronted in Hughes's Shakespeare, and there are menacing clouds (rape and murder are crucial to the "equation"), but there is no nihilism. Instead, there is relentless, if heartfelt, intensity and sincerity, even if both are probably more Hughes's than Shakespeare's.

Regarding Popa, Hughes the "Crow" poet refers to what I call sincerity as "simple animal courage" (*WP*, 222). Regarding Shakespeare's sincerity, Hughes tells us that he is a prophet and a shaman as well as a bard (*SGCB*, 85–92). When, long before *SGCB* appeared, Graham Bradshaw read the 1971 introduction to *A Choice of Shakespeare's Verse*, he noticed that for Hughes, and for Hughes's Shakespeare, skepticism is always only destructive, never even potentially healthy.[19] But if this is so, then the absence of even a trace of salubrious skepticism embeds the myth that Hughes ultimately arrives at in a sort of absolutism, if not dogmatism. There are manifold variations on his theme, but there are no genuine exceptions to it. Were it not for these variations, the whole enterprise would prove both confining and unhelpfully deductive. To be told by Hughes that he depends on a "vast *thesaurus* of a new language of signs," that there is a "purposeful *dexterity*" to his myth, that it is "an *intricate* piece of machinery" built up from a "kit of algebraic *components*," is to be reassured that while there is an "ideal order," there is also variety (*SGCB*, 19, 57, 43, 170, 190; my emphasis). But Hughes's absolutism persists. We get a sample of it at a point in the 1971 introduction where Hughes writes that "the *strongest single* determinant of a person's poetic imagination is the state of negotiations between that person and their idea of the Creator. This is *natural* enough, and *everything* else is *naturally* subordinate to it. How things are between man and his idea of Divinity determines *everything* in his life, the quality and connectedness of *every* feeling and thought, and the meaning of *every* action" (*WP*, 109; my emphasis). Even without italics, one is bound to feel the force of unwavering conviction here, conviction that both nourishes and mitigates absolutism. When Hughes reads Shakespeare he is, like Coleridge, supremely analytical, and he often brings his finely tuned poet's ear to what he calls Shakespeare's "verbal poetry" (*SGCB*, 478); still, he plunges head over heels into his relentless thesis. His mythography is pedagogical (again, compare Coleridge), and it is ethical; it is also ecstatic. Hughes reads Shakespeare as Hughes seizes Shakespeare; no wonder we cower and resist.

The man who wrote to Donya Feuer that he took it for granted that the reader of *SGCB* would be a "Shakespeare addict" first read Shakespeare from the late nineteenth-century Warwick edition that his mother gave him when he was a schoolboy at the Mexborough Grammar School. He told Richard Proudfoot that as a student he already knew "the four main tragedies by heart, and was pretty well acquainted with the rest."[20] Elaine Feinstein, one of Hughes's more recent biographers, tells us that Hughes "read and reread Shakespeare" while he served in the RAF.[21] From Cambridge, Hughes wrote to his sister Olwyn that he normally would "get up at 6, and read a Shakespeare play before 9" (*Letters*, 12; February 1952). Lucas Myers, an American who met Hughes at Cambridge, recalls that Hughes kept his "red Oxford rice paper edition of the complete works of Shakespeare in the top left hand drawer of his desk" when he worked as a reader at Pinewood Studios. He reached in to retrieve it when "he could no longer tolerate loading his mind with litter."[22] This would have been the infamous red Oxford Shakespeare to which Hughes refers in the *Birthday Letters* poem, "The Inscription." It appears to be this edition from which Hughes read Shakespeare to Plath "while she cooked their suppers" during their summer of 1956 honeymoon in Spain.[23] It might have been this edition into which, three years later, Hughes glued the "matted hairs" of a Yellowstone bear that had "lifted" his and Sylvia Plath's "larder."[24] Almost certainly, it was from this same edition that Hughes was still reading Shakespeare when in 1961 Sylvia Plath "ripped [it] to rags when happiness / Was invulnerable." ("The Inscription," *CP*, 1155). And it was unquestionably this edition that Hughes tells us was "Resurrected" ("The Inscription") in the form of another *Complete Works* that was probably given to Hughes by his lover, Assia Wevill.

These biographical traces provide a measure of evidence for Hughes's life-long devotion to Shakespeare, a devotion to which the verse anthology and then *SCGB* further testify. It may take more than the conviction that sustains Hughes's overarching fable to persuade readers that he has revealed the workings of Shakespeare's "perfect archetypal plot" (*SGCB*, 2); but that conviction is itself estimable, if not always in the eyes of those academics who have had a field day with *SGCB*. A witheringly sarcastic Terry Eagleton mocks Hughes as the Watson and Crick who has finally cracked "the Shakespearian code." Eagleton knows better: it is through "history, politics, [and] society" that we ought to "construct" Shakespeare.[25] Terence Hawkes is also dismissive of Hughes's anti-historicist universalizing (his "access to a transcendent and universally available 'human nature'") and of his "exciteable [*sic*] structuralism" ("a whole canon of texts is battened down to fit a specific template").[26] Although William Kerrigan, another academic, has reservations about Hughes's "too mythy book" and resists the "manic insistence" with which Hughes's "thesis is driven home," he allows as how it is at least "somewhat refreshing to submit myself to such unwavering belief." Moreover, while Kerrigan is most comfortable with the Hughes who examines Shakespearean particulars, he applauds him for his uncommon "Shakespeare-feel": "the capacity to think any piece of Shakespeare with all of Shakespeare in mind."[27] It fell to another poet, Tom Paulin, to sympathize unembarrassedly with Hughes's "vehement enthusiasm" and his "rhapsodic criticism." No less aware than Eagleton, Hawkes, or Kerrigan that Hughes's reading devolves into a "locked mythic patterning," Paulin finds Hughes "compelling" if not necessarily persuasive. He admires the "relentless hurrying drive" of Hughes's "communication" no less than the "unprecedented act of critical witness that spills out of an energy—a tragic energy—which has all but disappeared from current professional practice." This is so even though Paulin, too, acknowledges just how "fixed, reductive, tedious and obsessive the applied template of the myth eventually becomes."[28]

Hughes's initially mythic, eventually also tragic, equation has two literary back-stories. Unfolding in two movements conjoined by an explosive moment of transformation (a "controlled nuclear explosion" [*SGCB*, 344]), they provide

Hughes with his "key" to the "mature plays" (*SGCB*, 51). Movement one, which derives from Shakespeare's *Venus and Adonis* (1593), corresponds with Venus's desire for Adonis and his reaction to her. As Hughes's fable—if not quite Shakespeare's epyllion—has it, Adonis, although formerly Venus's apparently contented consort (see, for evidence, the Sonnets, where Southampton plays Adonis to Shakespeare's Venus), suffers an onset of what Hughes consistently calls "double vision." All of a sudden, when she approaches him, he can tolerate neither surrendering to her, nor worshiping her. In the past he had been at peace with her multiplicity (as Goddess of Complete Being), with her unified aspects as simultaneously Goddess of Love (at once mother and sacred bride, or Aphrodite) and Queen of Hell (of sex and death; hence, Persephone). However, Adonis's secularizing, moralizing, rationalizing, defensive ego prompts him to reject the daemonic part of the Goddess, by which he feels threatened. What he now finds intolerable within her, he also suspects must reside within himself. Since every figure in this scenario plays multiple roles or has multiple antecedents and offspring, we need to pause long enough to correlate Venus with the Virgin Mary, hence Adonis with Christ, her son and consort who will grow up to be the Jehovan Christ of the Reformation (who in turn does his best to demote Mary and destroy the Great Goddess). And so it goes: we are dealing with an old-style Catholic Mary/Goddess, with a suddenly R/reformed or Puritan Christ/Adonis, and, no less importantly, with a "fanatic" (*SGCB*, 90), Catholic Shakespeare, son of another Mary (Arden and Catholic). We could pause still longer, and so bring on stage Marduk (the destroyer of Tiamat, a First Mother), still another type of Adonis, but it is best simply to move on, having noted that Hughes operates, very ambitiously and simultaneously, on three levels—the inner: Shakespeare's nature; the outer: the English Reformation; and the all-embracing deep: the transcendental mythic equation. Does anyone else aspire to produce a comparably expansive reading of Shakespeare? Psychoanalytic and feminist narratives may pertain, but they are—perhaps out of timidity, perhaps modesty—considerably less ambitious.[29]

Whether Puritan fear rises up in Adonis/the hero because of what the Goddess actually does or because of a delusion on his part (see below), his double vision encourages him to split her in two and to try to reject her hellish part. Predictably, he cannot separate the woman he loves from the one he loathes any more than he can extricate himself from the loathsome part of his own soul, so he has to spurn her in all of her aspects. Rejected and enraged, she counterattacks—as Boar—and kills Adonis. No, Venus's—or the Queen of Hell's—re-embodiment as a murderous Boar is not what we "see" in *Venus and Adonis*, but then neither is another variant that Hughes pursues with only somewhat less ardor: the Boar as the irrational and inferior Rival Brother who usurps the power of his rational brother. Myth's complex root system reticulates underground. We continue to depend on Hughes's "divining rod" to track "the tunnels of the wild pig" (*SGCB*, 34).

Speaking of pigs, the Boar's "peculiarly hermaphroditic nature" gives rise to a breathtaking footnote in which Hughes describes it "as a sort of uterus on the loose—upholstered with breasts, not so much many-breasted as a mobile tub entirely made of female sexual parts, a woman-sized, multiple udder on trotters" with a mouth "like a Breughelesque nightmare vagina, baggy with over-production . . ." And, and!, as further alternately deadpan and madcap evidence for his argument, Hughes recalls that "[a]s a country boy, and the nephew of several farmers, Shakespeare enjoyed a familiarity with pigs that is not irrelevant to his myth" (*SCGB*, 11). Marina Warner shrewdly observes that Hughes himself ventriloquizes the irrational brother in footnoted "prose poem[s]" filled with "fleshy imagery," while higher up on the page, he speaks of DNA, equations, algebra, and the like in the voice of the rational brother.[30] Does the Hughes who evokes Shakespeare in rural Stratford speak for the poet laureate who spent his earliest years in the village of *Myth*olmroyd in the Yorkshire Pennines (and could what Kerrigan might call this "mythy" village name better hint at onomastic destiny—*nomen est omen*)?

Once the Boar accomplishes its murderous attack, Hughes's fable forks. In-sofar as it forecasts Shakespeare's tragedies, the murdered or possessed Adonis is reborn as Tarquin. Thus Hughes invokes the second backstory, *The Rape of Lucrece* (1594), in which Tarquin, having assaulted Lucrece (another Catholic avatar of the Goddess of Complete Being), understands that he has destroyed his own soul (this is Hughes's reading of *Lucrece*, lines 717–21). Insofar as Shake-speare's romances are concerned, Hughes moves on from what he calls the tragic to the transcendental plane. Along this alternate route, Adonis still dies, but he is absolved and redeemed and *reborn*—as the flower that springs from his blood near the end of *Venus and Adonis* (it is either a significant misreading or misremembering that allows Hughes to write that Adonis "is transformed *by Venus* into a flower" [*SGCB*, 52; my emphasis]). When Venus flies off with this flower between her breasts, the transcendental plane reopens what was closed off by the tragic plane, enabling a "death-by-the-Boar atonement and rebirth as a flower" (*SGCB*, 391). Following one fork, the Boar combines with Adonis to be-come Tarquin. Following the other, Adonis is recruited into a theophany. Either way, Adonis's agency is severely constrained. As Hughes writes, the "inevitability of the tragic idea which Shakespeare projects with such 'divine' completeness is that there is no escape from one choice or the other. Man will always choose the former [i.e., he will reject rather than submit to the Goddess], simply because once he is free of a natural, creaturely awareness of the divine indulgence which permits him to exist at all, he wants to live his own life" (*SGCB*, 393). As for submission, like Protestant grace, it is hardly even available as a choice, depending as it does on a "temporary blessing from the Goddess" (*SGCB*, 393).

We do well to remember that this chain of reflection began when Hughes was anthologizing Shakespeare's "top pressure poetry" (*WP*, 104). That astounding verse seemed to gather great force from the dark matter that is masculine sex nausea, a seminal instance of which is surely Adonis's unexpected rejection of Venus (recall that Ovid's Venus does win over Adonis). This renunciation is seminal because for Hughes, the pattern of rejection and subsequent Tarquinian attack recurs in one after another of Shakespeare's plays, more or less starting with *All's Well That Ends Well* and finally unfolding in its most complex form in *The Tempest*. Obviously, Hughes himself was a mythographer on a grand scale, and his mythography is flexible and ramifying, if it is anything. Those who begin to feel as though *Venus and Adonis* is spinning beyond recognition are focusing too narrowly on the poem's "story" to the neglect of its fable (of course this applies to the plays, *mutatis mutandis*). Such readers have forgotten the practical uses to which a busy poet/playwright puts a reusable template. And they have forgotten the way a Chaucer or a Shakespeare, a Mondrian or a Malevich (a Bach, Beethoven, or Schubert), worries a problem, works it first this way and then that, coming back to it again and again, exploring variations that just might lead to a resolution. Hughes assumes that Shakespeare fled from his wife back in Stratford-on-Avon; he maps this onto the Reformation repudiation of the Whore of Babylon and then "countersinks" the two in ancient myths of sacrifice, destruction, and (re)creation. He takes a view so long and broad (or deep) that we may not know whether to protest that anything goes or marvel that everything does. At times, we may be forgiven for feeling as though we are being subjected to what Tom Paulin calls Hughes's "Protestant guilt"—his personal guilt as well as the guilt that he feels on behalf of an England whose Reformation he is convinced has cost it its soul. Yet, when Hughes implies that this guilt is not Shakespeare's but Shakespeare's subject—that is, deeply troubled erotic relations in their political, ethical, and mythic dimensions—we may find ourselves more inclined to acquiesce to both Hughes's speculative biographizing and his unavoidable autobiographizing.

Although he never quite says so, Hughes himself seems to recognize that even putatively all-explanatory myths fail to reveal what motivates the "tragic explosion" that occurs inside of Adonis (*SGCB*, 1; subsequently inside of Angelo, Troilus, Hamlet, Othello, Lear, Timon, Leontes, *et al.*). Hughes is constrained to allow as how the "dramatic crisis, where Adonis becomes Tarquin, happens between the poems and not within them" (*SGCB*, 213). Off-stage. Out of sight. Unreported. Even on stage, in the plays, where the explosion takes place right before our eyes (think of Hamlet with Gertrude and Ophelia, of Lear with Cordelia, of Othello with Desdemona, of Leontes with Hermione), myth fails to explain immediate motive. In passing, Hughes notes that Shakespeare's "heroes loathe the Female because they loved her (and love her) too well . . . in some other, mythic dimension" (*SGCB*, 179). For an explicator with Hughes's amplitude and precision, this is tentative, and it is hardly explanatory. Because myth is ill-equipped to explain motive, or because motive tends to diminish myth, the combustible moments disclose a Hughesian Shakespeare unexpectedly prone "to *de*mythologize and even to secularize the whole dreadful complex" (*SGCB*, 212; my emphasis). At such moments, "Shakespeare translated the Mother and Father of all mythic conflicts—conflict between Goddess religion and Goddess-destroyer in all its ramifications—back into psychological terms, or rather back into the psycho-biological human mystery from which the religions and myth spring in the first place" (*SGCB*, 212–13). Although it may appear otherwise, Hughes is telling us that the "taproot" is neither psychology nor biology. It is "mystery." The source resists specification or reduction. It remains ineffable. For although Hughes would probably disagree, what else in the way of ultimate sourcing can we say about Macbeth than that his are "black and deep desires" (1.4.51), or about Gertrude, save that within her are "black and grained spots" (4.2.90)? Iago tells us straight out, "Demand me nothing. What you know, you know" (5.2.303). As we have seen, Hughes willingly foregoes the "upper temple complex of the realistic Shakespeare" for the "crypts and catacombs" of the mythic Bard (*SGCB*, 39). Indeed. But this only confirms that although Hughes is adept at answering "what" and "how," he is less able to say "why." To which in fairness it ought to be said that what for Hughes is a "knot of obsession" is for Shakespeare himself a "knot intrinsicate" (*Antony and Cleopatra*, 5.2.304).

Hughes the structuralist is committed to the "sequential unfolding" of Shakespeare's mature plays (*SGCB*, 43). Hughes the mythographer banks on their "ideal order," if not precisely the order that academic Shakespeareans assign to the plays (*SGCB*, 190). For example, the "seven tragedies divide naturally into two groups," and the first "group of four divides again into two groups of two" (*SGCB*, 227). It is hardly surprising that someone whose entire account of Shakespeare is predicated on an equation and two "patterns" (*SGCB*, 247) should arrive at a perfectly chiasmic reading according to which *Venus and Adonis* is a Catholic "source-myth" interpreted "from a Puritan point of view" and *Lucrece* is a Puritan "source-myth" interpreted "from a Catholic point of view" (*SGCB*, 83). This equipoise neatly corresponds with the Elizabethan moment, in which "the new Puritan spirit and the old Catholic spirit . . . were deadlocked" (*SGCB*, 75). But it complicates the picture of Shakespeare the "secret and passionate" Catholic, because Hughes also imagines a Shakespeare who is intellectually and sympathetically able to occupy contending positions (*SGCB*, 77). This versatile, ambidextrous Shakespeare is an artist who is for Hughes nothing less than a (Puritan) prophet *and* a (Catholic) shaman. The former, like the great Greek tragedians, embodies "a vision of sacred man, or of falling and fallen man in a sacred universe. Or of rational man confronting and challenging a sacred universe. In both the Greek world and Shakespeare's the archaic reign of the Great Goddess was being put down, finally and decisively, by a pragmatic, skeptical, moralizing, desacralizing spirit" (*SGCB*, 85). The latter, the shamanic Shakespeare, "gathers up the whole tradition of the despairing [Catholic/Goddess] group, especially the very earliest mythic/religious traditions, with all the circumstances of their present sufferings, into a messianic, healing, redemptive vision on the spiritual plane" (*SGCB*, 89). While this may seem like a lot to take on board, its structure, at least, should be familiar. The Shakespeare who is at one and the same time a "prophetic shaman of the Puritan revolution" and "a visionary, redemptive shaman of the Catholic" (*SGCB*, 91) remains the highly recognizable, omni-competent Shakespeare who stands for both/and. Here, in one of his many incarnations, is Coleridge's "myriad-minded" Shakespeare, the playwright whose approach to experience was founded on "complementarity," the Shakespeare "on both sides . . . equal and entire" (*SGCB*, 92).[31] It may take Ted Hughes hundreds of pages to unfold the sequence, but mature Shakespeare solves his own equation from the start, always, even "simultaneously, [writing] on the transcendental and tragic planes" (*SGCB*, 455).[32]

Shamanic and prophetic Shakespeare constitutes big-stakes Hughes analysis. But a very fine example of (apparently) lesser-stakes Hughes correlates equally well with the stock, both-sides-at-once Shakespeare that we have just encountered. Working in this instance not back down toward Earth from high up in the "sacred universe," but instead attentively and imaginatively reading the verses on the page, Hughes fixes on what the Greeks, George Puttenham, and subsequent rhetoricians call hendiadys. In the best academic discussion of Shakespearean hendiadys of which I am aware, George T. Wright reminds us that for the Latin grammarian Servius, hendiadys entailed "the use of two substantives, joined by a conjunction . . . to express a single but complex idea." It literally means "one through two," and it is all over *Hamlet* (there are at least sixty-six instances, by Wright's count).[33] Familiar examples include "the book and volume of my brain" (1.5.103), "the grace and blush of modesty" (3.4.41), or "this solidity and compound mass" (3.4.49). According to Frank Kermode, there is "a kind of unnaturalness in the[se] doubling[s]."[34] Wright points to the ways they make for "a deliberate violation of clear sense" (173). Because it blurs meaning, and especially when it keeps coming at us, hendiadys in *Hamlet* makes us feel "uneasy" (175); it functions not to resolve but to assert ambiguity (182).

Hughes sees things differently. To begin with, he approaches Shakespearean hendiadys the way he would approach a "riddle," a riddle that is, just like a miniature "Shakespearean moment" (*SGCB*, 1), "explosive."[35] Thus, in *All's Well that Ends Well*, when we read, "On the catastrophe and heel of pastime" (1.2.57), we need to puzzle out how a catastrophe is like a heel is like a pastime, how a pastime is like a heel, a heel like a catastrophe, and so on (*SGCB*, 144). It is as if a heel "could experience a nightmare, and like some kind of aerial receive and transmit all the tragedies possible to man" (*ES*, 32). A riddle, yes, but it is also a "gadget" (*ES*, 32), akin to Auden's verbal contraption: "a spark sets these two otherwise utterly freed and unrelated worlds of reference ["catastrophe" and "heel"] spinning around 'pastime' like electrons around a nucleus" (*ES*, 32). For Hughes, then, hendiadys is a sign of Shakespeare the "complicator" (*ES*, 27). If, for Kermode, hendiadys signals linguistic "tension or strain" (101), and if, for Wright, it warns us "how uncertain and treacherous language can be" (176), for Hughes, its "hybridization and crossbreeding" are signs of its "vigor," its "genetic resource[fulness]" (*ES*, 27). Treating hendiadys like a "hieroglyphic text" in the introduction to *Essential Shakespeare*, like what he aptly calls a "cryptoglyph" in *SGCB* (149), Hughes deems each instance of the figure "a sort of fractal of the whole play" in which it appears (*ES*, 35). It is at once exquisitely engineered, and it is "homemade, improvised." It "has a ramshackle air, like a prodigiously virtuoso pidgin" (*ES*, 35). To Ann Pasternak Slater and Craig Raine, Hughes wrote that such "pairing" could have the "effect on the reader" of "a momentary 'satori'—as they used to say in the Sixties" (*Letters*, 583; August 14, 1990, sounding for a moment like Allen Ginsberg on his "hydrogen jukebox"). Shakespeare's capacity to contain multitudes quickens a flash of spiritual understanding and correlates directly with Hughes's instinct to see the whole in all of its parts.

Beyond the formal and mystical competence of hendiadys lie political purposes consistent with the "both/and" or integrative aspirations of Hughes's

Shakespeare. Hendiadys, which is but one element in Shakespeare's "language of the common bond" (*ES*, 20), provides Hughes with evidence of Shakespeare's "masterful democratization of high language and low" (*ES*, 26). Hence it is anything but coincidental that this hendiadian language "arrived at the same moment as the Mythic Equation" (*SGCB*, 148): at both the micro- and macro-levels, Shakespeare expresses his "ethical concern . . . for an imaginative synthesis" (*ES*, 26). Anything but ambiguous, hendiadys, like the equation, points to harmonic patterning. The route that Hughes follows to this conclusion, while it is based on limited evidence and incomplete theater history, is worth following. The playwright who has it within him to inhabit the spirit of residual Catholicism *and* emergent Protestantism serves up language fit for the "educated aristocracy" *and* "the lowest pickpocket's 'trug'" in his audiences (*SGCB*, 139). His proto-democratic medium effects a linguistic resolution to psychic and social conflicts re-experienced by England's late twentieth-century Poet Laureate. By means of hendiadys, Shakespeare conjoins a new, recherché, high, or Latinate word with a familiar, low, English or Celtic word. Through his "little mechanism of translation," Shakespeare hands "catastrophe" up to "the Lords' enclosure" and "heel" down to the "nut-cracking crowd on the floor of the house" (*SGCB*, 143). This is to "mix and amalgamate" meaning (*SGCB*, 147). By condensing an entire play, a historical juncture, and a "sacred, mythic system" into a witty figure, Shakespeare models a kind of ethics of linguistics. Where Wright sees poetic "improvisation" that leads to "confusion" (171), Hughes sees "a crisis of improvisation" ("extempore, unpredictable . . . snatched and grabbed out of the listener's ears, his shirt front, his top pocket, his finger ends") that "illuminates that vast inner consistency of Shakespeare's articulated, noble system" (*SGCB*, 152).

Improvisation, consistency, and system. From *All's Well* to *The Tempest*, Hughes ascribes to Shakespeare a system that he insists is indisputably the playwright's own, its variations no less than its rules. An ungenerous way to say this is that Hughes conscripts Shakespeare to his own systems; where Hughes happens upon an exception, he reenvisions it as a variation (*Macbeth* and *Timon* provide striking variations). Short of taking Shakespeare moment by moment, and only moment by moment, it is hard to say how we can escape at least some degree of codification. It is just that Hughes persistently goads us to ask, "How much is too much?" One answer seems to be that a book on Shakespearean negotiation (say, Stephen Greenblatt's almost contemporaneous *Shakespearean Negotiations*) goes down more smoothly than one on a Shakespearean equation.[36] Myth has lost much of its purchase among academic Shakespeareans. Their accounts are, in most of their varieties, deeply suspicious of universalizing, especially from a masculinist point of view. Hughes universalizes, and writes from a man's point of view, even if his entire equation stems from a repudiated Ur-misogyny (the inaugural rejection of the Goddess). Laudably or vainly, Hughes is determined to see Shakespeare whole. This is how he fathoms the pattern, the archetypal plot, the substratum, the system. It enables him to recognize variations and corrections, newly emergent formulations and, preeminently, moments of transcendence.

To dwell on systems and equations, however, is to miss what is for Hughes a still more important matter. Recent, stimulating accounts of Shakespeare have been interested in the efficacy of his plays. They assess the theater's rambunctiousness, its penchant for endorsing the powers that be, or its ameliorative aspirations.[37] Hughes, too, writes about efficacy. But for him, Shakespeare's "passive ritual drama serves as something more than a communally organized social bonding." Shakespeare's drama "acts as a natural form of deep therapy, where the mythic plane holds the key to health, vitality, meaningfulness and psychic freedom on the outer plane [that is, the "realistic plane" where we are at best "half alive"]" (*SGCB*, 106). On a dramaturgical level, the logic of myth delivers Shakespeare's plots to satisfying endings that might otherwise, according to the logic of genre and heterosexual desire (what Hughes calls "human motivation"), feel arbitrary rather than inevitable (*SGCB*, 114). This is something many readers and playgoers can ratify. Because myth operates through and in the service of ritual, however, Hughes insists that it has healing power. By the time Shakespeare arrives at *The Tempest*, he has "solved the never-before-solved tragic problem of the Mythic Equation" (*SGCB*, 436). The predominant Shakespearean arc that Hughes plots with his equation has, then, a visionary aspect well in excess of its analytical coordinates. And Hughes invites us to put this aspect to the test.

As I have noted, the equation is first rehearsed offstage, in Shakespeare's two long narrative poems. It is set in motion on stage in what, since Frederick S. Boas, we often call the "problem-plays" (in Hughes's order, *All's Well That Ends Well*, then *Measure for Measure*, then *Troilus and Cressida*).[38] In *All's Well*, Shakespeare is first gripped by the equation. As it happens, this is also "the last play which is free from sexual disgust and it immediately precedes plays that are overwhelmed with a horror of sexual disease" (*SGCB*, 121). The arc reaches its terrible apogee in the major tragedies, in *King Lear* in particular, still more precisely in that play's "Down from the waist they are centaurs" speech (4.6.124). If there is more visceral evidence of sexual nausea in Shakespeare than Lear's "Fie, fie, fie! Pah, pah!" (4.6.129–30), then it only can be Othello's "cistern for

foul toads" (4.2.61). But the redemptive work that the Fool, Tom, and Cordelia perform on Lear transfigures this temporarily Adonis-turned-Tarquin into
an Adonis-turned-"saint on the transcendental plane" (*SGCB*, 261). Cordelia
may not survive the play but, unlike her antecedents—Lucrece, Ophelia, and
Desdemona among them—she lives long enough to transform the Adonis who
rejects her. *Antony and Cleopatra* furnishes the bridge to transcendence—that
is, to the romances and to the "solution of the Tragic Equation" (*SGCB*, 319)
that they enable. Shakespeare's reconfiguration of the Dido and Aeneas story sets
tragedy and transcendence into dialectical relation with one another; following
Hughes's metaphor, *Antony and Cleopatra* doubly exposes the two planes, or
superimposes the latter on the former (*SGCB*, 302). Antony on the tragic plane
is Roman, Herculean, Tarquinian. The redeemed Antony is Egyptian, and he
is Osirian (unconditionally in love with his Cleopatra/Isis but beset by Caesar/
Set). (As Hughes cannily observes, Eros is to Antony/Osiris as Enobarbus is
to Antony/Hercules [*SGCB*, 318].) Having crossed the bridge, Shakespeare is
ready to stage theophanic redemptions in which the tragic hero, he who rejected
the Goddess and was attacked by the Boar, is reborn not as Tarquin but as
Flower. Indeed, by the time he arrives at *The Tempest* (by way of Leontes, among
others), Shakespeare is ready to let on as how the equation has all along entailed
a paradox: Tarquin and the Tragic Equation alongside the Flower and transcendence constitute a paradox, not alternatives (*SGCB*, 455). Better still, with
Prospero having hunted the Boar/Caliban right "out of the Complete Works,"
the equation finally can be said to have been "dismantled" (*SGCB*, 462 and
469). For it is Prospero who "dismantles the crime of the usurping brother by
bringing Alonso and Antonio ashore helplessly at his mercy. . . . He dismantles
the double vision . . . [by separating] the loved and the loathed. . . . He has
purged himself of any shadow of the Boar, . . . rendered it impotent to harm
either his own rationality or Miranda's virginity, . . . subjugated it to slavery,
as Caliban. . . . And again, by sealing the betrothal of Miranda and Ferdinand
within the Masque, . . . he seems to have ensured that the double vision shall
not detonate the Tarquinian madness for Ferdinand, and that the Boar shall not
topple them into the inferno of the Equation" (*SGCB*, 469–70).

The first thing to be said about this ellipsis-laced quotation is that it is a
fair sample of five hundred pages of Hughes reading Shakespeare. Second, it
speaks again about efficacy and testifies to Hughes's deep convictions. One can
hardly escape feeling that Hughes himself has a profound stake in the healing
that he so wants Shakespearean drama to effect. Responding to his investment
in ritual, I emphasize "healing"; but Hughes always proffered another, equally

fervent, version of his story, one that is more juridical than therapeutic. First in the 1971 *Essential Shakespeare* introduction, then in a variety of his letters, and again in *SCGB*, Hughes imagines a momentous trial. Together, Hughes and Shakespeare litigate "the inevitable crime of Civilization, or even the inevitable crime of consciousness." This, the crime of the Reformation, puts Adonis "in the dock, accused, and Justice is being sought (by Shakespeare) for the different cultural tradition behind the outcry of his victim, the plaintiff, who speaks for the rejected (assaulted, murdered, escaped from murder) Goddess" (*SGCB*, 43).[39] Whether as ritual or trial, the *Complete Works* carries an enormous burden for Hughes. Like Edgar, Shakespeare aims to sweeten ("Sweet marjoram" [4.6.93]) what Tom Paulin calls the "stink" of "Protestant guilt." Still more ambitiously, Shakespeare just *might* help us to cleanse Civilization, with a capital C.

"Might" occasions a third observation about the lines that I have quoted, even as it recalls Hughes's integrity and reminds us of the still felt, late twentieth-century exigency of his enterprise. Hughes scrupulously admits his uncertainty (though not skepticism): Prospero only "*seems* to have ensured that the double vision shall not detonate." This, I think, is Hughesian fear, not irony; and it is a fear that Hughes ascribes to late Shakespeare, too (*SGCB*, 487). It is to acknowledge that because Prospero cannot reconcile the "loved and the loathed," he must sunder them. And Hughes is anything but blind to Prospero's dyspepsia. Caliban, "who was ready to love Prospero as much as he lusted for Miranda, and for whom the heavens open (and who weeps when they close), and who speaks the poetry of the natural world, possesses a sensibility and a nature that makes his master's seem stale and sour" (*SGCB*, 497). Still more to his credit, Hughes undermines the unreconstructed structuralist's fetish for tidy systems when, for all that he wants the equation to be solved, transcended, or dismantled, he worries aloud what would come to pass were Florizel (for whom we may also read Ferdinand) suddenly to "see the double vision and start everything over again" (*SGCB*, 410). In the final, sentence-long paragraph of the main text of *SGCB*, Hughes warns us that "the Boar is at large" (499) in Shakespeare's England and hardly less so in Hughes's.[40]

Although it gestated for twenty years, and although the Emory University collection includes a series of marvelous, elaborate, large folio-sized diagrams in which Hughes maps and remaps the equation's origins in *Venus and Adonis* and *Lucrece* (fig. 7.1), *SGCB* still feels like a convulsive outburst. The marginalia in neither Hughes's copy of the Signet *King Lear* (1963) nor in his Collins Clear-

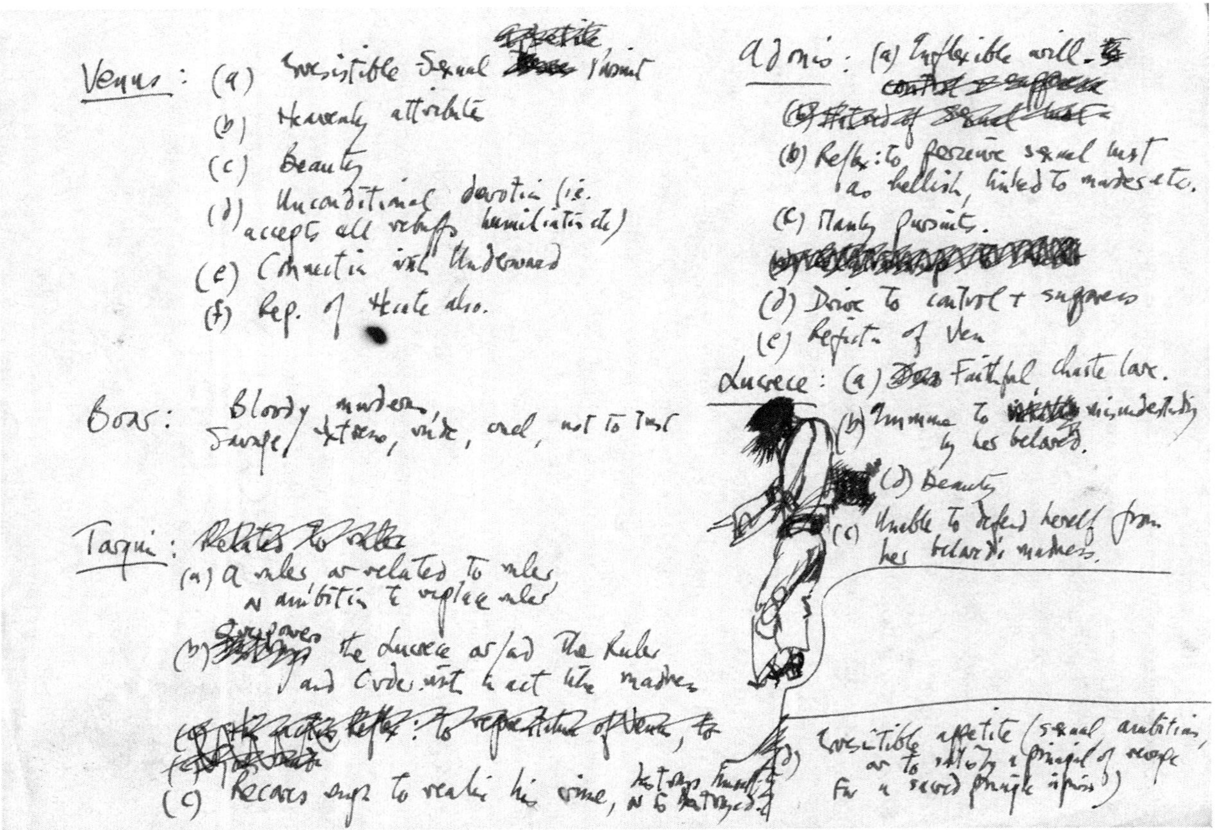

Figure 7.1: Ted Hughes's *Venus and Adonis* notes. Ted Hughes Collection (MSS 644). Courtesy of the Manuscripts, Archives, and Rare Book Library, Emory University. By permission of the copyright holder, Carol Hughes. Images of MS details © Estate of Ted Hughes and reprinted by permission of the Estate.

Type Press edition of *The Complete Works of William Shakespeare* (1923), both at Emory, do not even hint at Hughes the mythographer. (The inscription in Hughes's hand on the page facing the inside front cover of the Collins *Complete Works* reads, "Edward James Hughes," then faintly but again in purple ink, "1/1/49," and then in black ink, "Poet Laureate." Hughes succeeded John Betjeman as laureate in December 1984. I cannot say when he was marking up this edition.) Hughes's comments are mostly run of the mill. The Great Goddess is nowhere to be seen. Marginal Hughes is a realist and a psychologist. He is also a fine doodler—stylized heads and distorted human figures, along with line drawings of animals, spill over onto the columns of print. Perhaps these are a repository for the myths that govern *SGCB* and that inform Hughes's poems.

Still, for the most part, it is difficult to imagine anything more prosaic than what we find in Hughes's handwriting in the *Lear* paperback. He fills the inside front and back covers with a list of locations, starting with 1.1 and heading right through to the end of Act 5 (for example: "act I s. I Lear's Palace"; "s. II Edmund + Glos. at G's castle"; etc.). Between those covers, Hughes underlines hundreds of lines, sometimes in black ink, sometimes in blue, sometimes with red vertical lines down the side. He underlines Cordelia's two "nothings" and Lear's responses (1.1.89–92). To the right, he pens in "Dumbness." While this smidgen of commentary may hint at "the radiant dumbness of the truth" in *SGCB* (278), another snippet of Hughes's marginalia, just an inch further down the page, describes the gulf between Hughes the reader of the moment and the magnum-opus Hughes. To the right of Cordelia's "I love your Majesty / According to my bond, no more nor less" (1.1.94–95), Hughes writes "pedantry of." It is a long way from this sort of disparagement to the paragraph in *SGCB* in which Hughes equates Cordelia with Shakespeare's "worship . . . of simplicity. . . . Simplicity as the breath of the locked-up word of Divine Truth" (278).

There is a comparable distance between the Hughes we encounter in the margins of the Collins *Measure for Measure* and the Hughes of *SGCB*, where Angelo appears as an early incarnation of Adonis/Tarquin and Isabella as Venus/Lucrece. In his copy of the *Complete Works*, Hughes's Isabella has none of the hallmarks of his equation's Venus. Instead, she has the complex cognitive faculties and the conscience that myth-resistant readers attribute to her. Where Isabella tries to persuade the deputy to spare her brother, Hughes annotates: "She is on Angelo's side: is persuading herself: a self-deception. Argument rings hollow." Like "pedantry," this last phrase reveals the disparity between the mythographer and psychologist, a disparity evident in Hughes, if not in Hughes's Shakespeare ("I make the distinction . . . between great realistic poets, and great mythic poets—and define Shakespeare as a unique combination of the two" [*Letters*, 608; April 15, 1992, to A. L. Rowse]). The gap seems to close somewhat at the top of the next page, where Hughes, calling Angelo "Puritanical," foreshadows the Angelo required by the mythic equation, but it widens once again when, beside Angelo's first great, electrifying soliloquy, Hughes writes, "rationalizes his temptation." At the end of *Othello*, Hughes fills at least half of a blank page with unexceptionable, uninspired fragments ("Iago control figure"; "Not compelled by passion"; "Othello never loses our sympathy"; and "Simple child-heroism"; etc. [fig. 7.2]). The Hughes who annotates Angelo and Regan and Iago aligns more closely with Charles Dickens than Robert Graves.

Of course, there is no reason to think that it was Hughes's responsibility or intention either to entertain or to enlighten us in his jottings in his Shakespeare editions. If there are times when he catches us up—admiring Regan's "poise" at the end of *Lear* 2.1, or using the blank, bottom half of the page at the end of *Richard 3* to toss off a stunning apothegm—"[M]orality was an impulse not a system in Shakespeare"—more often than not, Hughes is simply underlining or doodling. Somewhat more surprising, in light of the widely acknowledged mythic dimensions of Hughes's poetry, is the fact that few Ted Hughes poems that refer explicitly to Shakespeare betray the mind-set that gives us *SGCB*. For Neil Corcoran, many of the preoccupations of *Crow* (1970), *Gaudete* (1977), and *Cave Birds* (1978) may be "comparable" to those Hughes found in Shakespeare, but there is very little correlation.[41] We might be primed for a dose of mythography in the *Lupercal* (1960) poem entitled "Cleopatra to the Asp" (*CP*, 87), but it is nowhere to be seen. For its part, "Prospero and Sycorax" (*CP*, 576) has a decidedly psychological, almost characterological, not mythological cast. Perhaps a more telling example is "An Alchemy" (*CP*, 279–82), an uncollected *Crow* poem that was first published in 1973, in Graham Fawcett's *Poems for Shakespeare 2*. Hughes's penchant for seeing the *Complete Works* whole is reflected in approximately sixty broken lines that skip from Aaron the Moor to Tamora, then to Lucrece, then Leontes, Angelo, Adonis, Richard, the Boar, an Ass, Titania, Hal, Portia, Moses's Serpent, Falstaff the Knight of Venus, Caesar, Helena the Healer, Ophelia, Othello, and Gertrude. This accounts for just the first third of the poem. The staccato articulation and the fleet cameos played by the "Boar's Moons," "Moon-browed Isis," Lilith, and Tiamat make for a Morse code articulation of the dense, critical Shakespeare tome to come. Poetic conventions license a pulsing series of abrupt juxtapositions ("Desdemona rising / The Nun of Vienna / From killing her swine"; "The lineal Boar / Who darkened darkness / And an Ass's horn / To gore Titania") that ignite unexpected sparks of

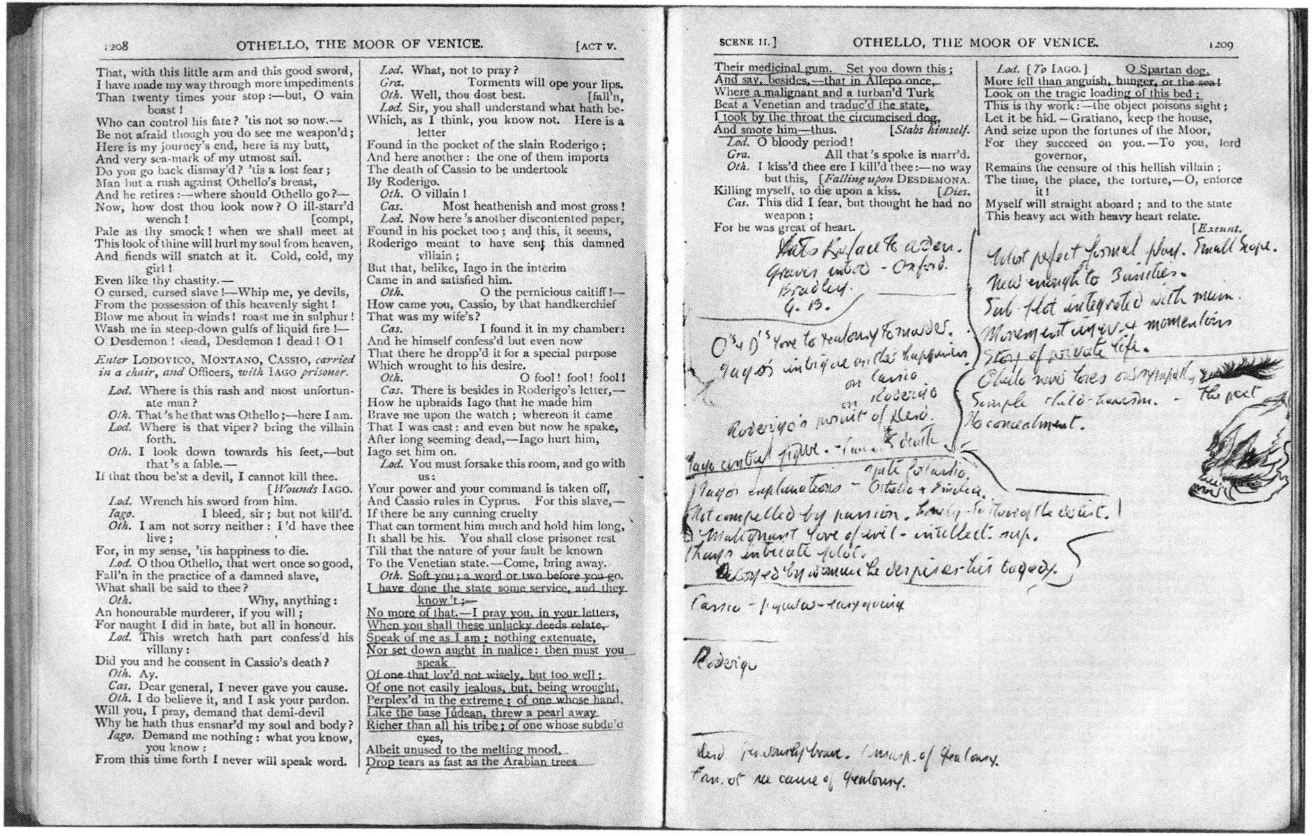

Figure 7.2: Ted Hughes's *Othello* marginalia. Ted Hughes Collection (MSS 644). Courtesy of the Manuscripts, Archives, and Rare Book Library, Emory University. By permission of the copyright holder, Carol Hughes. Images of MS details © Estate of Ted Hughes and reprinted by permission of the Estate.

association across the entire canon. But the careful ligatures that bind plots and characters into full-blown mythography would have to await *SGCB*, which, it so happens, lacks an index. It would have been a maddening job to produce one, but I like to think that some twenty years beforehand, Hughes had compiled an abbreviated poetic index to his then unwritten prose in "An Alchemy."

Given that Hughes himself acknowledged that in *Birthday Letters* (1998) he turned more confessional than in any of his prior verse, it is not surprising that the uses to which he puts *The Tempest* in the poem "Setebos" (*CP*, 1128–29) are more domestic (hence realistic) than mythic.[42] The question, "Who could play Miranda?" opens the poem. The answer is Sylvia. Ferdinand? "Only me," writes Hughes. Sylvia's mother, Aurelia Plath, comes on stage as Prospero. Later, Sylvia's father Otto appears as King Minos. The first stanza may tacitly correspond with the idyll that precedes Adonis's onset of "double vision" in *SGCB*—"Ariel / Entertained us night and day"; Caliban "showed us / The sweetest, the freshest, the wildest / And loved us as we loved"—but when a tempest disrupts the second stanza, Caliban "Revert[s] to type" and "the loved and the loathed" (*SGCB*, 469) retreat to their opposed corners. By the last lines of the poem, Hughes, in the form of Caliban (and the jester Trinculo and Lear on the heath, too), having "crawled / Under a gabardine, hugging tight / All I could of me," trembles beneath the "thunder and lightning" of Sycorax's laughter and the "bounding thunderbolt" that is "Prospero's head" hurtling down toward him. According to Hughes's retrospective account in "Setebos" (if not that of numerous Plath partisans), Ferdinand mercifully does not turn into Tarquin. But neither is there a theophany anywhere in sight.

A suite of thirteen Shakespeare poems collectively entitled "A Full House" and first published in an anthology entitled *Poems for Shakespeare* (1987; *CP*, 731–36) is noteworthy for its tone. Hughes is less earnest in this series than in *SGCB*, but he also turns sarcastic, bordering on caustic.[43] Readers of *SGCB* will recognize Venus in the first poem in the sequence ("Queen of Hearts"): she is "Venereal, uterine heat. / Smothering breast-fruit." But Adonis is reduced to a gasping "poor boy." When a "scythe-tusked boar" jumps out from under Venus's "skirts" his "mortal frailty" to tear, the boar takes the form of a cartoonish "Daddy . . . the god of war."[44] Then, in the last of this short poem's three stanzas, as in a number of the poems in "A Full House," a decidedly un-shamanic Shakespeare makes an appearance. In this case, "Willy's blood" (again cartoonishly?) in a "shower / Of fertiliser" nurtures the flower into which the "poor boy" morphs. Although it is difficult to determine Hughes's tone here, some sort of diminution must be signaled when Zeus and Christ devolve into "Willy." In

"King of Hearts," Hughes may evoke the supreme "God, Her / Of triple power," but he imagines Shakespeare as an unimposing, bourgeois Lear (or Gloucester), devising his will. Absent from this picture is *SGCB*'s Lear as "saintly imbecile" and sign of "Shakespeare's mythic intuition" (*SGCB*, 463–64). While cartooning, which is entirely foreign to *SGCB*, is by no means the predominant mode of "A Full House," it does mark the difference between what might be called a Hughes Shakespeare poem and his Shakespeare prose. We see this as well in "King of Spades": after Tarquin rapes Lucrece, in Humpty Dumpty fashion "Kingship itself / Was tumbled down." "The bubble of State / We see from this / Balloons from lips / That were made to kiss." Even if this is a helium, not a graphic, balloon, irony and wit have replaced prose-Hughes's urgency.

The matter of prose tone in contrast to verse tone carries over to the way Hughes addresses a final, distinguishing, both/and aspect of Shakespearean characterization. I am thinking of Shakespeare's Cleopatra, who can be both "my chuck" and a "great fairy," a "dame" or a "lass" or even a "strumpet" and yet the "serpent of old Nile"; also Shakespeare's Antony, who is both a "workman" and a "Herculean Roman," a "fool" and a "demi-Atlas." This is the Elizabethan hodgepodge that Shakespeare found so congenial and staged so convincingly. It is the characterological version of the sociolinguistic "common bond" that Hughes celebrates. But in his *SGCB*, Hughes sorts, he does not mingle; he sets aside the realistic so that he can concentrate on the mythic. Whereas Hughes's pursuit in *SGCB* is high-pitched and hermetic, in those of his poems in which Shakespeare figures, he is apt to turn colloquial or domestic, even indulgent (see "Ophelia," *CP*, 655). In his Hughesian prose incarnations, Othello is a Puritan Adonis, the Boar, and a "hot tyrant." For her part, "Desdemona takes on the two aspects of Sacred Bride and Divine Mother" (*SGCB*, 232). When we turn to "Knave of Spades," the tenth poem in "A Full House," we learn that Othello is a "fellow" and a "chap," and that Desdemona is "A light, light lass." I have raised the possibility that for Hughes to have explored motivation would have been for him to lessen the import, and the trans-historical resonance, of myth. Would a "lass" Desdemona lessen the ferocity of *SGCB*, even though a "lass" Cleopatra contributes to her "infinite variety"? Atop her monument, at a moment of theophanic apotheosis ("The crown of the earth doth melt" [4.15.64; see *SGCB*, 313–19]), Cleopatra is secure enough about her ambitions to mock them ("Wishers were ever fools" [4.15.38]). Although full of generosity and intensity, Hughes's monumental mythic embrace of Shakespeare typically lacks Cleopatra's, and so Shakespeare's, self-confidence. Not that poking fun at ourselves and our most cherished convictions comes easily to any of us, whether or not we are poets. Maybe it is just that Keats, who brings to his encounters with Shakespeare his own brand of enthusiasm and urgency, sets the bar high for those who follow him. Keats identifies himself with Antony and Cleopatra when he writes to J. H. Reynolds that Shakespeare "overwhelms a genuine Lover of Poesy with all manner of abuse."[45] This is, as I have said, at once self-inflating and self-deprecating; it is tinged with sadomasochism and silliness. Ted Hughes may have felt too vulnerable to risk foolishness in his commentary on Shakespeare. He knew that he would be (and he was) exposed to academic abuse because *SGCB* unembarrassedly reveals the breadth and depth of his joint allegiance to Shakespeare and to the Goddess of Complete Being *without* the protective shield of poetic license. As Hughes wrote to Seamus Heaney in 1998, "I sometimes wondered if that Shakes [*sic*] tome wasn't the poem I should have written—decoded, hugely deflected and dumped on the shoulders [of poetry?] that could carry it." (*Letters*, 704). Instead, with *SGCB*, Hughes took a risk that Keats's fairy mythology never required him to take.

CONCLUSION

If each writer canvassed in *The Great William: Writers Reading Shakespeare* arrived at different ratios of how to what—dwelling now on how Shakespeare says something, now on what he is saying—the *how* often took precedence. This is unsurprising. When Berryman says that he has "been sort of untouched by Shakespeare," he must be thinking of Shakespeare's *what*, because the Shakespearean *how* both consumed him and was immensely useful to him. Workmanship, method, technique, *poiesis*, prosody, these are the things that working writers contend with, and so are alert to, all of the time. Yes, when they read Shakespeare, they may occasionally be nonplussed. We have heard Keats lament that Shakespeare "left nothing to say about nothing or any thing"; Woolf asked "Why then [after Shakespeare] should anyone else attempt to write?"; and Berryman wrote to Mark Van Doren that work on his edition of *King Lear* "ruins me altogether for anything else." But in one way or another, Shakespeare usually comes across to writers as a lavish toolkit or an overflowing reservoir. He is a formidable but generous patron, even if Shakespeare the man often slips from sight. For Coleridge, at the same time that Shakespeare remains forever himself, he is an inhumanly disparate form—he "becomes all things." Hughes, who conjures a vividly imagined Shakespeare (starting with the "country boy" who knew his way around pigs) writing at a highly charged historical moment, is nonetheless mostly preoccupied with Shakespeare the shaman and prophet, a conduit for myth and ritual but hardly the subject of a biography. Even Ginsberg's Shakespeare, who apparently was beholden to an exasperated "boyfriend," recedes into the breadth of his poetic line and the minute particulars of his imagery. There are moments for Keats, and for Coleridge in particular, when Shakespeare stands for innate "universality" or for "some great & general truth inherent in human nature"; but when they are reading, typically, and appropriately for these writers, Shakespeare the man yields center stage to his diction and syntax, his verse and his prose. What holds sway are the "the volley & volume . . . of his words" (Woolf), his "virtuoso pidgin" (Hughes).

W. H. Auden addresses this more or less artificial method/matter distinction when he notes that the "basic assumptions in Shakespeare do not change very much. What does continually change is the development of his verse."[1] This is striking because on Wednesday evenings for eight successive months, Auden had been interpreting what he calls the "assumptions" of one play after the next, paying attention almost exclusively to the Shakespearean *what*.[2] It was only on Saturday afternoons, and only during the spring term, that he zeroed in on words and phrases; and even then, he commented more as a philologist than a poet.[3] And yet, like Charles Olson, Auden could present a clear, developmental account of Shakespeare's verse styles. He explains that early on, the plays are both Marlovian and lyrical. But soon, characters arise who do not fit these styles, so Shakespeare begins to explore "a new freedom with the *caesura* as well as with actual imagery" (315). Shakespeare deepens his prose style, and in time it "reacts back upon the verse" (315).[4] A "middle style" emerges in *2 Henry 4*. "Broken and shortened lines" now give actors "the opportunity to gesture. . . . It is a gestured verse" (317). What follows is Shakespeare's "maturest," still more free style, alone answerable to his most "subtle characters" (317–18). Auden appreciates Shakespeare's "fabulously good taste for words," his increasing use of "one part of speech as another," and his freedom with "mixed metaphors" (318). In the late works (which Auden compares to those of Milton, Ibsen, Verdi, Beethoven, and Goya), he finds an "enormous interest in particular kinds of artistic problems lovingly worked out for themselves, regardless of the interest of the whole work" (271). What catches Auden's attention are not the climaxes in these plays but "bridge passages" whose "virtues are virtues for the real connoisseur" (271). Marvelous "bye-writing" is what Keats called them. From these, "a writer wanting to learn his trade can find out how to write verse by studying them" (272).

I do not mean to suggest that writers who read Shakespeare are solely connoisseurs of exquisite craftsmanship.[5] In the "The Shakespearian City" section of *The Dyer's Hand and Other Essays* (1963) and in the lectures from which I have just quoted, Auden is a moralist, a philosopher, and a psychologist. If he is a formalist, it is only in the sense conveyed by these lines from his 1939 review of Mark Van Doren's *Shakespeare*: "in Shakespeare poetry and life are one. If we do not like poetry, he can mean nothing to us whatsoever. In the true sense of the word 'pure,' he is the purest poet who ever lived; that is to say, he explored all life through a single medium, that of language. His range of curiosity was unlimited, but he confined himself to one mode of understanding, the poetic. All the other ways of organizing experience, philosophical belief, or scientific research he never touched and gave no sign of wishing to touch. The dyer's hand was completely immersed in what it worked in."[6] For Auden, form and matter are spliced together, even if they almost never have perfectly equal values. Ted Hughes fastens onto Shakespearean hendiadys, finding in it a "fractal" of the play in which it appears as well as a figure that, by democratizing language, proves ineluctably political. Charles Olson speaks more literally as a craftsman and more cryptically as a poet when he says of the form and purpose of the language of *The Tempest* that Shakespeare "knows verse shall be as sharp and sweet as wood is made, of its grain, and use."

At one time or another all Shakespeare readers are caught up short by his extraordinary aptness, his uncanny felicity of expression. Whether the *mot juste* or the apposite phrase is one that Shakespeare borrowed or improvised, its syllabic measure and its semantic density embed it in our memories. "Unaccommodated man," "semblable coherence," "bald unjointed chat," "signifying nothing": these are among the many seemingly random phrases that lodge in *my* mind. There are also bravura Shakespearean lines. Recall that both Olson and Ginsberg seize on Iris's "Thy banks with pioned and twilled brims" in *The Tempest* (4.1.64; these are the first occurrences of *pioned* and *twilled* cited in the *OED*). Keats also underscores this line, although in his Johnson-Steevens edition, it is amended to "Thy banks with peonied and lilied brims." Often said to fancy Shakespeare at the level of the phrase, Keats nonetheless frequently rules beneath whole lines and entire speeches. In this instance, he underscores the first twelve lines of Iris's speech. This sort of admiration of a word, phrase, line or passage is hardly aestheticization *tout court*. Neil Corcoran has written that "Auden's Shakespeare criticism . . . is very much the criticism of a practitioner, and a quiet *ars poetica* may be read out of it." He then argues that Auden steadfastly refuses the "aestheticisation of ethics." This seems right, and something similar might be said of Olson, and of Ginsberg, for all of their apparent concentration on form. But this is not quite to say that Auden refused to "intertwine the social and aesthetic."[7] Writers like Coleridge and Hughes, Woolf and Ginsberg consistently and inevitably respond to ethics enmeshed in aesthetics, which is only to say that they acknowledge the necessary implication of the *what* in the *how*. The aesthetic is not a contaminant, and style has no meaning without substance (hence Robert Creeley's insistence that "form is never more than an extension of content"), although at any given moment they may not hold equal sway.

How, then, *do* we read Shakespeare? What, either cognitively or phenomenologically, occurs when we read his lines? Hughes certainly thinks that pleasure can be felt even when sense is obscure. *Utile* appears to trump *dulce* when Thoby Stephen "consumed" Shakespeare in his "large clumsy way," getting "the measure of the daily world" from Shakespeare, as opposed to when Virginia Woolf, for whom words were not useful but true, read Shakespeare.[8] Not that this disentangles Shakespearean method from meaning—form and content (dancer and dance) remain "intimate" if content is "what's being stated as it is being stated."[9] A thought gorgeously expressed means something different from a thought put dully (and we have seen that Berryman said that Shakespeare taught him how to try to be gorgeous!). There is no possibility of escaping style or of achieving a null style. When Coleridge writes of a reader's "pleasureable [*sic*] activity of mind," he means that we enjoy reading Shakespeare because our intellectual faculties are quickened by the pleasure we take in his language. At the same time, if a poet is only ever a great poet if a "profound philosopher," then our analytical exertions can and should not be confined to the formal analysis of Shakespeare's language.

The craft of a playwright no less than that of a wheelwright or shipwright pertains to both form and content. To speak of what is wrought is necessarily to credit parts and whole, balance and disproportion, poise and roughness, pleasure and functionality, mind and body (both Shakespeare's and ours). Writers reading Shakespeare incorporate what they read. Olson wants to tap what he calls the "celerity" of Shakespeare's verse. When Woolf writes of the mind "tumbl[ing] & splash[ing] among [his] words," it sounds as if she is referring to the minds, even to the rendering, of her own characters. When she imagines the "physical stuff" of her brain expanding, throbbing, and quickening as she reads, what she describes is a version of Coleridgean "intellecturition," which is itself an amalgam of thought and appetite. Ginsberg rehearses "the mouthing that Shakespeare presents for an actor"; Woolf calls attention to a "full mouthed rhetoric" in the plays; and Olson hears Falstaff's speech "seized where it issues from any of our mouths." Auden dwells on "the dyer's hand" and Hughes works his way through the *Complete Works* with his own "hand-torch and divining rod." Trying to fathom the mechanics of Shakespearean hendiadys, Hughes imagines clauses "snatched and grabbed out of the listener's ears, his shirt front, his top pocket, his finger ends." All of this Shakespearean prestidigitation sometimes was overwhelming, but it also was galvanizing. "When the ink has gone dry upon the pen," Woolf wrote, Shakespeare can "revive the sense of language." "Shakespeare usually recovers my prose," wrote Olson. "Just crazy today," he reported to Creeley when he was in the midst of reading *King Lear* and *Antony and Cleopatra*, "wild, crazy, excited by a whole series of sights, breaking."

If this rings true for a writer reading Shakespeare, it easily could be the response of any reader reading Shakespeare. Shakespeare's language has been lighting up readers for centuries. Even if at first blush many of us associate our most fully kinetic and emotionally resonant responses to his works with theatrical productions, it bears remembering that a reader's experience is anything but impoverished (although it is by no means "better"—this is not a *paragone*).

Readers get not just the vigor, speed, and thrill of Shakespeare's words, but also an incomparable opportunity that almost no performance, let alone film (recall the unrelenting verbal onslaught that is Kenneth Branagh's *Hamlet*) affords: the chance radically to decelerate the flood of words. "There is time . . . to make a note in the margin," wrote Woolf. In the theater, what Ginsberg calls "mouthing" is the prerogative of actors; but with a text in hand, it is Ginsberg's, indeed any reader's, privilege. The French say that they "assist" at a performance (*assister à*: to be at or see a spectacle, match, or concert). The reader who reads out loud, circles and underlines words, or writes in the margins assists, if you will, Shakespeare. One could even say that our readerly response to Shakespeare's words, our bliss, is as fully embodied as our response to his plays in the theater. We may lose something extraordinary that attaches to the theatrical experience— our bodily presence to actors' bodies and theirs to ours; but we gain something equally mysterious—our intellectual and bodily ("handy-dandy," which is form, which is content?) responses *immediately*, and over and over again at will, to Shakespeare's words. The writers in *The Great William: Writers Reading Shakespeare*, like many of us, grew up and grew old with their editions of the *Complete Works*. The words on the page have mouth feel and the volumes themselves have hand feel.[10] We can take them down from our shelves whenever we like, travel with them, lend them, mark them up. They are ours to shape or warp as no performance is ours, save those in which we ourselves may occasionally perform. This readerly, what I have called psychosomatic, experience is hardly one that we have with Shakespeare alone, but it is one that Shakespeare makes different. These seven writer-readers bear ample witness to this difference.

NOTES

Introduction

1. Of course, I am not the first to follow this route. For a wide-ranging and pathbreaking discussion of marginalia, see H. J. Jackson, *Marginalia: Readers Writing in Books* (New Haven, CT: Yale University Press, 2001). Jackson followed up *Marginalia* with *Romantic Readers: The Evidence of Marginalia* (New Haven, CT: Yale University Press, 2005). Jackson has also edited Samuel Taylor Coleridge's Shakespeare marginalia (see note 5, below). Among a number of single-author studies of Shakespeare reading, there are Páraic Finnerty, *Emily Dickinson's Shakespeare* (Amherst: University of Massachusetts Press, 2006); John Haffenden's introduction to *Berryman's Shakespeare: Essays, Letters, and Other Writings by John Berryman*, ed. John Haffenden (New York: Farrar, Straus and Giroux, 1999); and R. S. White, *Keats as a Reader of Shakespeare* (Norman: University of Oklahoma Press, 1987). On George Eliot, see Bernice W. Kliman, "Sucking Honey from Annotations: George Eliot and George Henry Lewes on Shakespeare," *Shakespeare Newsletter*, 49, no. 3 (1999): 59–78. Neil Corcoran's *Shakespeare and the Modern Poet* (Cambridge: Cambridge University Press, 2010), which is not a study of reading per se, includes highly rewarding pages on Yeats, Eliot, Auden, and Ted Hughes. The same applies to Kenneth Gross's review essay, "Poets Reading Shakespeare," *Raritan*, 28, no. 3 (2009): 105–31. General editors Peter Holland and Adrian Poole's wonderful, eighteen-volume Great Shakespeareans series (now available from Bloomsbury Arden) includes essays, again not strictly studies of reading, that start with Dryden, Pope, and Johnson, and move on to, among many others, Goethe, Coleridge, Hazlitt, Keats, Dickens, Hardy, Emerson, Melville, Marx, Freud, Eliot, Auden, and Beckett.

2. James Boswell's *The Life of Samuel Johnson, LL.D.* is cited in H. J. Jackson, *Marginalia*, 274, n. 7. For Berryman's lament, see *Berryman's Shakespeare*, 226–27.

3. In *Shakespeare and the Modern Poet*, Neil Corcoran writes of W. H. Auden that "there is a self-effacing modesty in his Shakespeare criticism, . . . complemented, though, by the serenity of his Shakespeare engagements, the sense they convey that no anxiety inheres in this encounter" (128).

4. Lawrence Lipking makes a distinction more theoretical than practical between marginalia (spontaneous and "wayward" fragments that barely rise to the level of coherent thought; what Poe called "nonsense") and marginal glosses (in which perplexities are explained and parts are related to the whole). See "Marginal Gloss," *Critical Inquiry* 3, no. 4 (1977): 612–13. Poe writes that "*marginalia* are deliberately pencilled, because the mind of the reader wishes to unburthen itself of a *thought*;—however flippant—however silly—however trivial." Just before the start of his "*farrago*" of his own marginalia, Poe quips that "just as the goodness of your true pun is in the direct ratio of its intolerability, so is nonsense the essential sense of the Marginal Note." Edgar Allan Poe, "Marginalia [part 1]," *US Magazine and Democratic Review*, 15 (November 1844).

Online at http://www.eapoe.org/works/misc/mar1144.htm (accessed September 7, 2014).

5. Samuel Taylor Coleridge, *The Collected Works of Samuel Taylor Coleridge: Marginalia*, ed. H. J. Jackson and George Whalley, vol. 12, pt. 4 (Princeton, NJ: Princeton University Press, 1998), 453. Hereafter cited in the text by part and page as *CM*.

6. John Keats, *The Letters of John Keats*, ed. Robert Gittings (London: Oxford University Press, 1970), 277.

7. *The Virginia Woolf Manuscripts: From the Henry W. and Albert A. Berg Collection of the New York Public Library*. Microform edition (Woodbridge, CT: Research Publications International, 1993), notebook vol. 26, entry 25. The only known recording of Virginia Woolf is a 1937 BBC radio broadcast from the series called "Words Fail Me." An edited version, entitled "Craftsmanship," appears in *The Death of the Moth and Other Essays* (London: Hogarth Press, 1942), 126–32.

8. *The Diary of Virginia Woolf: Volume Three, 1925–1930*, ed. Anne Olivier Bell (New York: Harcourt Brace Jovanovich, 1980), 300 (April 13, 1930).

9. John Berryman, *Berryman's Shakespeare: Essays, Letters, and Other Writings by John Berryman*, ed. John Haffenden (New York: Farrar, Straus and Giroux, 1999), 226. Further citations from Haffenden's collection appear parenthetically in the text. Van Doren (1894–1972) also taught Louis Zukofsky, Allen Ginsberg, John Hollander, and Richard Howard.

10. Ted Hughes, *Shakespeare and the Goddess of Complete Being* (New York: Farrar Straus & Giroux, 1992), 3.

11. Ted Hughes, *Letters of Ted Hughes*, ed. Christopher Reid (London: Faber and Faber, 2007), 607–08 (letter to Simon Jenkins, the editor of *The Times*; April 11, 1992). Writing five weeks later to Ben Sonnenberg, Hughes added that the crime against the goddess that he tries in his book "has by now virtually destroyed English Society, English Education, English individual life" (611; May 17, 1992).

12. Ibid., 609 (to A. L. Rowse; April 15, 1992).

13. Hughes, *Shakespeare and the Goddess*, 85–92.

14. John Berryman, *The Freedom of the Poet* (New York: Farrar, Straus and Giroux, 1976), 3.

15. Naropa Basic Poetics Class (March 6, 1980). Online at https://archive.org/details /naropa (accessed September 24, 2014).

16. D. H. Lawrence, by contrast, wrote that he "always felt an aversion from Hamlet: a creeping unclean thing he seems." Cited by Adrian Poole in his introduction to *Joyce, T. S. Eliot, Auden, Beckett*, ed. Adrian Poole, Great Shakespeareans, vol. 12 (New York: Continuum International Publishing Group, 2012), 4.

17. See "Charlotte Brontë" in *The Essays of Virginia Woolf: Volume 2, 1912–1918*, ed. Andrew McNeillie (London: Hogarth Press, 1994), 27.

18. Cited in *The Romantics on Shakespeare*, ed. Jonathan Bate (New York: Penguin Books, 1992), 166. Keats famously writes of "the camelion Poet" who "has no Identity—he is continually in for—and filling some other body"; but Coleridge's Shakespeare, though another Proteus, "yet still the God [is] felt to be there." See *The Letters of John Keats*, ed. Robert Gittings (London: Oxford University Press, 1970), 157; and Samuel Taylor Coleridge, *The Collected Works of Samuel Taylor Coleridge: Lectures 1808–1819*

on Literature, ed. R. A. Foakes, vol. 5, pts. 1–2 (Princeton, NJ: Princeton University Press, 1987), pt. 1, 69. Baudelaire's version of this trope is more vampiric: the poet is "commes ces âmes errantes qui cherchent un corps, il entre, quand il veut, dans le personage de chacun" ("like those wandering spirits that seek a body, he enters, when he likes, into the person of any man"). See "Les Foules" in *Petits Poëmes en Prose* (Paris: Michel Lévy Frères, 1869), 31. I owe this reference to Jeffrey Skoblow. The translation is mine.

19. I pursue this argument at greater length in my chapter on Olson. I have been quoting from Olson's ten-chapter, unpublished manuscript on Shakespeare (1954) and from "Quantity in Verse, and Shakespeare's Late Plays" in Charles Olson, *Collected Prose*, ed. Donald Allen and Benjamin Friedlander (Berkeley: University of California Press, 1997), 270–82.

20. Coleridge, *Collected Works of Samuel Taylor Coleridge: Lectures 1808–1819 on Literature*, 1.359.

21. Allen Ginsberg, *Composed on the Tongue*, ed. Donald Allen (Bolinas, CA: Grey Fox Press, 1980), 153.

22. Berryman, *Berryman's Shakespeare*, 338.

23. T. S. Eliot writes of Shakespeare "the *craftsman*" and of his "workmanship" in "Shakespeare and Montaigne" (1925) and in *Hamlet* (1919). Cited in Anne Stillman, "T. S. Eliot," in Poole, ed., *Joyce, T. S. Eliot, Auden, Beckett*, 84 and 86.

24. Woolf, *The Essays of Virginia Woolf: Volume 3, 1919–1924*, ed. Andrew McNeillie (New York: Harcourt Brace Jovanovich, 1988), 496.

25. Virginia Woolf, *A Sketch of the Past* (1939–40) in *Moments of Being*, ed. Jeanne Schulkind (London: Hogarth Press, 1985), 138–39.

26. But compare Coleridge: "At all points from the most important to the most minute, the Judgement of Shakespear is commensurate with his Genius" (*Collected Works of Samuel Taylor Coleridge: Lectures 1808–1819 on Literature*, 2.263).

Chapter One

1. See Janet Ruth Heller, *Coleridge, Lamb, Hazlitt, and the Reader of Drama* (Columbia: University of Missouri Press, 1990), 43–94.

2. Seamus Perry, "The Talker," in *The Cambridge Companion to Coleridge*, ed. Lucy Newlyn (Cambridge: Cambridge University Press, 2002), 103–25.

3. Samuel Taylor Coleridge, *Biographia Literaria*, 2 vols., ed. J. Shawcross (Oxford: Oxford University Press, 1901), 2:11. Hereafter cited parenthetically in the text by volume and page as *BL*.

4. Samuel Taylor Coleridge, *The Collected Works of Samuel Taylor Coleridge: Marginalia*, ed. H. J. Jackson and George Whalley, vol. 12, pt. 4 (Princeton, NJ: Princeton University Press, 1998), 866. Volume 12, pts. 1 and 4 are hereafter cited parenthetically in the text by part and page number as *CM* (e.g., *CM*, 4.868).

5. Samuel Taylor Coleridge, *The Collected Works of Samuel Taylor Coleridge: Lectures 1808–1819 on Literature*, ed. R. A. Foakes, vol. 5, pts. 1–2 (Princeton, NJ: Princeton University Press, 1987), 1.359. Hereafter cited parenthetically in the text by part and page as *CLect* (e.g., *CLect*, 2.319).

6. M. M. Badawi, *Coleridge: Critic of Shakespeare* (Cambridge: Cambridge University Press, 1973), 65.

7. Samuel Taylor Coleridge, *The Collected Works of Samuel Taylor Coleridge: The Friend*, ed. Barbara E. Rooke, vol. 4, pts. 1–2 (Princeton, NJ: Princeton University Press, 1969), 1.449 and 451. Hereafter cited parenthetically in the text by part and page as *Friend*.

8. Samuel Taylor Coleridge, *The Notebooks of Samuel Taylor Coleridge*, ed. Kathleen Coburn (and Anthony John Harding, vol. 5) 5 vols., each in 2 parts (New York: Pantheon; Princeton, NJ: Princeton University Press, 1957–2002), 3: note 3290. Hereafter cited parenthetically in the text by volume and note as *CN* (e.g., *CN*, 3:3290).

9. On the importance to Coleridge of a reader deriving "pleasure . . . from the activity of your own mind," see H. J. Jackson, "Coleridge as Reader: Marginalia," in *The Oxford Handbook of Samuel Taylor Coleridge*, ed. Frederick Burwick (New York: Oxford University Press, 2009), 283. Jackson is quoting from Coleridge's marginalia in George Frere's copy of the autobiography of Richard Baxter.

10. Perry, "The Talker," 112. Coleridge wrote that the "stimulus of Conversation suspends the terror that haunts my mind; but when I am alone, the horrors . . . almost overwhelm me." Cited in Thomas McFarland, *Romanticism and the Forms of Ruin: Wordsworth, Coleridge, and Modalities of Fragmentation* (Princeton, NJ: Princeton University Press, 1981), 111, n. 34.

11. Samuel Taylor Coleridge, *Collected Letters of Samuel Taylor Coleridge*, ed. Earl Leslie Griggs, 6 vols. (Oxford: Clarendon Press, 1956–71), 1:260 (cf. *CM*, 1.ciii). Hereafter cited parenthetically in the text by volume and page number as *CL*.

12. Kathleen Coburn, *Experience into Thought: Perspectives in the Coleridge Notebooks* (Toronto: University of Toronto Press, 1979), 13.

13. Ibid., 12 and 13; my emphasis.

14. On Boyer and bottoms, see Samuel Taylor Coleridge, *The Collected Works of Samuel Taylor Coleridge: Table Talk.*, ed. Carl Woodring, vol. 14, pts. 1–2 (Princeton, NJ: Princeton University Press, 1990), 326 and 326n. Hereafter cited parenthetically in the text by part and page number as *TT* (e.g., *TT*, 2.61).

15. Josie Dixon, "The Notebooks," in *Cambridge Companion to Coleridge*, 80 (see n. 2 above).

16. According to Thomas De Quincey, "Coleridge often spoiled a book; but, in the course of doing this, he enriched that book with so many and so valuable notes, tossing about him, with such lavish profusion, from such a cornucopia of discursive reading, and such a fusing intellect, commentaries so many-angled and so many-coloured that I have envied many a man whose luck has placed him in the way of such injuries; and that man must have been a churl . . . who could have found in his heart to complain" (*The Collected Writings of Thomas De Quincey*, ed. David Masson (Edinburgh: Adam and Charles Black, 1889), 2:314.

17. This, my later chapters show, is a question that Woolf, Berryman, and Hughes posed; it does not appear to have troubled Olson or Ginsberg.

18. Keats's Shakespeare, who "overwhelms a genuine Lover of Poesy with all manner of

abuse," is blessedly held at bay by Keats's sense of humor. This may have been Coleridge's way with Shakespeare's editors, but not with Shakespeare himself.

19. Compare *CM* 4.784 and 4.731, the latter for comment on Aufidius's speech, "so beautiful" but "least explicable from the mood & full Intention of the Speaker, of any in the whole works of Shakespear."

20. See Seamus Perry, *Coleridge and the Uses of Division* (Oxford: Clarendon Press, 1999), 225–46.

21. Ibid., 241 and 237.

22. H. J. Jackson, *Marginalia: Readers Writing in Books* (New Haven, CT: Yale University Press, 2001), 164.

23. Elinor Shaffer, review of *The Collected Works of Samuel Taylor Coleridge: Marginalia*, vol. 1, in *Studies in Romanticism* 21 (1982): 532–33. H. J. Jackson acknowledges some limitations to the Bollingen procedures in "Coleridge as Reader: Marginalia," 275–76.

24. Once again, Coleridge exercises his humor at an editor's expense.

25. Seamus Perry, ed., *S. T. Coleridge: Interviews and Recollections* (Hampshire, UK: Palgrave, 2000), 236.

Chapter Two

1. All citations from Keats's letters are drawn from *The Letters of John Keats*, ed. Robert Gittings (London: Oxford University Press, 1970). Hereafter cited parenthetically by page number in the text.

2. For a Keats who is "haunted" by *Antony and Cleopatra* and who must defend himself "against Shakespeare's overwhelming consciousness," see William Flesch, "The Ambivalence of Generosity: Keats Reading Shakespeare," *ELH* 62 (1995): 149–69. Flesch's essay is our most sophisticated and astringent account of Keats's belatedness in relation to Shakespeare and of the defensive tactics with which Keats experiments.

3. This sounds a lot like Emily Dickinson, as described by Thomas Wentworth Higginson in a note to his wife following a visit with the poet: "After long disuse of her eyes she read Shakespeare & thought why is any other book needed." Online at http://archive.emilydickinson.org/correspondence/higginson/jnl342.html (accessed August 21, 2014). In a letter to Joseph Lyman, Dickinson, whose eye doctor had just given her permission to read again, described the joy she felt being able to return to Shakespeare: "I thought I should tear the leaves out as I turned them. Then I settled down to a willingness for all the rest to go but William Shakespear. Why need we Joseph read anything else but him." Cited by Páraic Finnerty, in *Emily Dickinson's Shakespeare* (Amherst: University of Massachusetts Press, 2006), 141.

4. The speaker of Shakespeare's Sonnets is self-conscious about having a "dyer's hand," and Shakespeare himself, the son of a glover, was a popular entertainer and a worker, a play*wright*. For his part, Keats, the son of a hostler and trained as an apothecary, was said to be of the "Cockney School."

5. The *OED* gives as its primary definition, "Of ill omen, inauspicious; indicative or suggestive of future misfortune" but also "Of good omen, auspicious" and cites George

Peele's *The Famous Chronicle of King Edward the First*: "Let vs like friends pastime vs on the sands, Our frolike mindes are ominous for good." Online at http://www.oed.com .proxy-um.researchport.umd.edu/view/Entry/131206?redirectedFrom=ominous#eid (accessed October 9, 2014).

6. The portrait ended up hanging over brother George's mantelpiece in Louisville, Kentucky. See Denise Gigante, *The Keats Brothers: The Life of John and George* (Cambridge, MA: Harvard University Press, 2011), 79.

7. Cf. Virginia Woolf, in "Reading" (1919): "the windows being open, and the book held so that it rested upon a background of escallonia hedges and distant blue, instead of being a book it seemed as if what I read was laid upon the landscape not printed, bound, or sewn up, but somehow the product of trees and fields and the hot summer sky, like the air which swam, on fine mornings, round the outlines of things." *The Essays of Virginia Woolf: Volume 3, 1919–1924*, ed. Andrew McNeillie (New York: Harcourt Brace Jovanovich, 1988), 142.

8. All citations are taken from the facing-page French and English text in Proust's *On Reading*, trans. and ed. Jean Autret and William Burford (New York: Macmillan Co., 1971). Hereafter cited by page number in the text.

9. In a letter to her friend Ethel Smyth, written on July 29, 1934, Virginia Woolf wrote that "the state of reading consists in the complete elimination of the *ego*; and its the ego that erects itself like another part of the body I dont dare to name." See *The Sickle Side of the Moon: The Letters of Virginia Woolf, 1932–1935*, vol. 5, ed. Nigel Nicholson (London: Hogarth Press, 1979), 319.

10. In 1818, Keats wrote to John Taylor that "[p]ride and egotism will enable me to write finer things than any thing else could—so I will indulge it—Just so much as I am hu[m]bled by the genius above my grasp, am I exalted and look with hate and contempt upon the literary world" (280). Beth Lau notes the "apparent contradictions in Keats's alternate celebrations of selflessness and selfhood" in her chapter "John Keats," in *Lamb, Hazlitt, Keats*, ed. Adrian Poole, Great Shakespeareans, vol. 4 (London: Continuum International Publishing Group, 2010), 109–59, esp. 128–40.

11. See Helen Vendler, *Coming of Age as a Poet: Milton, Keats, Eliot, Plath* (Cambridge, MA: Harvard University Press, 2003), 63.

12. Walter Jackson Bate, *John Keats* (Cambridge, MA: Harvard University Press, 1963), 33.

13. I have inspected this volume, which David Luck, senior archivist at the London Metropolitan Archives, was kind enough to weigh for me. Keats and Reynolds were portaging a book that weighs 9.4 pounds.

14. Compare Coleridge: "I am deeply convinced, that no man, however wide his Erudition, however patient his antiquarian researches, can possibly understand, or be worthy of understanding, the writing of Shakespere." See *The Collected Works of Samuel Taylor Coleridge: Lectures 1808–1819 on Literature*, ed. R. A. Foakes, vol. 5, pts. 1–2 (Princeton, NJ: Princeton University Press, 1987), 1.78.

15. For Keats's copy of Hazlitt's *Characters of Shakespear's Plays* (London: printed by C. H. Reynell for R. Hunter, 1817), see *EC8 K2262 Zz817h. Houghton Library, Harvard University, Cambridge, MA, online at http://nrs.harvard.edu/urn-3:FHCL.HOUGH :4016065.

16. Cf. R. S. White, *Keats as a Reader of Shakespeare* (Norman: University of Oklahoma Press, 1987), 183.

17. Andrew Motion, *Keats* (New York: Farrar, Straus and Giroux, 1997), 109.

18. Bate, *John Keats*, 85.

19. See Jack Stillinger, *The Poems of John Keats* (Cambridge, MA: Harvard University Press, 1978), 64.

20. Randall McLeod, "UnEditing Shak-speare," *Sub-stance*, 33/34 (1982): 36. Further citations are noted parenthetically in the text.

21. Photographically reproduced in ibid., 30. Jack Stillinger (*The Poems of John Keats*, 588–89) provides a good account of the states of this poem. He thinks that the version that appears in Keats's Shakespeare Folio "probably . . . was written earlier than the letter text," but he warns that all possible orderings of the recoverable states "are rather too speculative."

22. McLeod does not mention that Keats also transcribed his sonnet "Bright Star" opposite the opening of "A Lover's Complaint" in the copy of Shakespeare's poems that he shared with Reynolds.

23. Caroline F. E. Spurgeon, *Keats's Shakespeare: A Descriptive Study* (1928; repr., Oxford: Oxford University Press, 1966).

24. Motion, *Keats*, Plate 62.

25. Ibid., Plate 64.

26. Keats's Whittingham edition, at Harvard University's Houghton Library, is also available online. See *The Dramatic Works of William Shakspeare*. London: Sold by Carpenter and Son [etc.], 1814–[1818]. *EC8 K2262 Zz814s. Houghton Library, Harvard University, Cambridge, MA. Online at http://nrs.harvard.edu/urn-3:FHCL.HOUGH:3425902. Keats's Folio marginalia are recorded in *John Keats: The Major Works: Including Endymion, the Odes and Selected Letters*, ed. Elizabeth Cook (Oxford: Oxford University Press, 2009), 333–36. *The Poetical Works of William Shakespeare* (London, 1806), 8vo, inscribed as a gift to Keats from Reynolds, is heavily marked in numerous handwritings. Spurgeon makes out marks and notes by Reynolds, also pencil markings by Richard Woodhouse, but she thinks that "the greatest amount of marking is by Keats; . . . he has scored them [sonnets] all down one side and has in addition marked again certain lines in them." See *Keats's Shakespeare*, 39. Frank Owings, Jr., in *The Keats Library: A Descriptive Catalogue* (London: Keats-Shelley Memorial Association, 1978), is much more circumspect (53).

27. White, *Keats as a Reader of Shakespeare*, 8 and 59.

28. Ibid., 63–68.

29. Motion, *Keats*, 193.

30. See my account Virginia Woolf's unfriendly response to annotators in chapter 3.

31. Spurgeon, *Keats's Shakespeare*, 29. Keats's impatience with Johnson is comparable to Coleridge's responses to Warburton and Theobald. Coleridge's expostulations are legion. Among them are "O genuine, inimitable (at least I hope so) Warburton! one in 5 Millions would be half a one too much." "O true Warburton! and the sancta Simplicitas of honest dull Theobald's Faith in him!" "Like all W's comments, ingenious in Blunder—he can never see any other Writer's Thoughts for the mist-making Swarm of

his own." See Samuel Taylor Coleridge, *The Collected Works of Samuel Taylor Coleridge: Marginalia*, ed. H. J. Jackson and George Whalley, vol. 12, pt. 4 (Princeton, NJ: Princeton University Press, 1998), 703, 710, and 720.

32. Spurgeon, *Keats's Shakespeare*, 31.

33. The lines in *Troilus and Cressida* read: "I stalk about her door / Like a strange soul upon the Stygian banks / Staying for waftage" (3.2.7–9).

34. Cf. White: "Self-annulment and self-assertion are equally important in Keats's view of the reader's activity" (*Keats as a Reader of Shakespeare*, 26).

35. Woolf, *Essays of Virginia Woolf: Volume 3, 1919–1924*, 438. Further citations from this volume and from *Volume 4, 1925–1928*, ed. Andrew McNeillie (London: Hogarth Press, 1994), are noted parenthetically in the text.

36. Roland Barthes, *The Pleasure of the Text*, trans. Richard Miller (New York: Hill and Wang, 1975), 14. See also *Le plaisir de texte* (Paris: Editions du Seuil, 1973). I have made minor changes to Miller's often-cited translation. Further citations appear parenthetically in the text.

37. Richard Miller translates "*replonge*" as "dip in again." With Virginia Woolf's "plunge" in mind, I have changed this to "plunge in again." Cf. Virginia Woolf: "To be able to read books without reading them, to skip and saunter, to suspend judgement, to lounge and loaf down the alleys and bye-streets" ("How Should One Read a Book?" [1926] in *Essays of Virginia Woolf*, 4:393).

38. "Chuck," a diminutive for "chicken," is the term of endearment that Macbeth also surprises us with when he tells Lady Macbeth, "Be innocent of the knowledge, dearest chuck" (3.2.46). Allen Ginsberg (see chapter 6) has a fine time mouthing *The Tempest*'s "I myself could make / A chough of as deep chat" (2.1.264–65).

39. Lau, "John Keats," 121 and 124. On Keats's attention to phrases, Lau provides citations from Reynolds, Cowden Clark, and Hazlitt through Matthew Arnold to Walter Jackson Bate and Jack Stillinger. Keats himself writes of the "fine isolated verisimilitude" that negatively incapable Coleridge "would let go by" (43).

Chapter Three

1. Woolf deemed even the desire to read susceptible to analysis. In her essay "Sir Thomas Browne" (1923), she describes that desire as being "always despotic in its demands"; but "like all other desires which distract our unhappy souls, [it] is capable of analysis." See *The Essays of Virginia Woolf: Volume 3, 1919–1924*, ed. Andrew McNeillie (New York: Harcourt Brace Jovanovich, 1988), 363–64.

2. See *Virginia Woolf Manuscripts: From the Monks House Papers at the University of Sussex*. Microform edition (Brighton: Harvester Press, 1985) and *The Virginia Woolf Manuscripts: From the Henry W. and Albert A. Berg Collection of the New York Public Library*. Microform edition (Woodbridge, CT: Research Publications International, 1993). All citations from Woolf's notebooks appear parenthetically in the text as MSS Sussex or MSS New York, by manuscript volume and entry number. See also Brenda R. Silver, *Virginia Woolf's Reading Notebooks* (Princeton, NJ: Princeton University Press, 1983).

3. Samuel Taylor Coleridge, *The Collected Works of Samuel Taylor Coleridge: The Friend*, ed.

Barbara E. Rooke, vol. 4, pts. 1–2 (Princeton, NJ: Princeton University Press, 1969), 2.48–49.

4. Virginia Woolf, *Passionate Apprentice: The Early Journals, 1897–1909*, ed. Mitchell A. Leaska (New York: Harcourt Brace Jovanovich, 1990), 178.

5. Citations from Virginia Woolf's diaries appear parenthetically in the text by date, volume, and page. See *The Diary of Virginia Woolf: Volume Two, 1920–1924*, ed. Anne Olivier Bell (New York: Harcourt Brace Jovanovich, 1978); *The Diary of Virginia Woolf: Volume Three, 1925–1930*, ed. Anne Olivier Bell (New York: Harcourt Brace Jovanovich, 1980); *The Diary of Virginia Woolf: Volume Four, 1931–1935*, ed. Anne Olivier Bell (New York: Harcourt Brace Jovanovich, 1982); *The Diary of Virginia Woolf: Volume Five, 1936–1941*, ed. Anne Olivier Bell (New York: Harcourt Brace Jovanovich, 1984).

6. November 14, 1940 (Woolf drowned herself on March 28, 1941). Cited in Brenda R. Silver, "'Anon' and 'The Reader': Virginia Woolf's Last Essays," *Twentieth Century Literature* 25 (1979/80): 357. Further citations by page number appear parenthetically in the text. Here is Emily Dickinson describing what it was like to read *Antony and Cleopatra* after eight months of following her doctor's order that she rest her eyes by not reading: "Give me ever to drink of this wine. Going home I flew to the shelves and devoured the luscious passages." Cited by Páraic Finnerty, in *Emily Dickinson's Shakespeare* (Amherst: University of Massachusetts Press, 2006), 141.

7. Virginia Woolf, *Passionate Apprentice: The Early Journals, 1897–1909*, 178. Further citations by page number from *Early Journals* appear parenthetically in the text.

8. Citations from Virginia Woolf's letters appear parenthetically in the text by date, volume, and page (by page only for consecutive citations from the same letter). See *The Flight of the Mind: The Letters of Virginia Woolf, 1888–1912*, ed. Nigel Nicholson, vol. 1 (London: Hogarth Press, 1975); *A Change of Perspective: The Letters of Virginia Woolf, 1923–1928*, ed. Nigel Nicholson, vol. 3 (London: Hogarth Press, 1977); and *Leave the Letters Till We're Dead: The Letters of Virginia Woolf, 1936–1941*, ed. Nigel Nicholson, vol. 6 (London: Hogarth Press, 1980). A curiously similar admission is made by Herman Melville in a letter to Everet Duyckinck (February 24, 1848): "Dolt & and ass that I am I have lived more than 29 years, & until a few days ago, never made close acquaintance with the divine William." Cited in Hershel Parker, *Herman Melville: A Biography, Volume 1, 1819–1851* (Baltimore, MD: Johns Hopkins University Press, 1996), 616.

9. Virginia Woolf, *A Sketch of the Past* (1939–40) in *Moments of Being*, ed. Jeanne Schulkind (London: Hogarth Press, 1985), 138 (my emphasis). Further citations by page number appear parenthetically in the text.

10. Virginia Woolf, *A Room of One's Own* (1929; repr., New York: Harcourt [Harvest], 1989), 47–48. Further citations by page number appear parenthetically in the text.

11. See *Catalogue of the Books from the Library of Leonard and Virginia Woolf taken from Monks House, Rodmell, Sussex and 24 Victoria Square* (Brighton: Holleyman & Treacher, 1975).

12. Hermione Lee, *Virginia Woolf* (New York: Knopf, 1996), 473.

13. Ibid., 744.

14. "Age cannot wither her, nor custom stale / Her infinite variety. Other women cloy /

The appetites they feed, but she makes hungry / Where most she satisfied" (*Antony and Cleopatra*, 2.3.245–48).

15. Woolf, *Essays, Volume 3, 1919–1924*, 496.

16. John Berryman, *Berryman's Shakespeare*, ed. John Haffenden (New York: Farrar, Straus and Giroux, 1999), xxxiv.

17. Woolf, *Essays, Volume 4, 1925–1928*, 325.

18. Virginia Woolf, *The Death of the Moth and Other Essays* (London: Hogarth Press, 1942), 34.

19. Flann O'Brien (writing as Myles na Gopaleen) describes a "book-handling . . . service which enables ignorant people who want to be suspected of reading books to have their books handled and mauled in a manner that will give the impression that their owner is very devoted to them." For those who pay for "*Le Traitement Superbe*," each "volume [will] be well and truly handled, first by a qualified handler and subsequently by a master-handler . . . suitable passages in not less than fifty per cent of the books [will] be underlined in good-quality red ink and an appropriate phrase . . . inserted in the margin." He then lists some phrases: "Rubbish!" "Yes, indeed!" "How true, how true!" "I don't agree at all." and "I remember poor Joyce saying the very same thing to me." See Flann O'Brien, *The Best of Myles* (1968; repr., Normal, IL: Dalkey Archive Press, 1999), 20–21.

20. In the version of "How Should One Read a Book?" that she published in *The Yale Review*, Woolf distinguished between "two processes in reading. One might be called the actual reading; the other the after reading. During the actual reading, when we hold the book in our hands, there are incessant distractions and interruptions. New impressions are always completing or cancelling the old." But later, "the whole book floats to the top of the mind complete. . . . The book takes on a definite shape. . . . Now one can think of the book as a whole." "Holding this complete shape in mind it now becomes necessary to arrive at some opinion of the book's merits, for though it is possible to receive the greatest pleasure and excitement from the first process, the actual reading, though this is of the utmost importance, it is not so profound or so lasting as the pleasure we get when the second process—the after reading—is finished, and we hold the book clear, secure, and (to the best of our powers) complete in our minds" (*Yale Review* 89, no. 1 [2001]: 50–51 [orig. pub. in October 1926]).

21. Alice Fox, *Virginia Woolf and the Literature of the English Renaissance* (Oxford: Clarendon Press, 1990), 104.

22. Woolf's phrase, "in the margin of the mind," makes one wonder if she knew of, or had even seen, Coleridge's annotations. Is there any of Coleridge in Colonel Tallboys?

23. Cited in Fox, *Virginia Woolf*, 110.

24. See my "Shakespeare in Praise of Mediocrity," *Hopkins Review* 7, no. 2 (2014): 192–202.

25. Writing in her diary about "the masterpieces," Woolf admits that reading them is "in its way as intense a delight as any; but for the most part pain" (*Diary*, June 16, 1925; 3:32).

26. Quentin Bell, *Virginia Woolf: A Biography* (London: Hogarth Press, 1972), 138.

27. Virginia Woolf, *Contemporary Writers* (London: Hogarth Press, 1965), 124. Stretch, we have seen, is what Shakespeare's language does to a reader (it "keep[s] one on the stretch almost to the exclusion of comment").

28. Virginia Woolf, *Mrs. Dalloway* (New York: Harcourt Brace, 1925), 80. For an attempt at translation, see Garrett Stewart, *Reading Voices: Literature and the Phonotext* (Berkeley: University of California Press, 1990), 271. Roland Barthes, *The Pleasure of the Text*, trans. Richard Miller (New York: Hill and Wang, 1975), 67.

29. Woolf, "How Should One Read a Book?" 50.

30. Virginia Woolf, *A Writer's Diary*, ed. Leonard Woolf (New York: Harcourt Brace Jovanovich, 1953), 44 (February 18, 1922).

Chapter Four

1. For "assault," see the note entitled "Again the sense the forms we have are conventions . . ." under the rubric "Charles Olson, Background to the Maximus Poems (Notes and Essays, 1945–1957)" in OLSON: *The Journal of the Charles Olson Archive* 5 (Spring 1976): 44.

2. For "archaic postmodern," see http://charlesolson.ca/archaic-postmodern (accessed July 31, 2014).

3. Charles Olson, "*Lear* and *Moby-Dick*," *Twice A Year* (Fall–Winter 1938): 165.

4. Charles Olson, *Call Me Ishmael* (New York: Reynal & Hitchcock, 1947), 52. Further citations appear parenthetically in the text.

5. Alex Calder argues against "supposing, with Olson, that Shakespeare is to Melville as steroids are to a weightlifter, a powerful additive whose ingestion enabled the author to heft *Moby-Dick* as the single masterstroke of a hampered career." See "Herman Melville" in *Emerson, Melville, James, Berryman*, ed. Peter Rawlings, Great Shakespeareans, vol. 8 (New York: Continuum International Publishing Group, 2011), 71.

6. Edward Dahlberg, *The Confessions of Edward Dahlberg* (New York: G. Braziller, 1971), 256.

7. Charles Olson, *Selected Letters*, ed. Ralph Maud (Berkeley: University of California Press, 2000), 24. Recall Keats's sonnet, in which he asks Shakespeare to "[g]ive me new Phoenix wings to fly to my desire."

8. Charles Olson, *The Maximus Poems*, ed. Charles F. Butterick (Berkeley: University of California Press, 1983).

9. One hears here Emerson's affirmation in "The Poet" (1844) that "America is a poem in our eyes; its ample geography dazzles the imagination, and it will not wait long for metres." See *The Selected Writings of Ralph Waldo Emerson*, ed. Brooke Atkinson (New York: Modern Library, 1950), 338. In Melville's own "Hawthorne and His Mosses" (1850), Olson would have read "that if Shakespeare has not been equalled, he is sure to be surpassed, and surpassed by an American born now or yet to be born." See *Shakespeare in America: An Anthology from the Revolution to Now*, ed. James Shapiro (New York: Modern Library, 2014), 132.

10. *Charles Olson and Frances Boldereff: A Modern Correspondence*, ed. Ralph Maud and Sharon Thesen (Middletown, CT: Wesleyan University Press, 1999), 64.

11. Ibid., 66.

12. "Projective Verse," in Charles Olson, *Collected Prose*, ed. Donald Allen and Benjamin Friedlander (Berkeley: University of California Press, 1997), 247. Further citations appear parenthetically in the text as "PV."

13. *The Complete Correspondence of Charles Olson & Robert Creeley*, ed. George F. Butterick (volumes 1–8) and Richard Blevins (volumes 9–10) (Santa Rosa, CA: Black Sparrow Press, 1980–1996). Further citations appear parenthetically in the text as CO/RC by volume and page number.

14. Charles Olson, *The Collected Poems of Charles Olson*, ed. George F. Butterick (Berkeley: University of California Press, 1987). Further citations appear parenthetically in the text as *CP*.

15. Olson's "of course" suggests that he was sensitive to what Creeley might perceive as self-serving.

16. Robert Creeley, *Tales out of School: Selected Interviews* (Ann Arbor: University of Michigan Press, 1993), 30.

17. "Human Universe," in *Collected Prose*, by Charles Olson, ed. Donald Allen and Benjamin Friedlander (Berkeley: University of California Press, 1997), 156. Further citations appear parenthetically in the text as "HU."

18. This letter is in the University of Connecticut Olson collection.

19. "Quantity in Verse, and Shakespeare's Late Plays," in Olson, *Collected Prose*, 270–82 (see n. 17 above). Further citations appear parenthetically in the text as "QV."

20. When Ted Hughes tracks the fierce Reformation clash between Catholicism and Protestantism across Shakespeare's mature and late plays, he describes the playwright of the last plays as "the magus of a Gnostic, Hermetic ritual." See *Shakespeare and the Goddess of Complete Being* (New York: Farrar Straus & Giroux, 1992), 331. The sacred verse that Olson finds in these plays expresses what is for Hughes their deep-structure rituals and myths.

21. "On Poets and Poetry," in Olson, *Collected Prose*, 253 (see n. 17 above).

22. Compare Virginia Woolf: "When one reads the mind is like an aeroplane propeller invisibly quick and unconscious—a state seldom achieved." *The Diary of Virginia Woolf: Volume Five, 1936–1941*, ed. Anne Olivier Bell (New York: Harcourt Brace Jovanovich, 1984), 151.

Chapter Five

1. "John Berryman, The Art of Poetry No. 16," *Paris Review* 53 (Winter 1972): 177–207. Online at http://www.theparisreview.org/interviews/4052/the-art-of-poetry-no-16-john-berryman (accessed August 6, 2014).

2. See John Berryman, *The Dream Songs* (New York: Farrar, Straus and Giroux, 2007). All citations are from this edition.

3. John Berryman, *Berryman's Shakespeare: Essays, Letters, and Other Writings by John Berryman*, ed. John Haffenden (New York: Farrar, Straus and Giroux, 1999), xxxiv. Further citations appear parenthetically in the text as *BS*.

4. "Poets Reading Shakespeare," *Raritan: A Quarterly Review* 28, no. 3 (2009): 127.

5. John Roe writes that "Shakespeare entered Berryman's poetry through Berryman's intense study of his works." For example, Shakespeare's plays gave Berryman "the confidence to . . . experiment with pronoun usage, career dizzily around words, and mix high and low like never before." See "John Berryman," in *Emerson, Melville, James, Berryman,*

ed. Peter Rawlings, Great Shakespeareans, vol. 8 (London: Continuum International Publishing Group, 2011), 148 and 153.

6. John Haffenden, *The Life of John Berryman* (London: Routledge & Kegan Paul, 1982), 72. Further citations appear parenthetically in the text as *Life*.

7. John Berryman, MSS 43, Shakespeare (Project), box 1, folder: Shakespeare Notes, in The John Berryman Papers in the Literary Manuscripts Collections, Manuscripts Division, Elmer L. Andersen Library, University of Minnesota. Hereafter cited as *Papers*.

8. "Down & Back," in *John Berryman: Collected Poems, 1937–1971*, ed. Charles Thornberry (New York: Farrar, Straus and Giroux, 1989), 177. Further citations appear parenthetically in the text as *CP*.

9. E. M. Halliday, *John Berryman and the Thirties* (Amherst: University of Massachusetts Press, 1987), 65.

10. Berryman's frank self-diagnosis calls to mind the equally unsparing passage from Coleridge's Prospectus for *The Friend* that I quoted in chapter 1: "I have employed almost the whole of my Life in acquiring, or endeavouring to acquire, useful Knowledge by Study, Reflection, Observation; . . . at different Periods of my Life I have not only planned, but collected the Materials for, many Works on various important Subjects: so many indeed, that the Number of my unrealized Schemes, and the mass of my miscellaneous Fragments, have often furnished my Friends with a Subject of Raillery. . . . I am inclined to believe, that this Want of Perseverance has been produced in the Main by an Over-activity of Thought, modified by a constitutional Indolence, which made it more pleasant to me to continue acquiring, than to reduce what I had acquired to a regular Form. Add too, that almost daily throwing off my Notices and Reflections in desultory Fragments, [and] . . . the Conviction, that, in Order fully to comprehend and develope any one Subject, it was necessary I should make myself Master of some other, which again as regularly involved a third, and so on, with an ever-widening Horizon."

11. In 1825, Coleridge wrote to the Reverend Edward Coleridge, "Montague has undertaken to arrange engagement with his publisher for an edition of Shakespeare by me." This edition would include "properly critical notes, prefaces, and analyses, comprizing the results of five and twenty years' study." Of course, Coleridge's Shakespeare edition never materialized. See M. M. Badawi, *Coleridge: Critic of Shakespeare* (Cambridge: Cambridge University Press, 1973), 204.

12. Ted Hughes attended Rylands's Shakespeare lectures in 1952. To his sister Olwyn, he wrote, "One Mr Rylands, who was last year a slow motion dissecting xperiment [*sic*] on Pope, is talking of—speech & action in Shakes' Plays. . . . [H]is lectures are big acts but funny, and lively." See Ted Hughes, *Letters of Ted Hughes*, ed. Christopher Reid (London: Faber and Faber, 2007), 12 (February, 1952).

13. E. M. Halliday, *John Berryman and the Thirties*, 147.

14. Paul Mariani, *Dream Song: The Life of John Berryman* (Amherst: University of Massachusetts Press, 1996), 80. Further citations appear parenthetically in the text as *Mariani*.

15. John Berryman, *Papers*, MSS 43, Prose: *King Lear*, box 1, folder: Rockefeller Correspondence. Subsequent quotations in this paragraph are from, respectively, MSS 43, Correspondence, box 8, folder 1; and MSS 43, Correspondence, box 30, folder: Guggenheim.

16. John Berryman, *Papers*, MSS 43, Correspondence, box 30, folder: Guggenheim.

17. *Papers*, MSS 43, Correspondence, box 30, folder: Guggenheim; for excerpts, see *BS*, *lix*.

18. *Papers*, MSS 43, Shakespeare (Project), box 2, folder: Preface.

19. John Berryman, *The Freedom of the Poet* (New York: Farrar, Straus and Giroux, 1976), 3. Further citations appear parenthetically in the text as *FP*.

20. Quotations in this paragraph are from John Berryman, *Papers*, MSS 43, Shakespeare (Project), box 1, folder Shakespeare Notes.

21. Halliday, *John Berryman in the Thirties*, 74.

22. John Berryman, *We Dream of Honour: John Berryman's Letters to His Mother*, ed. Richard J. Kelly (New York: W. W. Norton, 1988), 34. Further citations appear parenthetically in the text as *Letters*.

23. *The Diary of Virginia Woolf: Volume Two, 1920–1924*, ed. Anne Olivier Bell (New York: Harcourt Brace Jovanovich, 1978), 143 (November 16, 1921).

24. Richard J. Kelly and Alan K. Lathrop, eds. *Recovering Berryman: Essays on a Poet* (Ann Arbor: University of Michigan Press, 1993), 81. Further citations appear parenthetically in the text as *RB*.

25. Eileen Simpson, *Poets in Their Youth* (New York: Farrar, Straus and Giroux, 1990), 97.

26. Berryman, *Papers*, MSS 43, Correspondence, box 8, folder: W. W. Greg; and *Papers*, MSS 43, Correspondence, box 8, folder: *King Lear* A, respectively.

27. Berryman, *Papers*, MSS 43, Teaching Notes, box 3, folder Miscell.

28. Harry Thomas, *Berryman's Understanding: Reflections on the Poetry of John Berryman* (Boston, MA: Northeastern University Press, 1988), 82.

29. Robert Lowell, quoted in ibid., 68.

30. Simpson, *Poets in Their Youth*, 97.

31. Ibid., 20.

32. Ken Gross has written beautifully about passages in *The Dream Songs* that channel "the words of *King Lear* at their most chaotic, most cut off from the stability of a given character, rhetorical strategy, or dramatic gesture" ("Poets Reading Shakespeare," 129).

33. Thomas, *Berryman's Understanding*, 7.

34. Simpson, *Poets in Their Youth*, 41.

35. Berryman, *Papers*, MSS 43, St. Pancras' Brazier, folder 1.

36. Ibid., folder 5.

37. John Roe intriguingly, if cryptically, suggests that we approach *The Dream Songs* "as if it were itself an edition of *King Lear*" ("John Berryman," 167). Anne Barton writes that "without 'Dr Dryasdust,' there would have been no 'flying horse.'" See her "John Berryman's Flying Horse," *New York Review of Books* 46 (September 23, 1999): 67.

Chapter Six

1. "Between 1808 and 1819, Coleridge offered a total of eight courses of lectures which were either wholly or partially devoted to considerations of Shakespeare." See Charles Mahoney, "Coleridge and Shakespeare," in *The Oxford Handbook of Samuel Taylor Coleridge*, ed. Frederick Burwick (Oxford: Oxford University Press, 2009), 499.

2. *The Letters of T. S. Eliot: Volume 3, 1926–1927*, ed. Valerie Eliot and John Haffenden (London: Faber & Faber, 2012), 622.

3. "The Development of Shakespeare's Verse," Hayward Bequest, King's College, Cambridge, HB/P/7 1937–41. Eliot also delivered these lectures at Bristol University in 1941. Their title comes from the uncorrected carbon copy in Harvard's Houghton Library.

4. W. H. Auden, *Lectures on Shakespeare*, ed. Arthur Kirsch (Princeton, NJ: Princeton University Press, 2002). See my Conclusion.

5. Neil Corcoran, *Shakespeare and the Modern Poet* (Cambridge: Cambridge University Press, 2010), 123.

6. Allen Ginsberg's journal, cited in Bill Morgan, *I Celebrate Myself: The Somewhat Private Life of Allen Ginsberg* (New York: Viking, 2006), 105.

7. *Jack Kerouac and Allen Ginsberg: The Letters*, ed. Bill Morgan and David Stanford (New York: Penguin, 2010), 70.

8. *The Selected Letters of Allen Ginsberg and Gary Snyder*, ed. Bill Morgan (Berkeley, CA: Counterpoint, 2009), 7.

9. Allen and Louis Ginsberg, *Family Business: Selected Letters between a Father and a Son*, ed. Michael Schumacher (New York: Bloomsbury, 2001), 85.

10. *The Letters of Allen Ginsberg*, ed. Bill Morgan (Philadelphia, PA: Da Capo Press, 2008), 323.

11. Naropa History of Poetry class, recorded June 18, 1975. See the Naropa Poetics Audio Archives, online at https://archive.org/details/naropa (accessed November 15, 2014).

12. See the transcription in the Allen Ginsberg Papers Collection, Special Collections Library, Stanford University, M733, box 19, folder 8. Naropa Institute, founded in 1974, later became Naropa University. In 1980, Ginsberg told his students that Sonnet 73 was Kerouac's favorite (Naropa Basic Poetics class, recorded March 6, 1980).

13. Naropa Basic Poetics class, recorded January 7, 1980 (see n. 11 above). When the *Paris Review* interviewer Ted Berrigan told Jack Kerouac that Ginsberg "once said that he learned how to read Shakespeare, that he never did understand Shakespeare until he heard you read Shakespeare to him," Kerouac responded, "Because in a previous lifetime, that's who I was." "Jack Kerouac, The Art of Fiction No. 41," *Paris Review* 43 (Summer 1968). Online at http://www.theparisreview.org/interviews/4260/the-art-of-fiction-no-41-jack-kerouac (accessed May 5, 2015).

14. See the Allen Ginsberg Papers Collection, M733, box 28, folder 4. It was only six months earlier that "Professor" Ginsberg began teaching Shakespeare at Naropa.

15. "Rashness," as we have seen, was Virginia Woolf's word for approaching Shakespeare (via her brother Thoby) with a mix of presumption and deference.

16. Ginsberg, no doubt provocatively, started pushing Rimbaud on Trilling in 1945. And Trilling resisted stalwartly. There followed years of contention between Trilling and Ginsberg. One minute, Ginsberg was deferential; the next, he would refuse to back down. Trilling was consistently and admirably frank with Ginsberg. Although "Howl" met with much acclaim, Trilling told Ginsberg that he found it "quite dull," "without any music . . . no real voice here." As for Ginsberg's dream about Trilling's bed, it may be noted that Diana Trilling's relationship with Ginsberg was vexed in its own right, not only during his Columbia years but for forty years thereafter. In her 1959 essay, "The Other Night at Columbia: A Report from the Academy" (*Partisan Review* 26 [Spring 1959]: 214–30), she finds that the girls in attendance at a well-attended Ginsberg, Or-

lovsky, Corso reading are not pretty and that the men show no "promise of masculinity." To her credit, rather than dismiss the Beats, she aligns them with liberal intellectuals. Although at first she is impatient with Ginsberg and his poetry, perhaps in spite of herself, she is moved by it. See Mark Shechner, "Ginsberg and Trilling: The Columbia Connection," *Michigan Quarterly Review* 46, no. 4 (2007): 652–66; and Robert Genter, "'I'm Not His Father': Lionel Trilling, Allen Ginsberg, and the Contours of Literary Modernism," *College Literature* 31, no. 2 (2004): 22–52.

17. Allen Ginsberg, *The Book of Martyrdom and Artifice: First Journals and Poems, 1937– 1952* (Cambridge, MA: Da Capo Press, 2006), 140–42.

18. Ibid., 432.

19. Samuel Taylor Coleridge, *The Collected Works of Samuel Taylor Coleridge: The Friend*, ed. Barbara E. Rooke, vol. 4, pts. 1–2 (Princeton, NJ: Princeton University Press, 1969), 2.16.

20. Samuel Taylor Coleridge, *The Notebooks of Samuel Taylor Coleridge*, ed. Kathleen Coburn (and Anthony John Harding, vol. 5) 5 vols., each in 2 parts (New York: Pantheon; Princeton, NJ: Princeton University Press, 1957–2002), 3:3247.

21. Ginsberg, *Book of Martyrdom and Artifice*, 186 and 188 (my emphasis). Given that Keats's letters later made an appearance along with Shakespeare's plays in Ginsberg's dream, it bears remembering that in his 1817 letter to Benjamin Robert Haydon, Keats (also twenty-one years old) tentatively fancied Shakespeare his "Presider."

22. *Jack Kerouac and Allen Ginsberg: The Letters*, 36.

23. Barry Miles, *The Beat Hotel: Ginsberg, Burroughs, and Corso in Paris, 1958–1963* (New York: Grove Press, 2000), 85.

24. Cited in Morgan, *I Celebrate Myself*, 55.

25. "Allen Ginsberg, the Art of Poetry No. 8," *Paris Review* 37 (Spring 1966): 24–30. In the course of this interview, Ginsberg explains that he "got hung up on Cézanne around 1949, in my last year at Columbia, studying with Meyer Shapiro" and that "the last part of *Howl* was really an homage to art but also in specific terms an homage to Cézanne's method." In a strophe near the end of the first section of "Howl," he writes: "who dreamt and made incarnate gaps in Time & Space through images juxtaposed, and trapped the archangel of the soul between 2 visual images and joined the elemental verbs and set the noun and dash of consciousness together jumping with sensation of Pater Omnipotens Aeterna Deus." See *"Howl" and Other Poems* (San Francisco: City Lights Books, 1965), 16.

26. In addition to the Naropa Poetics Audio Archives, some transcribed tapes of Ginsberg's classes may be found at The Ginsberg Project's blog (http://ginsbergblog.blogspot .com/) and at Stanford University's Ginsberg archive.

27. Eve Kosofsky Sedgwick, *Between Men: English Literature and Male Homosocial Desire* (New York: Columbia University Press, 1985), 28–29 and 36.

28. Had Ginsberg read William Empson on the Sonnets? On Ginsberg, purportedly the poet of "defiantly undisciplined utterance and emotional crisis," in praise of Auden, "the high church, high culture, establishment formalist," see Aidan Wasley, *The Age of Auden: Postwar Poetry and the American Scene* (Princeton, NJ: Princeton University Press, 2011), 33–48 (pp. 35–36).

29. Ted Hughes also was moved by the Sonnets' "naked self surrender," their "unflinching, total vulnerability." See *A Choice of Shakespeare's Verse* (1991; repr., New York: Farrar, Straus and Giroux, 2007), 202.

30. See *The Selected Letters of Allen Ginsberg and Gary Snyder, 1956–1991*, ed. Bill Morgan (Berkeley, CA: Counterpoint Press, 2008), 224.

31. Ginsberg calls the line from Sonnet 116 "a very funny line." See the transcription of the Naropa History of Poetry class at http://ginsbergblog.blogspot.com/search/label /Michael%20Drayton (accessed November 15, 2014).

32. See the transcription in the Allen Ginsberg Papers Collection, Special Collections Library, Stanford University, Collection M733, box 19, folder 8.

33. See the letter from Ginsberg that William Carlos Williams inserted into *Paterson*, revised edition prepared by Christopher MacGowan (New York: New Directions, 1992), 173.

34. "Improvised Poetics," Allen Ginsberg in discussion with Michael Aldrich, Edward Kissam, and Nancy Blecker, November 26, 1968; reprinted in Allen Ginsberg, *Composed on the Tongue*, ed. Donald Allen (Bolinas, CA: Grey Fox Press, 1980), 36.

35. From the record jacket of *Allen Ginsberg Reads "Howl" and Other Poems*, Fantasy Records 7006 (1959); reprinted as "Notes Written on Finally Recording 'Howl,'" in *On the Poetry of Allen Ginsberg*, ed. Lewis Hyde (Ann Arbor: University of Michigan Press, 1984), 81. Ginsberg, who was corresponding with Olson in the late 1950s, knew "Projective Verse" (1950) well. Breath, as we have seen, figures largely in Olson's manifesto; for example: a line of verse "comes . . . from the breath, from the breathing of the man who writes, at the moment that he writes." See Charles Olson, *Collected Prose*, ed. Donald Allen and Benjamin Friedlander (Berkeley: University of California Press, 1997), 242; also Charles Olson, *Selected Letters*, ed. Ralph Maud (Berkeley: University of California Press, 2000), 258–61.

36. For Ginsberg's lectures on the songs at the end of *Love's Labor's Lost*, see the Naropa Poetics Audio Archives tapes of his Basic Poetics class on January 7, 1980, and his History of Poetry class on June 18, 1975.

37. At the University of Wyoming in 1971, largely on acoustic grounds, Ginsberg compared "Atta boy! Atta boy!" (the last line of Williams's "To Greet a Letter Carrier") with the Second Page's "With a hey, and a ho, and a hey nonino" in *As You Like It*. See "Poetic Breath, and Pound's *Usura*," in *Allen Verbatim: Lectures on Poetry, Politics, Consciousness*, ed. Gordon Ball (New York: McGraw-Hill, 1974), 165–66.

38. See "An Exposition of William Carlos Williams' Poetic Practice," a 1975 Naropa lecture reprinted in *Composed on the Tongue*, 123. From Blake, Ginsberg would have known that "[t]o Generalize is to be an Idiot To Particularize is the Alone Distinction of Merit." See Blake's annotations to *The Works of Sir Joshua Reynold* at http://www.blakearchive.org /exist/blake/archive/erdman.xq?id=b12.8 (accessed September 2, 2014).

39. Ezra Pound, *The Cantos of Ezra Pound* (New York: New Directions, 1996), 461 (this Canto dates from 1948). In "The Human Universe" (1951), Ginsberg would have found Olson making a case for "particularism." See Charles Olson, *Collected Prose*, ed. Donald Allen and Benjamin Friedlander (Berkeley: University of California Press, 1997), 156.

40. See *Palladis Tamia: Wit's Treasury* (London 1598), in *The Bedford Companion to Shakespeare: An Introduction with Documents* (Boston: Bedford Books, 1996), 32.

41. "Introduction," *Love's Labor's Lost,* in *William Shakespeare: The Complete Works,* ed. Stephen Orgel and A. R. Braunmuller (New York: Penguin Books, 2002), 208. Shakespeare made the same connection. See *Julius Caesar:* "all that I live by is with the awl. I meddle with no tradesman's matters, nor no women's matters" (1.1.21–22).

42. This 1970 Penguin Books edition of *The Tempest,* edited by Northrop Frye, is now in the Stanford University Ginsberg archive. Tapes of the four classes on *The Tempest* may be accessed at https://archive.org/details/naropa.

43. "Craft Interview with Allen Ginsberg," in *The Poet's Craft: Interviews from the New York Quarterly,* ed. William Packard (New York: Paragon House, 1987), 34. Did Ginsberg recall "activity of mind" or "perpetual activity of attention" from *Biographia Literaria?*

44. Ginsberg, "Improvised Poetics," 32 and 38. For his Naropa students, Ginsberg listed eleven items under the rubric, "SOME DIFFERENT CONSIDERATIONS IN MINDFUL ARRANGEMENT OF OPEN VERSE FORMS ON THE PAGE." Number six is "Units of mouth phrasing (pause within the same breath) (Ginsberg, Olson)." See *Composed on the Tongue,* 153. In his History of Poetry class on accentual and quantitative measure, Ginsberg tells his students that he will "bring in some recordings of Pound voweling his own quantitative *Cantos.*" See http://ginsbergblog.blogspot.com/2011/09/history -of-poetry-5-accentual-and.html (accessed September 2, 2014). Marjorie Perloff writes about a 1993 National Poetry Foundation conference at the University of Maine at Orono. She and Ginsberg were lodged in the same inn at which, late in the evenings, Ginsberg would turn "to his real preoccupation: the analysis of prosody. Around midnight, he would appear in the lounge and engage whoever was present in a series of language games, centering on the metrics of Ezra Pound. I soon became one of Allen's partners in crime. He would recite a line from the *Cantos* and I would help him figure out how to scan it." See her "Allen Ginsberg," *Poetry* 202, no. 4 (2013): 351.

45. "Quantity in Verse, and Shakespeare's Late Plays," in *Selected Writings of Charles Olson,* ed. Robert Creeley (New York: New Directions, 1966), 34–35. Although Ginsberg called Olson a "heavyweight influence" (*Allen Verbatim,* 162), when it came to breaking with the iambic pentameter line, it was Ezra Pound who was his pathfinder. See Ginsberg, "Poetic Breath, and Pound's *Usura,*" 162 and 172.

46. Ginsberg, "An Exposition of William Carlos Williams' Poetic Practice," 122.

47. Ginsberg, "Improvised Poetics," 40, 33, and 39; and "Poetic Breath, and Pound's *Usura,*" 172.

48. Helen Vendler, *Soul Says: On Recent Poetry* (Cambridge, MA: Harvard University Press, 1995), 10.

49. Allen Ginsberg, *Kaddish and Other Poems, 1958–1960* (1961; San Francisco: City Lights Books, 2010), Fiftieth anniversary edition, 11. All citations are from this edition.

50. Othello compares Desdemona to a "cistern [cesspool] for foul toads" (4.2.61); standing beside the sleeping Desdemona, about to kiss then kill her, he says: "I'll smell it on the tree" (5.2.15).

Chapter Seven

1. I quote from T. S. Eliot's introduction to G. Wilson Knight, *The Wheel of Fire: Interpretations of Shakespearian Tragedy* (1930; London: Routledge, 2001), *xx* and *xvi.*

2. W. H. Auden, *W. H. Auden: Collected Poems*, ed. Edward Mendelson (New York: Random House, 1976), 325.

3. G. Wilson Knight, *The Wheel of Fire: Interpretations of Shakespearian Tragedy*, 14; on the "mystic vision" of the final plays, see page 15. Ted Hughes would also have known Northrop Frye's *A Natural Perspective: The Development of Shakespearean Comedy and Romance* (1965), about which C. L. Barber once wrote that Frye "is not proving a theory in the ordinary sense, but pursuing a vision." See *Shakespeare Quarterly* 22, no. 1 (1971): 69. Neil Corcoran recalls Yeats's "At Stratford-on Avon" (1901) and Leslie Fiedler's *The Stranger in Shakespeare* (1972), "a study of Shakespeare 'at the mythic level.'" See Corcoran's *Shakespeare and the Modern Poet* (Cambridge: Cambridge University Press, 2010), 218 and 220. My chapter on Ted Hughes is a revised version of an essay that appeared in *New England Review* prior to the publication of Corcoran's superb book.

4. Ted Hughes, *Shakespeare and the Goddess of Complete Being* (New York: Farrar Straus & Giroux, 1992). Further citations appear parenthetically in the text as *SGCB*.

5. Louis Zukofsky, *Bottom: On Shakespeare* (Berkeley: University of California Press, 1963), 15.

6. Ted Hughes, *Letters of Ted Hughes*, ed. Christopher Reid (London: Faber and Faber, 2007), 146 (June 19, 1959). Further citations appear parenthetically in the text as *Letters*.

7. Ted Hughes, *Papers*, MSS 644, box 105, folder 1. There are two major Ted Hughes archives. One is located at the Manuscripts, Archives, and Rare Book Library, Robert W. Woodruff Library, Emory University. Further citations by manuscript, box, and folder in the Emory collection appear parenthetically in the text as *Papers*. The other Hughes archive, which concentrates on the last years of his life, is in the British Library. One significant Shakespeare artifact at the BL is the 1968 shooting script for Peter Brook's film of *King Lear*, annotated throughout by Hughes. Brook commissioned Hughes to "rewrite" the play, to make it (in Hughes's words) "something plain, simple—not measured & musical." Hughes thought that it was an "impossible thing" to do, but in October of 1968 he said that he enjoyed the effort. After Brook decided not to use Hughes's version, Hughes wrote that the "project has fizzled out as far as I'm concerned. I got completely sick of it, had bad dreams about it etc, & finally I've pulled out. It was a mistake to get involved." See *Letters*, 285–86.

8. Quotations in this paragraph are, respectively, from Hughes, *Papers*, MSS 644, box 99, folder 6; and box 105, folder 7.

9. Ibid., MSS 644, box 105, folder 7.

10. Ibid., box 99, folder 1.

11. Ibid.

12. The first two quotations are from ibid., box 106, folder 3; and folder 1.

13. See Ted Hughes, *Winter Pollen: Occasional Prose* (New York: Picador, 1995). Further citations appear parenthetically in the text as *WP*.

14. Ted Hughes, *The Essential Shakespeare* (New Jersey: Ecco Press, 1991), 38. Further citations appear parenthetically in the text as *ES*.

15. See Virginia Woolf, "*Twelfth Night* at the Old Vic" (1933), in *The Death of the Moth and Other Essays* (London: Hogarth Press, 1942), 34.

16. Hughes, *Papers*, MSS 644, box 99, folder 1.

17. Letter from Carol Hughes to author, June 10, 2008. In a 1991 letter to Ann Pasternak Slater and Craig Raine, Hughes writes that he has been "lying very low" because he "contracted shingles" (*Letters*, 591).

18. In 1930, G. Wilson Knight wrote of a "strain" of "almost unhealthy horror of sexual impurity" in Shakespeare's plays, "the unnecessarily savage disgust at the physical aspect of sex unless hallowed by a spiritual and faithful love" (*Wheel of Fire*, 282).

19. See Graham Bradshaw, "Hughes and Shakespeare: Visions of the Goddess," in *The Achievement of Ted Hughes*, ed. Keith Sagar (Athens: University of Georgia Press, 1983), 65.

20. The quotations are, respectively, from Hughes, *Papers*, MSS 644, box 91, folder 5; and box 106, folder 1.

21. See Elaine Feinstein, *Ted Hughes: The Life of a Poet* (New York: Norton, 2001), 19–20.

22. See Lucas Myers, *Crow Steered Bergs Appeared: A Memoir of Ted Hughes and Sylvia Plath* (Sewanee, TN: Proctor's Hall Press, 2001), 44.

23. See Diane Middlebrook, *Her Husband: Hughes and Plath—A Marriage* (New York: Viking Penguin, 2003), 83.

24. See "The 59th Bear," in *Ted Hughes: Collected Poems* (New York: Farrar, Straus and Giroux, 2003), 1103. Further citations appear parenthetically in the text as *CP*.

25. Terry Eagleton, "Will and Ted's Bogus Journey," *Guardian*, April 2, 1992, 26. Of course, Hughes's reading of Shakespeare is steeped in the religious conflicts of the Reformation, in their spiritual if not so much their ideological import.

26. Terence Hawkes, "A porker-wise Bard," *The Times Higher Education Supplement*, June 19, 1992, 32.

27. William Kerrigan, "Ted Hughes on Shakespearean Mysteries," *Raritan* 13, no. 3 (1994), 147–56.

28. Tom Paulin, "Protestant Guilt," *London Review of Books*, April 9, 1992, 10–11.

29. Janet Adelman's compelling *Suffocating Mothers: Fantasies of Maternal Origins in Shakespeare's Plays, "Hamlet" to "The Tempest"* (New York: Routledge, 1992) comes to mind.

30. Marina Warner, "Shakespeare and the Goddess," in *Signs & Wonders: Essays on Literature & Culture* (London: Chatto & Windus, 2003), 254 (first published in the *Times Literary Supplement*, April 17, 1992).

31. For "complementarity," see Norman Rabkin, *Shakespeare and the Common Understanding* (New York: Free Press, 1967), 11–28. Joel B. Altman gets at the both/and nature of Shakespeare's dramaturgy by pointing to the rhetorical tradition of posing questions and arguing them *in utramque partem*—on both sides of the question. See his *The Tudor Play of Mind: Rhetorical Inquiry and the Development of Elizabethan Drama* (Berkeley: University of California Press, 1978).

32. Corcoran finds that Hughes's reconciliatory Shakespeare is fundamentally at odds with his subversive Shakespeare—the "healer" and the "guerilla" are "fractured at [Shakespeare's] very core" (*Shakespeare and the Modern Poet*, 197). Hughes would have argued that the redemptive visionary and the angry prophet were fused—hybridized, he might have said—in Shakespeare, perhaps in himself, as well. Hughes acknowledges Shakespearean (and historical) oppositions, but his dialectical conception moves toward, even when it does not arrive at, synthesis.

33. George T. Wright, "Hendiadys and *Hamlet*," *PMLA* 96, no. 2 (1981): 168 and 173. Further citations appear parenthetically in the text.

34. Frank Kermode, *Shakespeare's Language* (New York: Farrar, Straus and Giroux, 2000), 102. Further citations appear parenthetically in the text.

35. See the 1991 introduction to *The Essential Shakespeare*, 32; Hughes reworks this material in *SGCB*.

36. Stephen Greenblatt recommends Hughes's "brilliant pages on *Venus and Adonis*" in the notes to *Will in the World: How Shakespeare Became Shakespeare* (New York: W. W. Norton, 2004), 404.

37. Just one example among many is Jeffrey Knapp's *Shakespeare's Tribe: Church, Nation, and Theater in Renaissance England* (Chicago: University of Chicago Press, 2004).

38. See Frederick S. Boas, *Shakespeare and His Predecessors* (New York: Charles Scribner's Sons, 1900), 344–408.

39. Responding to Eric Griffiths's damning review of *SGCB* in *The Times*, Hughes wrote that "I present Shakespeare's mature plays, from *All's Well That Ends Well* to *The Tempest*, as the successive hearings of a court case, which I follow up through a detective investigation. This is specifically the trial of the English (Puritan Protestant) mind. The criminal's victim is his best beloved (his mother, wife, daughter). Shakespeare is a severe judge. In fact, he exacts Divine Judgment" (April 16, 1992).

40. In a letter to Ben Sonnenberg dated May 17, 1992, Hughes wrote that *The Tempest* is a "play of fundamental despair, fundamental bafflement with the given elements of mankind, fundamental tolerance of what has to be hideous, contradictory and ultimately self-destructive. At the same time, paradoxical delight in the perverse beauty of it all." "I say nothing about this in the book, or not much" (*Letters*, 612).

41. Corcoran, *Shakespeare and the Modern Poet*, 225.

42. For subtle examples of Hughes's (Shakespearean) "mythical method" in *Birthday Letters*, see ibid., 231–37.

43. Responding to Hughes's "horse-like magical vehicle" named Ariel in the 1992 laureate poem, "A Unicorn Called Ariel," Corcoran finds it "hard to judge if Hughes intends any humour." About the Shakespearean elements in Hughes's "laureate poems," Corcoran writes that they "fail to sustain much interest" (ibid., 238–39).

44. This is darkly cartoonish, if it recalls Sylvia Plath's "Daddy" (Otto Plath).

45. John Keats, *The Letters of John Keats*, ed. Robert Gittings (London: Oxford University Press, 1970), 40.

Conclusion

1. W. H. Auden, *Lectures on Shakespeare*, ed. Arthur Kirsch (Princeton, NJ: Princeton University Press, 2000), 313. Further citations appear parenthetically in the text. Auden delivered this lecture on May 14, 1947 at the New School for Social Research in New York.

2. One of the unchanging basic assumptions that Auden identifies pertains to the tragedies and is as ardent as Ted Hughes's "tragic equation": "all of Shakespeare's tragedies might be called variations on the same tragic myth, the only one which Christianity possesses, the story of the unrepentant thief, and anyone of us is in danger of re-enacting it in

his own way." See W. H. Auden, *The Dyer's Hand and Other Essays* (1962; New York: Vintage Books, 1968), 175–76.

3. Recall that Coleridge deemed his lectures a more appropriate venue for "illustrating great principles than for any minute examination." The latter, as we have seen, he conducted in his marginalia.

4. Here, too, Olson and Auden dovetail with one another. In Olson's unpublished manuscript (dating from the 1950s), he comments on the way late Shakespeare's "phrasings . . . pass over into following lines and come to their ends rather at caesuras." As for prose, Olson argues that Shakespeare found his way to his "Second Verse" form by "cut[ting] back" to the "vernacular" by means of Falstaff's prose.

5. Henry James turns readerly connoisseurship into authorial solipsism in his introduction to *The Tempest*. James stands in awe before a Shakespeare who, "frankly amused with himself," performs "for *himself*, for himself above all." "The neighbours may gather in the garden, the nightingale be hushed on the bough; it is none the less a private occasion, a concert for one, both performer and auditor, who plays for his own ear, his own hand, his own innermost sense, and for the bliss and capacity of his instrument." See William Shakespeare, *The Tempest*, ed. Sidney Lee (New York: Sproul, 1907), xv, xvii, and xviii.

6. See *The Complete Works of W. H. Auden, Prose: Volume II: 1939–1948*, ed. Edward Mendelson (Princeton, NJ: Princeton University Press, 2002), 30. Cited by Neil Corcoran in *Shakespeare and the Modern Poet* (Cambridge: Cambridge University Press, 2010), 123–24.

7. Corcoran, *Shakespeare and the Modern Poet*, 144–46.

8. See Virginia Woolf, "Craftsmanship," in *The Death of the Moth and Other Essays* (London: Hogarth Press, 1942), 126 and *passim*.

9. I again quote Robert Creeley (see chapter 4). In his well-known essay, "The Heresy of Paraphrase," Cleanth Brooks also uses the word *intimate*: "The relationship between the intellectual and the non-intellectual elements in a poem is actually far more intimate than conventional accounts would represent it to be." See *The Well Wrought Urn: Studies in the Structure of Poetry* (New York: Harcourt, Brace & World, 1947), 204.

10. On holding books, and our hands and bodies in relation to them, see "Take It and Read," in Andrew Piper, *Book Was There: Reading in Electronic Times* (Chicago: University of Chicago Press, 2012), 1–23.

INDEX

Page numbers in italics refer to figures.